Teaching Children English

CAMBRIDGE TEACHER TRAINING AND DEVELOPMENT

Series Editors: Ruth Gairns and Marion Williams

This series is designed for all those involved in language teacher training and development: teachers in training, trainers, directors of studies, advisers, teachers of in-service courses and seminars. Its aim is to provide a comprehensive, organised and authoritative resource for language teacher training and development.

Teach English – A training course for teachers
by Adrian Doff

Trainer's Handbook
Teacher's Workbook

Models and Metaphors in Language Teacher Training –
Loop input and other strategies
by Tessa Woodward

Training Foreign Language Teachers – A reflective approach
by Michael J. Wallace

Literature and Language Teaching – A guide for teachers
and trainers
by Gillian Lazar

Classroom Observation Tasks – A resource book for language
teachers and trainers
by Ruth Wajnryb

Tasks for Language Teachers – A resource book for training
and development
by Martin Parrott

English for the Teacher – A language development course
by Mary Spratt

Teaching Children English – A training course for teachers of
English to children
by David Vale with Anne Feunteun

Teaching Children English

A training course for teachers of English to children

David Vale with
Anne Feunteun

CAMBRIDGE
UNIVERSITY PRESS

Published by the Press Syndicate of the University of Cambridge
The Pitt Building, Trumpington Street, Cambridge CB2 1RP
40 West 20th Street, New York, NY 10011-4211, USA
10 Stamford Road, Oakleigh, Melbourne 3166, Australia

© Cambridge University Press 1995

First published 1995

Printed in Great Britain by The Cambridge University Press

A catalogue record for this book is available from the British Library

Library of Congress cataloging-in-publication data

Vale, David.
  Teaching children English: a training course for teachers of
  English to children / David Vale with Anne Feunteun.
       p.   cm. – (Cambridge teacher training and development)
  Includes bibliographical references and index.
  ISBN 0 521 42015 6 (hc) – ISBN 0 521 42235 3 (pb)
    1. English language – Study and teaching – Foreign speakers.
    2. Children of immigrants – Education – Language arts.
    3. English teachers – Training of.   I. Feunteun, Anne   II. Title.
  III. Series.
  PE1128.A2V35   1995
  428'.007 – dc20   94-20664
                                              CIP

ISBN 0 521 42015 6 hardback
ISBN 0 521 42235 3 paperback

Contents

Thanks

We would like to give special thanks to:

Bill Stanford and François Knuchel of Language Resources, Japan, who shared so many of their creative ideas as teacher trainers.

Ken Jackson and Stephen Mullaney for sharing their gifted view of the teaching of children.

María Sara Rodríguez for her dynamic input on the creation and organisation of teacher training materials.

The many hundreds of teachers we have worked with on our training courses in Europe, Asia and Latin America. Without their input and feedback this book could not have existed.

The children, whose imagination and creativity make teaching English worthwhile.

Thanks also to Elizabeth Serocold, Annemarie Young, and Peter Donovan of Cambridge University Press; Diane Hall and Marion Williams.

Acknowledgements

The author and publishers would like to thank the following:
Korky Paul and Valerie Thomas for *Winnie the Witch*, 1978, by kind permission of Oxford University Press.

Drawings by Darin Mount and Sue Wollatt

INTRODUCTION

1   Who this book is for

Teaching Children English is a training resource book for teachers of English to young learners, aged seven years and over. The course addresses three main groups of teachers:
Teachers with some existing EFL experience and training, who have little or no experience of teaching English to children.
Teachers with experience of teaching children, but with little or no experience of teaching EFL.
Trainee teachers who are training to teach EFL, including EFL to children.
The book is intended for native and non-native English speakers. For non-native teachers, the tasks within the book give extensive opportunities to develop, where necessary, confidence and language competence within an activity-based environment.
The book is also intended as a resource for trainers.

2   Course contents

The book has two main parts – Part One, the *Training course*, contains all the activities, tasks reading texts and discussion questions for teachers in training. Part Two, the *Trainer's notes*, provide both general guidelines and step-by-step notes for the trainer. At the end of the book there is a *Resource file* of activities (See page 4 of this Introduction). There is also a list of further reading.
There are ten units, each dealing with a specific aspect of teaching methodology and classroom practice. We have used a *theme-based approach* for the *task content* of each unit. In other words, each unit contains *stories, rhymes, songs, practical tasks* and *language tasks*, etc. related to a specific theme – which illustrate the methodology and classroom practice issues in question.

Each unit is presented as an integrated segment of an overall training programme. The following is a list of topics:

Unit 1   Establishing common ground: attitudes and approaches to teaching children
Unit 2   Starting points: starting lessons in a language course
Unit 3   Building up a teaching sequence
Unit 4   Adapting EFL techniques to teaching children
Unit 5   A balanced teaching diet
Unit 6   Storytelling, comprehension, errors and correction
Unit 7   Classroom management and organisation
Unit 8   Visuals and other teaching aids
Unit 9   Content and curriculum
Unit 10   Observation, assessment and records

The chart below illustrates the main activities and key study areas:

Unit	Study area	Tasks include
1	Attitudes and approaches to the teaching of English to children	Mini-creatures: making a spider mobile word games based on the spelling of *communication* three ways of using a *snail* for teaching purposes
2	Starting points: an overview of three teaching approaches	Circus: preparing the first lesson, making masks, starting activities examples of TPR and *action songs* designing a tune for an action song and singing it
3	Building up a teaching sequence: an overview of two approaches	Potatoes: using a story as the central point of a unit – *The Giant Potato*: storytelling potato games potato (puppet) role play language development related to the story potato bingo potato chant
4	Overview of teaching techniques: examples from EFL and mainstream primary education	Islands: designing a board game and using it in the teaching situation action games – a *TPR* task, *island* song/action rhyme, island games

Unit	Study area	Tasks include
5	A balanced teaching diet: focus on balancing activities to give variety, pace, and interest; the relationship between EFL and mainstream education	Bridges/the colour green: making and testing *bridges* the *Three Billy Goats* storytelling developing a language focus from the theme discussion/reading task on the relationship between educational ideals and teaching realities developing a balanced teaching diet study corners in the classroom
6	Storytelling, comprehension, errors and correction: validity of approaches and techniques in EFL and mainstream education	Activities related to measuring: group-dynamics activities storytelling: *Jack and the Beanstalk* extension activities from this story/study corners in the classroom use of error and correction techniques
7	Classroom management and organisation	Activities relating to the storytelling of *Goldilocks and the Three Bears*: organising the three bears' house tasks related to organisation of space in the classroom tasks related to control and discipline use of a simple *observation grid*
8	Visual and other teaching aids	Festivals/special days/Hallowe'en activities: making *festival* visual aids and using them masks, lanterns witch rhyme/*Winnie the Witch* casting a spell illustrated lesson plans
9	Content and curriculum: review of training course content; developing this into a short activity-based curriculum for children	*This is the House that Jack Built*: a language curriculum related to cross-curricular tasks evaluation of an existing curriculum – producing a *curriculum poster* supplementing a curriculum
10	Observation, assessment and records	A wanted poster: working with *profiles* reading task – *assessment* developing an assessment/evaluation procedure and materials

As the above table shows, the book emphasises an *activity-based approach* to the teaching of English to children. However, it is not our intention to **impose** a particular approach in this book. Therefore, all ideas or approaches contained within this book, however dogmatic in style, should be treated as points of reflection for teachers' **own** beliefs. We want to encourage teachers to consider the relevance of their present teaching methods/approaches, as well as those included in the book, to the needs and interests of **their** pupils and **their** teaching situation.

Introduction

The contents of the book represent a range of key issues that have been raised by teachers and trainers in programmes and courses we have organised in Europe, Asia and Latin America. In these programmes we have seen that each new training group adds its own experience to the course content. Particular needs are raised, and differing conclusions are reached. This book, therefore, is not seen as an exhaustive programme of study. Instead, the contents provide a foundation and framework around which a training programme can be tailor made to suit the individual character of a training group, and its specific requirements.

Resource file

This book also contains a Resource file (from page 233). This is not intended as a complete list of ideas, tips, materials and recipes. However, since many teachers do not have easy access to resource centres we have outlined potential extension activities for the topic, task or theme of each of the ten units. This file functions as a practical guide to the manner in which extension activities can be developed in a language/primary class-room around a specific theme.

3 How to use this book

Training format

The course is designed so that it may function in the following ways:

As a training text to be used by a trainer working with groups of teachers. For the trainer, there are additional notes on how to use the book in the section called Trainer's notes, starting on page 127.

As a training text to be used by teachers studying on their own. In this case, teachers will need to read the accompanying Trainer's notes. In a *self-access* situation, we suggest that individual teachers discuss and share the *group/pairwork* activities within the book with their teaching colleagues. We consider the *sharing* of ideas with colleagues as an essential part of the learning process.

Study procedure

It is important for teachers to feel comfortable in the training situation, and to adapt the ideas in this book to suit their own style of teaching and teaching circumstances. In general, each study session within the book is broken down into four stages:

1 **Planning and preparation,** e.g.
   establishing the study agenda/targets
   collecting resources and materials
   organising the working space

2 **Participatory tasks,** e.g.
   group-formation activities
   practical tasks
   discussion tasks
   storytelling
   language teaching tasks

3 **Feedback and assessment,** e.g.
   group discussion and assessing/reporting on completed activities
   planning future activities
   setting new targets

4 **Concluding activities,** e.g.
   recording opinions in a journal or on a poster
   group-formation activities

In addition, teachers may be expected to complete *outside tasks,* e.g. trying out new ideas in their own classroom, observation of other teachers and further reading.

Recording

In this book, we suggest that teachers keep a *journal* of their studies, e.g. a record of teachers' discussions and reflections on the sessions, with particular reference to the relevance of the activities in their own teaching contexts. (See Trainer's notes page 133.) This could obviously take the form of a loose-leaf file. However, more appropriately in terms of working with child-centred materials, teachers might consider building up an *illustrated journal* (e.g. in a 'Big Book') of course studies. Where feasible, we recommend that teachers work co-operatively on their journal with a partner or small group.

Further reading

Extensive background reading on child psychology, child development, child education theory, etc. lies outside the scope of this book. However, where appropriate there are short reading tasks related to the child, or teaching children. Although these passages usually present a specific point of view, they are not intended to be prescriptive.

How to use this book: additional notes for the trainer

The Trainer's notes in this book are intended as a resource, and as points of reference for the trainer. They take into account the wide range of circumstances that a trainer might find him- or herself working in, and the variety of experience that a trainer might have.

The teachers' needs

From our experience, teachers require support in the areas shown in Tables 1–3 below. These tables outline typical points raised by teachers, and give examples of training course content used in response to these needs:

Table 1	**Teachers with EFL experience, but with no experience of working with children**	
Teachers say they need	**Trainer and training content focus on**
Tips for teaching children	Awareness of the needs of children
	Awareness of the value of child-centred activities
Solutions to discipline problems	Guidelines for classroom management
Keys to manage large classes effectively	Guidelines for class control
	Guidelines for pace and variety within a lesson
Ready-made patterns for lessons	Ways to integrate EFL methods to the teaching of children
	Awareness of the potential relationship between a *language curriculum* and a *mainstream education curriculum*
Games and songs for children	Guidance related to resource materials
Ways to keep children interested	Confidence and reassurance activities
Ways to enliven dull coursebooks	Information related to resource materials

Table 2	**Teachers with experience of teaching children, but with little or no experience of teaching EFL**	
Teachers say they need	**Trainer and training content focus on**
EFL teaching techniques	Guidelines on EFL techniques
	Ways to integrate primary methods to the teaching of EFL to children
	Awareness of the potential relationship between a *mainstream education curriculum* and a *language curriculum*
More English (non-native speakers)	Linguistic reassurance and training (non-native teachers)
Knowledge of English grammar and language structure	Language awareness activities
Confidence to get results	Confidence and reassurance activities
Ways to find time to fit English into a full timetable	Opportunities to share and exchange ideas with other teachers
Resource materials	Guidance and information related to resource materials

Table 3	Student teachers who are training to teach EFL, possibly to children	

Teachers say they need	Trainer and training content focus on
Experience and practice working with children	Observation of live teaching sessions
Hands-on teaching experience/simulation	
Lots of ideas and tips	Work on video of classroom teaching
Solutions to discipline and ways to manage large classes effectively	Guidelines for, and practice of classroom management
	Ways to integrate EFL methods to the teaching of children
	Awareness of the potential relationship between a *language curriculum* and a *mainstream education curriculum*
Models and examples of good teaching practice	Experience teaching English across the curriculum
Recipes for lessons	Guidance and information related to resource materials
	Confidence and reassurance activities

The training tasks

Bearing in mind the above needs, this book contains a wide variety of input and practical activities for the teachers. This content is outlined on pages 2–3 of this Introduction. There are five main types of tasks:

Practical tasks These provide a wide range of cross-curricular experiences. They include *art and craft, science, technology, maths, music, storytelling, drama,* and *PE* activities. The aims of these activities include:
– giving teachers first-hand experience of the sort of tasks that children enjoy doing;
– reassuring teachers that, through this first-hand experience, they will be able to adapt and use the tasks with their classes;
– demonstrating the value of practical tasks as *social, motivational,* and *language teaching* tools in the learning situation;
– providing a *spiral* input. In other words the teachers will be learning in a similar manner to the way they may wish to teach.

Observational tasks These ask teachers to view a teaching situation, or read information on practical teaching content. The aims include:
– providing points of reference for teachers with respect to specific aspects of classroom practice;
– providing resource information with respect to specific teaching content, techniques and approaches.

Teaching tasks These ask teachers to prepare and try out teaching content and techniques within the training classroom. Ideally, teachers may go on to try out new ideas and techniques with groups of children, and give feedback on the results. The main aim here is to give teachers confidence and reassurance with respect to their teaching content, skills and methods.

Discussion tasks Broadly speaking, these fall into two categories:
- discussion before taking part in an activity. In this case the main aim is to raise the teachers' awareness of the points in question;
- discussion or feedback following the completion of a task. Here there are two main aims:
  1 to encourage an active sharing and exchanging of information within the training group;
  2 to give teachers further confidence and reassurance with respect to their teaching ideas.

Recording tasks These tasks encourage teachers to find attractive and motivating ways of recording work done in a specific training session. This is another example of providing a *spiral* input (see **Practical tasks** above) in the training situation. In addition, teachers are asked to keep a personal journal of their training course. Here teachers can be encouraged to illustrate their journals, and to work co-operatively with fellow teachers to produce an attractive record of their studies.

Note: See pages 129–132 of the Trainer's notes for further information on the management of tasks.

The role of the trainer

A training situation where the trainees are themselves teachers, or student teachers, is especially demanding. Teachers are usually extremely emotionally committed to their work and may be reluctant to consider new ideas or approaches. This is especially true if teachers are used to practising (and learning) in a more or less traditional manner. Furthermore, it may be difficult to teach concepts in the manner that **you**, the trainer, understand them within a short training course since these are usually taken on board over a long period of time. Teachers need the opportunity to experience them at first hand. They also need the time to reflect on how new concepts affect their own thinking and principles within their own teaching situation. In addition, they need time to put them into practice in their own classrooms.

Therefore, for the purpose of managing the content of this book, we see the trainer as a facilitator, an organiser, a motivator, a supportive voice – and believe that he/she should be open to accepting alternative ways of teaching which may conflict with his/her own beliefs.

Practice and theory

The contents of this book are essentially of a practical nature. Teachers may wish to discuss some of the theoretical implications of the activities they complete. In this case, time should be allocated for such discussion, and appropriate reference books made available. A list of possible further reading is provided on page 274 of this book for this purpose.

Reflection and assessment

We recommend putting time aside regularly for the purposes of reflection and assessment, in particular for teachers to consider how the course content may affect their own teaching. In section 4 of Unit 10 (see page 123) of this book, we discuss the role of *profiling* in assessment. If you would like to use profiling as an ongoing assessment procedure, it is sensible to make the necessary arrangements for doing so at the beginning of the course, rather than when you reach Unit 10.

Similarly, on extended training programmes, we have found that teachers often raise issues they wish to see (or they would like to have had included) within their training programme, at the end of the programme, when it may be too late to influence the content of the course they are attending. We therefore recommend that, even within a busy training schedule, time for assessment, review and reflection is included and built into the schedule on, for example, every other training day.

In addition, at the beginning of the course, we have found it extremely useful to encourage the teachers, as a course requirement, to establish a regular *written dialogue* with another teacher on the training course (if possible, not a teaching colleague from the same school), or to keep a personal diary of their training experience. Teachers may write what they wish, for example, they could comment on course content, comment on how they felt during the day, comment on the training location, food, etc.

A letter board, or *post box*, is a convenient exchange/collection point for such correspondence. Although all letters are obviously private, teachers, through a written dialogue, may wish to keep the trainer informed of issues that affect training content and approach. Similarly, we believe that time invested by the trainer in the exchange of supportive words with teachers on an intensive training programme is time well spent.

1   Establishing common ground: attitudes and approaches to teaching children

1.1   Establishing key issues related to the teaching of children

- You are about to start your training course. What do you want the course to deal with? Think of the four most important issues related to teaching English to children. You have five minutes. Work individually and write down these four issues, or questions, on four separate slips of paper. When you have finished, hand them to your trainer, who will display them alongside the rest of your group's suggestions.
- Stand up. Select the **four** most important statements that are on display. (They need not be the ones you have written.)
- Work with a partner. Share the statements you have collected. You have ten minutes to discuss and select the **four** most important out of the eight statements you have collected between you.
- With your partner, join another pair of teachers. Share the statements you have selected. You have ten minutes to discuss and select the **four** most important out of the eight statements you now have in your group.
- With your group, join another group of four teachers. Share the statements you have decided on. You have ten minutes to discuss and select the **four** most important out of the eight statements you now have in your group. When you have finished, report your final selection to the whole group. Choose two teachers: one to write the final selections on the board, the other to copy them onto a sheet of A4 paper and to photocopy it for the rest of the group.

This activity will most likely have demonstrated the diversity of expectations which each teacher may have, even though all of you are attending the same course. It is therefore very important to establish common ground with respect to the attitudes you may have, and the approaches you may favour in the teaching of English to children.

1.2 Attitudes: what are your views on teaching English?

● Work with three other teachers. Read and complete the statements below. Discuss your answers.

	Children learn English because	Adults learn English because	I (am going to) teach English to children because
a) b) c)			

● When you are ready, share your responses with others in your training group.

1.3 A 'practical' challenge: a spider mobile

The practical activities in this book relate to various areas of the primary school curriculum. These tasks aim to:
- give you a first-hand opportunity to do the sort of tasks that you may require the children in your class to do;
- raise your awareness of specific language teaching points that may be generated by a practical task;
- raise your awareness of, and give you practice with, a range of useful classroom instruction language;
- give you the opportunity to work closely and co-operatively with the others in your training group.

Preparing instructions for the spider mobile

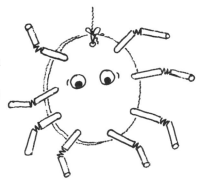

● Look at the diagram alongside of a spider mobile. (This is an example only, and should not necessarily be copied.)

● Work individually and write a set of instructions for an eight-year-old audience (at near-beginner level) for making the spider mobile.
● Now work with three or four others. Take turns within your group to give and show the instructions you have produced. Share ideas and

produce one consensus set of instructions (for an eight-year-old audience) on a sheet of A3 paper, and illustrate them.

Practical task: making the spider mobile

● Discuss the materials you need. Find these materials or suitable substitutes. Follow the instructions you have prepared and make one spider mobile within your group, as a group activity. Share skills and resources.

Discussion

● When you have finished, discuss:
  1 how you made the language of instruction clear to an eight-year-old audience;
  2 how you might exploit these instructions in an EFL classroom;
  3 how you felt as *learners* during the making of the mobile;
  4 how you might exploit the making of a spider mobile as a language teaching activity in an EFL classroom;
  5 how you might adapt this activity to suit an eleven-year-old audience rather than a class of eight year olds.

1.4 Spiders across the curriculum and the needs of children

A cross-curricular analysis

The chart below shows the tasks primary teachers might do on the topic of *spiders/mini-creatures* and a potential language focus that each activity might generate for *language teaching* purposes.

Curricular area	Example activity	Example language focus
Art and craft	Making a spider mobile Making glue and salt webs	Parts of the body: A spider has … Colours and shapes
Music	A tune for a spider rhyme	Singing the rhyme
Science	Close observation of spiders Sorting mini-creatures by the number of legs	Present simple: *Spiders eat/don't eat …*
Maths	Working with the number *8*	
Geography		
Drama and movement		
Hygiene		

- Complete the chart with more examples.
- Indicate the activities in the table you think you would be able to do with your children in English in the language classroom.
- Indicate the activities in the table that would best be done in L1.
- Discuss the possibilities of liaising/linking work in English with work carried out in L1 within the mainstream curriculum.

(You can refer to the topic web on page 234 if necessary.)

A 'needs' spidergram: reflection and feedback

- Work with a partner or within a group of four/six. You (or half your group) complete Spidergram A on page 267. Your partner (or the rest of the group) completes Spidergram B on page 271. Please do **not** look at both spidergrams while you do this activity.
- When you have finished, compare and discuss your results with your partner and the rest of your training group. For example, discuss the action a teacher might take for each of the needs of children you have listed.

1.5 Discussing *communication*

Discussion

Work with a partner. Write the word *communication* in the centre of a page. Form a *mind map* of words/activities that encourage authentic communication between children. Start with this:

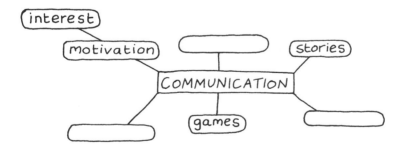

Now look at this example of a *step* word game:

1 interest
      topics for children
            novelties and games
                  Story and rhyme
2 enthusiasm   energy
      magic
        curiosity
           young
            group activities
               Songs

- Start with the word *communication*. In five minutes, share ideas and create as many *steps* as you can. The words/steps must relate to approaches or strategies that *encourage* or *discourage* authentic communication in the children's language classroom.
- When you have finished, compare your *communication steps* with others in your training group. Under the headings below, make a table on the board that includes the words and phrases you have produced.

Factors, approaches, strategies and attitudes that encourage authentic communication	Factors, approaches, strategies and attitudes that discourage authentic communication

Reading task: 'Teaching approaches'

- Work in a *base* group of three or six teachers. In each group appoint:
  T1 (and T4) who will read and summarise Lesson Plan A below;
  T2 (and T5) who will read and summarise Lesson Plan B below;
  T3 (and T6) who will read and summarise Lesson Plan C below.
  The whole training group now reorganises into three *expert* groups:
  - Group 1 (*Lesson Plan A* group), consisting of the T1 (and T4) members from each base group;
  - Group 2 (*Lesson Plan B* group), consisting of the T2 (and T5) members from each base group;
  - Group 3 (*Lesson Plan C* group) consisting of the T3 (and T6) members from each base group.

- Expert groups now read and discuss their lesson plans. When finished, return to your base groups to share notes and discuss the strong and weak points of each of the teaching plans. Use the following questions to start your discussion:
  1 How do you imagine the classroom is organised for each lesson plan?
  2 Which lesson plan do you associate with:
     - the way **you** learned a language?
     - the way you **teach** English to children?
     - the coursebooks you know for teaching English to children?

LESSON PLAN A

Presentation. Draw a snail on the board. Identify the snail and main parts of the snail's body. Get the children to repeat after you.

T: *This is a snail.*
Class: *This is a snail.*
T: *The snail has a round shell.*
Class: *The snail has a round shell.*
T: *The snail has a long body.*
Class: *The snail has a long body.* etc.

Drill. When finished, give the children word cues, and get them to say the complete sentences about the snail, e.g.

T: *Snail.*
Class: *This is a snail.*
T: *Shell.*
Class: *The snail has a round shell.* etc.

When the class is confident, choose individual children to say the complete sentences.

Pairwork. Organise the children in pairs. Ask them to repeat this activity in their pairs. Go round and listen for mistakes. Correct them where necessary.

Writing. Write the sentences on the board. Ask the children to copy them into their exercise books. Alternatively, leave gaps in the sentences and ask the children to complete the gaps and to write the whole sentences in their books, e.g.

This is ....
The snail has ....
The .... a long .... etc.

LESSON PLAN B

Presentation. Organise the class so that the children can work individually. Make sure that they all have a pencil and a piece of paper. Give them the following instructions for drawing a snail. You may draw on the board as you give the instructions to make sure that everyone understands:

T: *Start at the centre of the page, like this. Draw a very, very small circle, like this. Now draw a bigger circle, like this, around the small circle. Now draw a bigger circle, like this. Now draw a bigger circle, like this. Now draw a line, like this, under the circles. And two little things, like this.* etc.

Continue until the whole snail has been drawn.

Ask the children to describe the snails they have drawn. You give the examples. First, ask them to listen. Then ask them to repeat after you, or to complete your sentences, e.g.

T: *This is a snail. It has a round shell. It has a long body. It has two antennae. It has two eyes. It has a little nose. It has a little mouth. Now you try with me. This is a ...*
Class: *Snail.*
T: *It has a round shell. Everyone.*
Class: *It has a round shell.*
T: *Good. It has a long ...*
Class: *Body.* etc.

Repeat this activity until the children are confident and they can more or less pronounce all the words correctly. Next, point to the snail you have drawn on the board and ask the class questions about it. You may accept short answers, or encourage complete sentences.

T: *What's this?*
P: *Snail.*
T: *Good. This is a snail. Repeat, everyone.*
Class: *This is a snail.*
T: *And what does the snail have? Does it have three antennae?*
P: *No.*
T: *No, it doesn't. It has two antennae. Repeat, everyone.* etc.

Pairwork. When the children are confident with the language, organise the class in pairs. Ask them to ask and answer questions about the snails they have drawn. Go round and correct mistakes and help with the language and pronunciation.

Writing. Get ideas from the class and write up five or six sentences about the snail you have drawn, e.g.

This is a snail. It has a long body. It has a round shell. It has ..., etc.

Ask the children to write six similar sentences about the snails they have drawn.

LESSON PLAN C

Activity

- Organise the class into a semicircle. Show the children the pictures and posters of snails that you have brought in. Describe the snails in the pictures. Confirm the names of the parts of the body you taught last time. Use lots of gesture and mime to help put across the meaning of your description. Are the snails all the same size? What about the shells? What about the colour of the snails? Encourage the children to look carefully at the pictures. Find out if the children have seen snails around their home.
- Organise the class into groups of four or five. Tell the groups that they are going to make one monster snail in their group. They can use any colours they want. They can make it the shape they want. It is *their snail.* Assign roles within the group:
  - Appoint a *tidy monitor* (C1), whose role it is to collect materials for the group, and to make sure that everything is clean and tidy after the activity.
  - Appoint a *noise controller* (C2), whose role it is to make sure that, if necessary, his or her group speaks quietly.
- When the children finish, ask them to display their snails, for example on the wall.
- Ask the children to describe the snails they have made. You give examples. Refer to one of the snails as you speak:
  T: *This is a fantastic, monster snail. It has an enormous square shell. It has a long, long, blue body. It has five wavy antennae. It has six tiny green eyes.* etc.
- Repeat your example, moving from snail to snail, leaving out key words and encouraging the group whose snail it is to provide the missing information.

T: *This is a fantastic, ...*
G1: *... monster snail.*
T: *It has an enormous ...*
G2: *... round shell.* etc.

Rehearsal stage. Choose a pupil to stand by his or her snail and to point to parts of the model. You and the class describe the parts. Repeat this step several times.

- Finally, organise the class into new groups of four or five. Each group stands beside a snail. Appoint a *teacher* for each group. The teachers point to parts of the snail. The remaining children in the group describe it. You go round and help with the language. Encourage the children to help each other if they have problems. Discourage the children from merely repeating after you. Give children the complete examples to listen to, leave the group, and allow them time to practise. Return later to check on results.

Writing. Choose a confident volunteer (C1). Get ideas from the class and encourage them to help C1 to write up five or six statements or words about one of the snails they have made. Allow errors in this first draft and praise the result. If you wish, write an error-free version beside the children's work. Encourage the class to spot the differences.

- Organise the children in pairs or threes. Ask the children to write (on the board or in their exercise books) similar statements about the snails they have made. Encourage them to help each other. Give help if children ask you. You will work on producing more accurate written language next time.

1.6 Summary

Work with a partner or in a group of three to:
- share the reading of the following extract;
- discuss what **you** understand by an *activity-based approach*.

Keep your discussion notes concerning an *activity-based approach*. Read them again after you have finished the reading assignment in Unit 2.6, pages 27–35.

Traditional EFL approaches usually imply that the language presented on a textbook page is the learning aim. The result is that (in the case of teaching adults) a similar content is taught to all the students at the same time for a similar purpose. If this approach is transferred to the teaching of children, it assumes that all the children are able to, and motivated to, learn the same language, for the same purpose, at the same time. It may certainly be more **convenient,** from the teacher's point of view, to **teach** the same language content to all the children at the same time, from the same page in the same book. However, the validity of such an approach is extremely doubtful when one considers the wide range of ability, interest and motivation that is likely to exist within, for example, an average class of twenty eight-year-old children. Moreover, if our aim is for the individual child to be at the centre of the learning that takes place, then we must search for alternative ways of teaching English.

One possibility is to adopt an activity-based approach. Here the starting point is a practical task (or song or children's story/rhyme), the *content* of which would be *valid* to the children in their own mother tongue. Where this task is completed in the language classroom, one job for the teacher (or activity-based coursebook) is to select a clearly defined language point that is generated as a result of the completion of the task. For example, if nine-year-old pupils carry out a survey on the colour of eyes and hair among children in their class (and their parents), the language point could centre on *have/has:*
Ten children have brown eyes.
How many children have green eyes?
I have green eyes. My mother has brown eyes, etc.
Here, the *activity-based* approach offers the opportunity for children to work on a practical task, and succeed at their own level, incorporating their own abilities and experience. The results, created by the children, of this practical task can be used as the context within which language practice can take place.

The above contrasts strongly with language-based starting points such as *This is a pencil. Is the pencil green or red?* If translated into the children's mother tongue, this *task* is unlikely to be considered as valid content (or as a sensible question) for a normal nine-year-old child.

However, there is a range of problems that could confront the language teacher who wishes to use an activity-based approach. These might include:
inadequate resources for practical tasks
difficulty in organising the classroom space
lack of available time
lack of available storage or display facilities
lack of experience in the use of practical tasks as starting points for
    language practice
imposed language-based teaching materials, etc.

Despite the problem areas, it is worth keeping in mind that all normal nine-year-old children, when given the opportunity to live in an L2 environment, and interact with L2 speakers of their own age, will successfully acquire the L2, **without** a teacher, usually within a six-month period. It is a rare teacher who can honestly say that all normal nine year olds in his/her class will become successful users of English. It is our belief that by including an activity-based approach within the language classroom, the teacher is offering children many more opportunities for **success**. It follows that children who feel they are succeeding in practical tasks will gain the confidence to take risks, in order to succeed with the language that is inherent in the tasks.

1.7 Round-up: spider games and rhymes

Your trainer will direct this activity.

2 Starting points: starting lessons in a language course

2.1 Alternative ways of starting a language course

Introduction: expectations for the first English class

- Sit in groups of three. T1 takes the role of teacher, T2 the role of parent, and T3 the role of child. Share ideas, and complete the chart:

Expectations for the first English class

Teacher	Parents	Children

- When you have finished, join with another group and share the information you have written.
- In your groups of six, discuss the following from the point of view of a teacher:
  1 how you might feel if half the class cannot **say** anything at the end of Lesson 1, or, at the start of Lesson 2, seem to have forgotten everything they could say in Lesson 1;
  2 your course of action if in the first lesson some children will not repeat words you want them to, or speak only in L1;
  3 your course of action if some children misbehave during the first class;
  4 your course of action if some children do not participate during the first class.
- Share a summary of your group's points of view with the rest of your training group.

Starting a language course

In the language classroom, some teachers start their young learners' language course by using *ice-breaking* activities. Others may start with page 1 of the coursebook, or may spend a lot of time explaining what is going to happen in the children's own language, or may choose formal activities which set the tone of discipline and control for the year. What about you?

Imagine you are preparing the first lesson in a young learners' language course. Try these three starting points with the rest of your group. When you have finished, comment on how you felt as a *new learner* and as a *teacher* during each of the activities:

A) Sit in rows or in a semicircle. Follow your trainer's instructions.
B) Stand or sit in a circle. Use a bean bag or a ball provided by your trainer. Follow your trainer's instructions.
C) Stand in a large *circus ring*. Follow your trainer's instructions.

2.2 Group formation and the learning community

- Read the following text. Then work with a partner. Your partner is doubtful of the value of group-formation activities. Convince him/her of their value.

In any learning situation, where individuals are required to act and interact with others, there are many potential social and emotional (affective) constraints and pressures that may interfere with effective learning. For example:
- a highly successful business person may be embarrassed at his/her poor performance in English, and become reluctant to speak for fear of making a fool of him/herself;
- a self-conscious teenager may not wish to speak out in a new language in front of twenty pairs of critical ears;
- a shy eight year old may be unable to say a word for fear of making a mistake in front of a strict teacher and laughing classmates.

The result of lowering these *affective barriers* is that easier learning takes place. It has often been demonstrated that a relaxed learning environment supports the learning process. Moreover, when learners feel relaxed and at ease with their classmates, it encourages a wider sharing and exchange of ideas. In this atmosphere, learners gain the confidence to lend and receive support from peers, to take risks with new language in front of the class, and to relate to the teacher without the fear of possible ridicule and correction. Furthermore, a supportive atmosphere may lead towards more co-operative work among the pupils. Here, learners, working within a supportive group, process new language within the group, thus greatly facilitating the work of the teacher.

In the light of the above, it is surprising that very few books deal with the importance of establishing positive relationships among the children in the class (and between the teacher and pupils) at the beginning of a language course. In addition, factors such as motivation, confidence, interest, social grouping, and specific learning difficulties of the individual pupils within a class are mainly overlooked. The apparent need to teach *Hello, my name is ....* in the first or second lesson seems to take precedence over the value of providing a relaxed learning environment in which **all** the pupils may participate successfully, with the support of their peers, at their own level.

We therefore suggest that it is highly desirable to integrate activities into the learning situation which have the purpose of *forming the group* and creating a supportive learning community. Such *group-formation* activities build up support and trust as a course progresses. Individuals within the class gain the confidence to take risks – such as trying out new language, new ideas and new roles. Equally importantly, *friendship* and *fun* are major players in the learning process. As an example of this, if we as adults look back on the teaching and learning we remember most from our primary school days, most of us cite *fun, interest, enjoyment* as factors that promoted our learning, and recall such moments as those that have stayed in our memories.

Group-formation activities are seen therefore not merely as *ice-breakers*. They are activities that require, for example, the individuals within the group to work co-operatively, to act together, to support each other, to make physical contact with each other, to lend and receive trust – in highly enjoyable, non-competitive situations. Although activities such as exchanging names or completing information gaps are commonly used at the beginning of a language course, we do not see this type of task as *forming the group*, or adding much positive input to the overall group dynamics. There is a big difference between getting to know the names of other members of the group, and being able to risk, confidently, making a mistake in front of twenty or so peers without embarrassment, fear, or loss of face.

We appreciate that many teachers (and trainers) may regard group-formation activities as, at best, taking up valuable class time. At worst, they may view these activities as embarrassing for all concerned. Furthermore, there is a tendency to omit group-formation activities as a language course (or training programme) progresses. The assumption here is that the learners already know each other and do not therefore need additional formation. However, it is our experience that group formation within any learning community needs continual reinforcement, and that group-formation activities lead to a positive learning environment. Conversely, learning sessions that do not include group-formation activities may develop into a completely different learning atmosphere and be less effective in terms of results for the learner.

We have included group-formation suggestions throughout this book. In all cases, the *content* of the group-formation activities complements directly the areas of study involved and can be adapted to the teaching of children.

- Now stand in a small circle with a group of four or five teachers. Follow your trainer's instructions.

2.3 Practical task: the first page, the first lessons

The first page in the coursebook

This unit relates to the overall theme of *circus*. Work with three or four others:
- Look at the five cartoon frames below, which contain pictures of *Coco the clown, Angela the acrobat, Sam the strongman, Julie the juggler* and *Ricky the ringmaster.*

- Fill in the speech bubbles with typical greetings or a simple dialogue, e.g. *Hello, my name is Coco. What's your name?*

- Make a clown's mask or simple stick puppet.

- Colour and use it to introduce yourself to other teachers in your training group.

- Do you know of any language teaching books for children that use each type of activity above in the first lesson?
- Discuss with your group how **you** would start the first lesson of a language course.

The first lessons

- The topic is still *the circus*. Work in groups of four. Discuss and tick any of the following activities that you think are the most appropriate as *early stages* in a language course. You may add to the list with your own ideas.
    1 Pairwork practising *Hello, my name is X. What's your name?*
    2 Teaching the alphabet in English.
    3 Matching pairs of words (e.g. *Coco ↔ clown*).
    4 Helping children to make a list of English words they already know.
    5 Making a red nose out of a table tennis ball. Pretending to be a clown and making friends with the audience (i.e. rest of class).
    6 Bingo game using names of circus people/jobs as key bingo words.
    7 Roleplay of circus people: each character introduces him/herself by name and with an action.
    8 Writing similar sentences to the one(s) on the coursebook page.
    9 Total physical response (TPR)/action game activity, e.g. *Pick up a custard pie. Smile. Throw it at your friend. Laugh. Oh-oh. She's going to throw a custard pie at you. Duck. Too late. Wipe your face.*

10 A chant or song involving names of circus jobs.
11 Looking at a map of the English-speaking world and identifying the countries where English is spoken, use the map and imagine the route a circus might take.
12 Teaching the colours and the numbers.
13 Drawing and naming food children may want to eat at the circus.
14 Starting a 'circus area' or display in the classroom.
15 Making circus 'puppets'.

● Now work in a new group of four. Make a list of different kinds of puppets that children might make in the classroom, which can be used with the topic of circus. Choose one type of puppet material and make a *circus set*. Use your puppets to introduce yourself and to practise any **two** of the above activities.
● Work in groups of five. Discuss how you could further develop the use of these puppets with nine- to ten-year-old beginners in the language classroom.

2.4 Follow-up: circus across the curriculum

● Work in groups of five or six. Imagine (if necessary) that you teach nine year olds in a primary school. Discuss how you might develop the theme of circus across the curriculum in L1 (i.e. the children's native language), e.g.
  – make a *topic web* with the word *circus* at the centre;
  – include curriculum areas such as maths, art, crafts, technology, science, music, geography, history, physical education, drama and movement (refer to page 235 of the Resource file for ideas if necessary);
  – agree with your group how much of this work you could do in L2 (i.e. English) as part of a language course where the children are getting three one-hour lessons per week. In each case, specify:

Activity	Preparation and materials required	Potential language focus generated by the activity	Time needed

- Work with a partner within your group. Choose one language focus you have written in the table above where you feel that puppets could be used to practise/develop a short dialogue. Write this dialogue, which should overtly include the language point you have chosen, and practise it with a partner using simple *finger puppets*, or the clown puppet/mask you have already made.

2.5 Concluding activities

In this book, we suggest a range of group-formation activities that conclude each unit. These activities can be adapted to your own teaching situation.

- Work together with four other teachers. Work out a tune for this *circus* action song:
  Clap your hands,
  Touch your toes.
  Turn around, and put a finger on your nose.
  Flap your arms,
  Jump up high.
  Wiggle your fingers and reach for the sky.
- When you are ready, check with the other groups and agree on the best tune.
- Stand in a *circus circle*. You are all clowns. Sing the song with the rest of your group and add all the appropriate gestures.

2.6 Reading assignment

The following section is a reading task. It supports an *activity-based approach* to teaching children. This assignment may be completed outside the training room, or carried out as a *shared reading task*, working with a partner or small group.

- Before reading, write your own brief notes/answers to the following:
  - What do you understand by the term 'activity-based learning of English'? How is it different from 'language-based learning'?
  - What do you think is the importance of language *input* with respect to learning a language?
  - When children learn their first language, a rich and varied language input is an extremely important factor for their language development. Is this also true if children learn a second language? If so, how can this rich input be provided?
  - Most normal children aged between seven and ten become effective communicators in English (as an L2) after four to six months of living in an English-speaking environment. This is achieved without formal teaching of the new language. What implications does this

have for the teaching of English for three one-hour lessons per week in a language classroom?

Teaching English to children – an activity-based approach

INTRODUCTION

In recent years, much of EFL methodology and curricula have been developed for the purpose of teaching highly motivated adults or exam-driven teenagers. General EFL teacher-training courses, therefore, may not always be relevant to the teaching of children. It is therefore essential to give additional support and guidance to teachers who are teaching English to children for the first time. The teaching approach is necessarily different. Many of the techniques and attitudes that are essential for the teacher of children seem to conflict with general EFL methodology.

We feel that teachers of children should consider integrating/using an activity-based approach within their language classroom, since such an approach seems to have much to offer in terms of the overall needs of the child. For example:
- children study activities which have practical educational value;
- children are motivated and interested in what they are studying;
- children are introduced to a wide range of natural English. This language is meaningful and understandable, because the activities are meaningful and understandable;
- children are taught in English;
- children are not introduced to English language in an artificially pre-determined sequence of grammatical structures or functions; the input from the teacher, and their learning about their world, is in English;
- children can be taught in mixed ability groups: children with more English will speak more about the activity they are doing, and help lower-level classmates at the same time;
- the learning focuses on the individual child: each child is encouraged to acquire language at his or her own pace and own manner.

PRIORITIES FOR TEACHERS OF CHILDREN

A key priority for teachers is to establish a good working relationship with children, and to encourage them to do the same with their classmates. The teacher's role is that of parent, teacher, friend, motivator, co-ordinator, organiser. The skills for these roles have more to do with understanding children's development, children's needs, children's interests, the children themselves – than with EFL methodology alone.

Young learners have specific learning needs. It is not sufficient to provide children, whether native or non-native speakers, with a programme of study which merely focuses on language, or indeed on any other isolated skill. Instead, it is necessary to offer a whole[1] learning situation in which language development is an integral part of the learning taking place, and not the only end product. Moreover, it is extremely difficult to know what children in any given (language) lesson can or will learn. What **is** known is that children learn best when they are involved, and when their work is valued. They learn best when they are the *owners* of their work – when they have the opportunity to experience and experiment for themselves.

GOOD TEACHING PRACTICE

Good teaching practice is not limited to teachers of one nationality. It is not limited to one particular approach and series of techniques. It is important for teachers to have an opportunity to reflect on what happens in the classroom within a variety of teaching contexts and approaches, including those that are *activity based*. Teachers can then decide for themselves how such approaches relate to **their** way of teaching children.

AN ACTIVITY-BASED APPROACH

Language activities for the sake of teaching language alone have little place in the children's classroom. For example, it makes little sense to ask children *Can you see a boy and a girl in the picture? Can you fly?* where the purpose of these questions is merely to teach *can/can't*. Children do not normally learn language one structure or six new words at a time. They are able to learn language whole, as part of a whole learning experience. It is the responsibility of teachers to provide this whole learning/whole language experience. Therefore, rather than impose a language-based course of study on young learners, where children are exposed only to small and pre-determined chunks of language, it would seem to be of far more value to encourage children to acquire language through an activity-based curriculum. Such a curriculum can provide a language-rich *environment/input* for the child, while at the same time reflecting the actual interests and needs of the young learner. For example, let us assume that the language point you wish to teach is *can/can't*. Within an activity-based approach, a possible teaching sequence might be:
1 Introduce children to a range of small creatures, encouraging them to add their own examples.

[1]The term *whole* is used in this context to refer to the provision of activities which are of value to the overall educational and social development of the child, and not merely to develop English language skills.

2 Ask children to sort the creatures according to specific *can/can't* criteria (e.g. fly, swim, sting, buzz, walk, wriggle, dig).

3 Create an individual/class chart to record this information.

4 Encourage/support/teach the children to describe the results, focusing on *can/can't*.

While this task is taking place, the teacher is also exposing the children to a very wide range of language in the form of instruction, comment and description related to small creatures. This will be absorbed by each child at his/her own pace, without the pressure or need to produce it for display.

At the same time, this practical task will be supporting the development of the children in more general terms, such as:

– supporting cognitive development in terms of subject matter (e.g. science, art, geography);
– developing observational and recording skills;
– promoting awareness of the environment;
– focusing on co-operative work and socialisation;
– supporting emotional needs, for example, in terms of providing a situation in which children will proudly display their work.

An activity-based approach does not, however, prevent the teacher from establishing clear language objectives. The relationship between the topics being studied and the language to be focused upon (or to be covered according to the school curriculum) can be clearly demonstrated. For example, where the topic is *measuring (personal height, weight, ability to jump, hop,* etc.) the following chart illustrates the relationship between the main activity (measuring) and the language:

Main activities & topics	Skills practised include	Physical response language	Language input from teacher	Potential language output from the children
Measuring & personal measurements	Measuring distance, height, etc.; recording results of measuring	*stand up* *reach up* *stretch* *higher* *wider* *relax* *sit down*	Registration language; instructions, questions, comments & descriptions related to measuring activities and to classroom management	numbers *0-9* *eye* *hair* *foot* *hand* *centimetres* *me* *her* *him* *yes/no* verb *to be:* *I'm (142 centimetres) tall*

From early bird 1, Teacher's Book (David Vale, Cambridge University Press)

Similarly, the chart below demonstrates this relationship for an art and craft topic that includes *making a beetle mobile:*

Main activities & topics	Skills practised include	Physical response language	Language input from teacher	Potential language output from the children
Beetles & beetle games	Making a beetle; playing beetle games; numbers; parts of the body	*draw* *cut* *glue* *pick up* *say*	Registration language; instructions, questions, comments & descriptions related to making beetles and playing beetle games and to classroom management	parts of the body numbers: *21-30* *long (longer)* *big (bigger)* *small (smaller)* *round* *dice* *a/the* *my turn* *your turn* *her turn* *his turn* verb *to have: has a (small round head,* etc.)

In other words, not only are the **language** needs of a traditional EFL curriculum being covered, but at the same time the children are being exposed to, in terms of relevant input, a wide range of language as part of a whole learning experience **in English**.

AN EXAMPLE FRAMEWORK FOR TEACHING IN ENGLISH

An activity-based approach requires a clearly defined teaching framework. In the example shown below, the children are guided along a learning pathway which starts with input and active understanding, continues with first-hand experience of a practical task, and ends in speaking (and writing). This particular framework consists of three learning (teaching) phases:

1 **A preparation (or familiarisation) phase** which includes a series of *physical response* activities with the key language needed for the *main activity*. In this phase the children are exposed to key language and respond to it, but do not necessarily have to produce it. This phase creates a feeling of confidence and success with a limited amount of relevant language. It motivates and supports the young learner in the following *main activity* stage.

2 **A main activity phase** in which the children complete a practical topic. In the first example (see the chart above), the children

complete a variety of measuring tasks and record their results. This task is relevant to the stage of cognitive development of, for example, eight- or nine-year-old children. It is a maths/science activity which links to similar work children of this age might be doing within their mainstream education. In addition, the co-operation required to carry out this task and record results in chart form supports the social development of the child. In other words, the task is of value in *whole learning* terms, where *whole* takes into consideration the *whole child*. This activity is not merely an excuse for practising a predetermined language structure. Instead, the children will have understood and followed a series of instructions, comments, etc. from the teacher **in English** (children will already be familiar with key words related to these instructions through the above preparation phase activities), as well as having carried out the task and recorded results. These results provide a context and purpose, created by the child, for language production and practice in the ensuing *follow-up* phase.

3 **A follow-up and consolidation phase** in which the teacher uses the confidence and experience gained by the children in the two previous phases to encourage them to speak (and, if appropriate, record in writing/drawing). The children will, for example, give information about their personal involvement in a task, and the results achieved. During this stage the teacher may focus on specific language points. So, referring to the example of measuring, by using the *numbers* and *units* they will have learnt, the children, at beginner level, will most likely be able to say:
   - how tall they are: *(I'm) one, four, two centimetres tall* (i.e. 142);
   - how far they can reach: *one, six, nine centimetres* (i.e. 169);
   - how far they can jump, hop, etc.

In other words, the children will process a wide range of English throughout the activity, and will be able to respond to a variety of classroom questions and instructions that arise within the context of measuring:
T: *Who's the tallest in the class?*
S: *Tomiko.*
T: *Who's the shortest?*
S: *Maria.* etc.
This speaking may be supported by additional *practice* activities (e.g. word games, child-friendly language games, pre-reading tasks, etc.) in a workbook or similar. The table on the next page shows the teaching framework suggested for this topic.

INPUT PHASE	HANDS-ON (main activity)	PHASE	FOLLOW-UP PHASE
Lesson 1: preparation activities	**Lesson 2: measuring activities (1)**	**Lesson 3: measuring activities (2)**	**Lesson 4: follow-up activities**
Warm-up: play *Chinese whispers* or *pass the bean bag* for names	Warm-up: review and develop the *action game*. Use Class Cassette	Warm-up: develop the *action game*. Use Class Cassette	Warm-up: review and develop the *action game*. Use Class Cassette
Present new language: *numbers 0-9*	Check homework: check and display photos	Check homework: record results on the blackboard	Check homework: use Class Cassette
Introduce the physical response (*action game*) text. Use Class Cassette	Present new language: *colours of eyes and hair*	Present new language: *common measuring items*	Complete the results: *Workbook* review and recording activities
Game: *stand on numbers* or *Twister* with numbers	Activity: children measure heights. Record results on class chart	Activity: measure jumps and hops. Record results on class chart	Language practice: giving information about the results
Review: the children say how old they are	Language practice: short, true answers about the results	Language practice: short, true answers about the results	Homework: show parents their completed *Workbook page*
Homework: bring in a passport size photo	Homework: children measure other members of their families	Homework: complete and tidy up *results* page	Round-up: sing *One Little Indian*
Round-up: the children *make numbers* using their bodies	Round-up: writing numbers on partner's backs	Round-up: sing *One Little Indian*. Use Class Cassette	

This basic pattern for teaching and learning can be used to teach selected parts of the everyday curriculum, or of specific topics and projects – *in English.*

PUTTING THE CHILDREN'S NEEDS FIRST

In the EFL classroom there is a lot of pressure on the teacher to produce immediate, tangible results. Teachers worry about their own performance; parents want to hear their children speak English; administrators need concrete evidence of progress. Teachers therefore feel responsible if specific new structures and new words are not *learned and produced* every lesson. This is potentially a very harmful state of affairs since silence does **not** mean that the children are ignorant or not learning. Indeed, there is evidence that, in a total immersion situation, for example, many children go through a *silent period* during which they are processing their language environment.

Moreover, if teachers insist on accurate production as evidence of achievement from children, they will encourage a considerable percentage of children to fail. Children who have tried their best and failed to produce the result the teacher wants will often lose confidence and interest. They will feel, quite wrongly, that English is too difficult for them – and stop trying. Children should therefore be allowed to learn at their own pace, and language learning targets should not be forced upon them because of an external and non-flexible language syllabus.

Those who favour an activity-based approach feel that children gain in confidence and motivation by studying English in an activity-based environment, where the main objective is the successful completion of a practical task in English. Since the focus is initially on the practical task, children can be encouraged to work out for themselves what they want to say about their own work, at their own level. They can be allowed to make *language* mistakes without the fear of failure. In this way, a teacher is laying the foundations for a successful language learner. Most children will speak in the classroom – and speak well – when they are ready to speak, and have something they wish to speak about.

ERRORS AND CORRECTION

The long-term aim of teaching English is for the pupils to speak English confidently, correctly and fluently. However, it is neither reasonable nor desirable to have this expectation at the beginning of a language programme. Young learners may have ten or more years of language study ahead of them. In the early stages of a language course for children, it is important to establish priorities for the child as a learner. These include:
- building confidence;
- providing the motivation to learn English;
- encouraging *ownership* of language;
- encouraging children to communicate with whatever language they have at their disposal (mime, gesture, key word, drawings, etc.);
- encouraging children to treat English as a communication tool, not as an end product;
- showing children that English is fun;
- establishing a trusting relationship with the children, and encouraging them to do the same with their classmates;
- giving children an experience of a wide range of English language in a non-threatening environment.

Moreover, the correction of errors in the early stages of a language course may foster the following **negative** aspects:
- children lose confidence from fear of making mistakes;
- children become reluctant to take risks: they only say what they know they can say;

- children become dependent on the teacher for correction;
- the need for accuracy interferes with the need to communicate.

There are certainly times when children **do** want to know how to say something correctly, and there are times when correction may be necessary. Teachers need to judge the importance of errors and correction with respect to the other factors that affect the success of learning for children. Experience has shown that errors made in the early learning days do not become so ingrained that the children themselves cannot be guided to recognise and correct them – when they have enough experience of the language to make such correction meaningful and productive.

GROUP SUPPORT

Speaking a foreign language requires the learner to take risks. To make mistakes in front of many others can be a daunting experience for young learners. Until children feel comfortable and secure in the class they may learn very little. This sense of security takes time to develop and needs to be built up throughout the year. Lessons should always therefore incorporate activities which encourage group support, fun and friendship. Furthermore, to make the most effective use of class time these activities can be adapted to fit in with the theme or language of the particular unit that is being studied.

USING THEIR BODIES

It is very important for children to have the opportunity to use their hands and their bodies to express and experience language. In an everyday context in an English-speaking country, children are normally exposed to a variety of physical and intellectual experiences of language. In the foreign learning situation where children may have as little as one hour per week of English, it is vital to include physical activities where the main focus is on the *physical response* or *physical activity*, and not the spoken word.

The importance of providing physical and practical learning opportunities cannot be overstressed. For children, this type of input is a crucial stage in the learning pathway. With respect to activity-based study, where children are working in a language-rich environment, many of the *preparation* activities should necessarily incorporate physical response. This provides a foundation of active understanding of the English that will be needed for any given topic or project.

Similarly, course material should encourage children to **do** a range of practical activities or tasks that require dextrous as well as intellectual skills. These tasks will give the language a practical context that has obvious meaning to children. The results of the tasks – whether a chart, a badge, a beetle, or a collection of bottles – form a natural language text, created and *owned* by the children themselves. The teacher can then go on to exploit and practise selected aspects of this language text.

THE AGE OF THE LEARNER

An activity-based approach can be used successfully with children of all ages and nationalities. The activity content can be chosen from activities which are common throughout the primary school years. The content can, if necessary, be adapted to the country and culture of the children. Taking *measuring* as an example, six year olds may need a lot of guidance in order to be able to use a ruler and standard units of measurement. On the other hand, most ten year olds are able to estimate measurements in advance, and measure extremely accurately with a variety of measuring tools. However, the task of measuring is relevant to both age ranges. The language that is generated from the activity is also relevant to both age ranges. The role of the teacher is to make sure the activity content is exploited to suit the developmental age of the children in the class. The teacher also needs, where necessary, to ensure that this content is adapted to the children's cultural experience.

THE PACE OF LEARNING

Children do not all learn at the same pace or in the same manner. Pace within a lesson is a matter of experience, and sensitivity to individual needs. The temptation is often to work too fast through materials, rather than to exploit the ability and interest of the children. It is not necessary, for example, for all the children to complete all the activities that a book suggests. Moreover, when children have successfully mastered an activity, it may well be more useful to build on this success than to move on to the next unit.

It is also important to incorporate many changes of activity within one lesson. This means that the children should be introduced to language and content through a variety of steps and activities. Some may involve movement, others may be more passive. Since the attention span of young learners can be extremely short, change of pace (and approach) within a teaching sequence is vital.

In terms of *overall* pace through a course, this very much depends on the teacher and the class. One of the strong features of activity-based materials is that learning is not tied to a linear sequence of structures and functions. Teachers are able merely to leave out that which they feel is too easy, too difficult, or not relevant to their particular class.

Part 1

SUMMARY

In terms of the language teacher, an activity-based approach may require a change in attitude and teaching strategy. Traditionally, EFL has focused on the value of the language. Activity-based learning focuses on the value of the activity. The latter approach would seem to favour the needs of the child – and these needs are a very important factor to consider when teaching children.

- Go back to the notes/answers you prepared **before** reading the text. Have you changed your opinions at all?

3 Building up a teaching sequence

3.1 Starting points

A) PLAY POTATO ALPHABET

Stand in a small circle with a group of four or five teachers. Follow your trainer's instructions.

B) PLAY HOT POTATO

Form large circles of six to ten teachers. Follow your trainer's instructions.

C) PLAY PASS THE POTATO

Stand in equal team lines of about six to ten teachers per line. Follow your trainer's instructions.

D) PLAY VEGETABLE SOUP

Follow your trainer's instructions.

Follow-up/discussion

At the end of these games, sit with a team of four or five others:
● Discuss what activities you might do, in a mainstream educational curriculum, related to the topic/theme of potatoes (and vegetables) with eight- to ten-year-old children, e.g. *making potato animals and a potato zoo, potato printing, making a potato or carrot vehicle*, etc.
● List what you feel are the best **four** activities.
● Select two of these, and state a possible *language focus* for them. This language focus should be appropriate for the first year of a language course for children. Here is an example:

Activity	Language focus
Potato animals/potato zoo	Names of animals Present simple tense: *Lions eat meat. Tigers come from Asia. A cheetah has spots.* etc.
Potato printing, decorating an invitation card	Colours, shapes, *inviting a friend to your party*

- Reflect carefully on which cross-curricular activities can/cannot be carried out feasibly within a language lesson in the teaching situations you are familiar with.
- Consider the differences (if any) between developing a language focus as a result of completing a practical activity and doing a practical activity as an 'extension task' once a language point has been taught. In other words, is there any difference between teaching the present simple tense as a language point from a coursebook and then, if time is available, following this up with the making of a 'potato zoo', and making a potato zoo with the children and then, as a consequence of the need to describe the animals in the zoo, teaching the present simple tense?

As a conclusion, discuss your ideas with other groups in the training room.

3.2 Introducing new vocabulary

Micro teaching

- Work in groups of six. One member of your group takes the role of teacher (T), the remainder of your group takes the roles of nine-year-old pupils (P1–P5). Look at the drawings of the five *key vocabulary* items below.

- Within your group, P1-P5 make quick, A4 size copies of each drawing above onto separate sheets of paper, i.e. they do one drawing each, so that your group will have one complete set of pictures. T will use these as *flashcard* teaching aids for introducing vocabulary.
- T collects in the five flashcards your group has prepared. Follow this teaching procedure:
  1 T shows the five flashcards to the *pupils* in your group. T asks each pupil to draw/copy **one** of these flashcards onto a small blank piece of paper, making sure that the group produces a complete set. When finished, T asks the pupils to put their own pictures into their pockets for later. (Although a seemingly minor point, it is very important for pupils to put their own pictures away at this stage.)
  2 T gives out *his/her* five flashcards (at random) to the pupils, making

one pupil responsible for *one picture*. T names the picture as he/she gives it out. Ps listen only.

3 T names the flashcards. Ps hold up the appropriate flashcard. They don't speak.

4 Ps exchange flashcards and hold them up. T names the flashcards. Ps point to the appropriate picture. They don't speak.

5 Ps exchange flashcards. T then names them. Ps put their hands up when they hear their word. They don't speak.

6 Ps choose/exchange a new flashcard. T names them. When they hear their words, Ps do a simple mime or gesture to represent the picture/item on the flashcard. Ps choose/exchange flashcards and repeat this step, then they hand the flashcards back to T.

7 Ps take out **their own** pictures from their pockets. T names each of the pictures. Ps hold them up when they hear their word.

8 Ps work co-operatively, exchanging pictures and teaching each other how to say their words. T is available in the background to support learning if necessary.

Feedback/discussion

Work in groups of five or six. Discuss the teaching procedure you have followed. Include the following questions in your discussion:

1 Could you use this technique for presenting other sets of vocabulary?

2 What types of vocabulary could **not** be easily presented in this way?

3 What are the limitations or restrictions of this technique with young beginners in the language classroom? For example, how would you adapt this technique for teaching groups of 15 or 35 pupils?

4 Would this technique be suitable for mixed-ability classes?

5 Would this technique need to be adapted for older children, say, eleven year olds?

6 How would you imagine the classroom layout for introducing vocabulary in this way?

3.3 Total 'potato' response activity/action games

Introduction

Either play a quick game of *Simon says* with your training group, or sing *This is the way* ... (See pages 262 and 261.)

Both *Simon says* and *This is the way* ... are traditional examples of *action games* or *action songs*. They are based on a short sequence of instructions or descriptions which are acted out, involving lots of physical response. Children often link a (physical) response with the spoken word when they are acquiring their first language. Within language teaching, this type of teaching and learning has taken on the title of *TPR* (*Total Physical Response*).

We have included a variety of action games (TPR experiences) within the book, at least one for each unit . In each case the language content of the action game complements the theme or content of the unit – and has usually been *named* accordingly – hence total *potato* response.

Practice

Stand in a space in the room. Follow your trainer's instructions.

At the end of the activity, work with a team of four or five others. Comment on, or discuss these points:

1 How many teaching steps were there in this activity? What were they?
2 What, if any, is the relationship between the content of this text and the vocabulary you have worked with in the previous tasks?
3 This activity precedes a *storytelling*. Assuming that the content of this TPR activity is relevant to the story, what do you think the content or theme of the story will be?
4 Could this activity threaten the *status* of the teacher?
5 How much classroom space is needed for this activity? Could it be adapted to suit large classes and/or classrooms where movement of the pupils is very difficult to organise?
6 In this activity, the trainer used a *team leader* for each group. If you did this same activity with children, would you use *team leaders*? If so, would their role differ?

3.4 The 'giant potato story'

Introduction

Think of your favourite story as a child. Write down the key lines for (an extract of) the story. Draw a picture to illustrate it. Tell the story (in English) to a partner.

Reading and listening to stories provides one of the richest sources of language and creative thought input for children and adults alike. For children, fantasy, magic, adventure, beauty are all introduced in a way that they can identify with – and understand. Stories play a key role in the language development of children and are a constant source of enjoyment. The stories used in this book are integrated with the other tasks in any specific unit. The aims of this storytelling are to:

– give you the opportunity to practise *active* storytelling;
– give you the opportunity to feel the value of stories as a *learner* as well as a teacher;
– show the value of stories as the *starting point*, *central point* or *springboard* for a range of activities that may also include a *language teach-*

ing focus. (However, the language in the story may **not** necessarily be the main language focus.)

Active storytelling

- Work in groups of five or six. Follow your trainer's instructions.

Follow-up

- Work together in your group.
  Use up to six blank OHP transparencies (or A4 sheets of paper if necessary) and a variety of coloured pens. Divide the story into six main parts (maximum). Share ideas and expertise and illustrate the story on the transparencies. Write key lines from the story under your illustrations.
  When you have finished, take turns to re-tell the story using the transparencies.
- Discuss with your group:
  - how you felt during these storytelling activities;
  - what you learnt from this activity;
  - how you might organise your classroom space for this activity;
  - the practical use of this activity in your language classroom;
  - what the possible next steps would be in the teaching sequence;
  - the practical uses of this activity in the primary classroom as part of an L1 topic on *vegetables* or *potatoes*.
- Finally, using the chart below as an example and resource (but not necessarily to copy), produce a cross-curricular *topic web*, with *potato* at the centre. (Refer to page 236 for ideas if necessary.)
- Display your group's poster and share ideas with those of other groups.

Subject	Activity	Example language focus
Maths	Counting and weighing	Numbers; *how much/many?*
Geography	Potato maps	Names of countries, nationalities
Art	Potato printing, decorating a card	Colours, shapes, writing invitations
Craft	Potato land	Buildings, directions
History	Where potatoes came from	Past tense, countries, nationalities
Technology	Making a potato vehicle	Parts of a vehicle, *how far ...?*
Drama	Potato puppet roleplay	Dialogue for giant potato story
Physical education	Potato races, pass the potato	Imperative, instructions
Home education	Potato recipes	Imperative, instructions, tastes

3.5 Reading task: potato puppets

- Sit in groups of five. Read individually the following lesson notes.
- When you have finished reading, discuss with your group:
  1 ways of creating a stage for puppet activities;
  2 how you might use (include potential difficulties of) this activity in your language classroom;
  3 other uses (and other types) of puppets, e.g. sock puppets as language presenters in a roleplay;
  4 how puppets may allow children to take roles which they might otherwise feel embarrassed to accept;
  5 how puppets may provide authenticity and motivation in a potentially dull language practice.
- What might the possible next step(s) be in a teaching sequence in your classroom situation?

Lesson notes

1 MAKING THE PUPPETS

Organise the children into teams of four or five if possible, or pairs. Appoint a leader for each pair/team. Leaders collect potatoes, cocktail sticks, and the scrap materials you and the children have prepared to dress and decorate the *potato family* with.

- Pairs/groups make their potato puppet family, using cocktail sticks for arms/legs, beads for eyes, etc.

Language focus
Family words, relationships, describing people (i.e. potato puppets)
While the children are working, go round and confirm the key *family* vocabulary such as *Mr, Mrs, son, daughter, father, mother, pet cat*, etc. Help and encourage the children to develop within their pairs/teams the descriptions of their potato family, for example: *This is Mrs Fry's daughter, Barbara* (or *This is Barbara Fry*). *She's ten years old. She's tall and thin*. If

appropriate, teach this language more formally to the whole class, perhaps using a set of potato puppets, or by drawing a family tree on the board, and eliciting/teaching the language.

When ready, encourage confident pairs/teams to describe their potato families to the whole class.

Optionally, help/ask the children to write a short family description for their potato family. This can be copied into their exercise books.

---

2 ACTING THE 'GIANT POTATO' ROLEPLAY

The children remain seated in their pairs/teams. Make sure that each group has completed its set of *potato family puppets*.

Create a stage, for example on a table top, for the puppet play. Set the scene: decide where the house is, where the garden is, where the giant potato is planted, where the characters are, etc.

Choose pupils to manipulate the puppets and take the roles of the main characters, plus one for the narrator. The remaining children are observers. The *puppets* act out the story. You speak appropriate dialogue/narration lines as the children/puppets silently act out their roles. Example dialogue:

Barbara: *This is for you, Dad. It's from Peru ...*
Peter: *What's in it?*
Mrs Fry: *What's in it?*
Mr Fry: *A ... very strange, very, very strange ... potato.*
Narrator: *Mr Fry plants the potato. He waters it. The rain pours down. The potato starts to grow. It grows bigger and bigger and bigger.*
Mr Fry: *Christina, please come here. Help me.*
Mrs Fry: *Coming ...*
Mr Fry: *OK. Pull. Harder, harder.*
Narrator: *They pull harder and harder, but nothing happens.*
Mrs Fry: *Peter. Come here. Help us.*
Peter: *Coming,* etc.

Repeat this step: choose new pupils to take the (puppet) roles of the main characters and encourage the remainder of the class to take the role of the narrator. This time, make sure the pupils demonstrate the *movement* involved, for example, the position of each of the characters relative to the house, to the giant potato and to each other as the story progresses. The class observe and listen carefully to the dialogue. The *acting* pupils don't need to speak at this stage.

Choose new pupils to take the character roles. Repeat the activity. The non-acting pupils listen carefully to the dialogue.

The class work in their pairs/teams. Groups rehearse the roleplay, using their potato puppets. You go round the class and help with the language if needed. Encourage the pupils to develop their lines. Discourage them from merely repeating after you. Give the pupils complete examples to listen to, leave the group, and allow them time to rehearse. During this stage, the pupils may work co-operatively to produce (with your help) and write out a script for their roleplay. Return later to check on results.

Groups perform their roleplay for the rest of the class. This is a free stage. Don't correct errors.

Language focus

A *Members of the family* Using the puppets, check that the pupils can identify the members of the family, and their relationship to each other (e.g. *Who is Mr Fry's son? What is Mrs Fry's daughter's name?*, etc.).

B *Please come here, help me/us ... Coming.* Encourage short pair practice exercises for this.

C *This is for you, (Dad). It's from (Peru). What's in it?* Encourage short pair practice exercises for this.

D (if appropriate to the class/ability of the class) Focus on *pull harder and harder, but nothing happens.*

E (if appropriate to the class/age/ability of the class) *The overall dialogue.*

Elicit and choose children to write the dialogue lines up on the board. Groups compare this dialogue with their own. They copy both into their exercise books.

3.6 Bingo: using key 'potato' vocabulary

Within a young learners' EFL class, games such as bingo are often used as *fillers*: special treats or rewards for good behaviour, rather than as a key part of a balanced lesson. Indeed, in a learning situation where time is often very limited, it is very advantageous to integrate the content of a game into the overall lesson or unit aims. The following teaching plan for *bingo* provides a further consolidation and review link in the teaching sequence for the giant potato story.

● Read the lesson notes, then follow the instructions below them.

Giant potato bingo – lesson notes (for use with children)

1 Ask all the pupils to tell you words they can remember from the story. Write these up on the board. Ask them to copy any five of these words into their exercise books. While the pupils are doing this, write all the words they have written on the board onto small pieces of paper, one word per piece of paper. (You may also ask children who finish first to help you.)

2 Play *bingo*. Put the complete set of words you have prepared into a bag or box. When the pupils are ready, P1 picks out words from the bag, and you call them out. The winner is the first pupil to have all five of his/her words called out. If you play more than one game, the first pupil to match his/her five words becomes the caller for a repeat game, and you become one of the bingo players.

● Work in a group with four other teachers.
Discuss any changes or additions you might like to make to the above procedure.
Appoint a *teacher* (T) for your training group. T co-ordinates the activity and you play bingo.

3.7 Concluding/group-dynamics activity

- Work in teams of five or six. Choose Rhyme A or Rhyme B.

Rhyme A
Hokey, pokey, winky wum,
How do you like your potatoes done,
Mashed or fried they taste just yum!
Hokey, pokey, winky wum.

Rhyme B
Salt, vinegar, pepper, mustard,
Baked potatoes hot and buttered,
Apple pie with cream and custard,
Salt, vinegar, pepper, mustard.

- In your team, work out an imaginative tune for your rhyme, and sing it. Discuss how you would teach it to a class.

3.8 Summary – a unit outline

- Work in a group of five or six. Read the skeleton Unit Outlines (A and B) below. They relate to the activities/theme covered in this unit and are intended for a class of twenty eight/nine-year-old children who have been studying English for about forty hours.
- Compare the sequence of activities you have completed in the training room with the unit outlines. Note any differences.
- Discuss which outline **you** consider more appropriate to the teaching situation you are familiar with.
- Discuss the time/number of lessons needed for each unit outline.
- Discuss whether you think it is feasible/desirable to integrate parts of Unit Outline A with parts of Unit Outline B (or vice versa).

Outline of language-based unit (A) for the Giant Potato story
1 Play the cassette of the Giant Potato story twice.
2 Teach the new words.
3 Do *listen and repeat* practice with the story-lines.
4 Teach the structures.
5 Question and answer practice about the story (whole class).
6 Pair practice: question and answer about the story.
7 Extension activity: roleplay of the story
   – teach the dialogue,
   – act it out,
   – write the dialogue.
8 Short comprehension test of the story (multiple-choice/gap-filling activities).
9 Finish with the chant *one potato, two potatoes* ...

Outline of activity-based unit (B) for the Giant Potato story

1 Bring in potatoes. Children handle, draw and describe them.
2 Introduce (recognition only) key words from story.
3 Action game introducing more of the key language from the story.
4 Active (dramatised) storytelling by teacher of the Giant Potato Story.
5 Extension activities related to potatoes and the story:
   drawing (illustrating) the story on transparencies
   printing with potatoes
   making potato faces/people
   eating potatoes
   enactment (mimed/key word roleplay of the story)
   potato rhyme (*one potato, two potatoes*)
6 Display work done.
7 Feedback and language focus based on results of activities.
8 Guided writing/recording of the results of the activities.

4 Adapting EFL techniques to teaching children

4.1 Starting points

Group-formation activities

A) ROW YOUR BOAT

- Sit in four parallel lines facing the board, on the floor or on chairs. Hold hands with the teacher(s) next to you. Imagine you are in a boat. You are on a treasure island. You are rowing down a wide stream. Sing this song.
  Row, row, row your boat, gently down the stream.
  Merrily, merrily, merrily, merrily,
  Life is just a dream.
  Remember to row in harmony with others in the boat as you sing.
- Repeat the song as a *round*, i.e.
  The front row of teachers (in the boat) sings the first line. The remaining teachers listen.
  The front row of teachers sings the second line. The second row of teachers sings the first line. The remaining teachers listen.
  The front row of teachers sings the third line. The second row of teachers sings the second line. The third row of teachers sings the first line. The remaining teachers listen, and so on.

B) FIVE FAT SAUSAGES

- Sit in circles of five or six. Imagine you are around a camp fire on an island. T1 holds an imaginary frying pan above the fire. There are five fat, delicious, sausages in the pan. The remaining teachers in the group chant this rhyme:
  Five fat sausages frying in the pan,
  (T2's name) ate one, and then there were four.
  T2 must grab an imaginary fat sausage from the pan at that moment in the rhyme, while all the other Ts in the circle try to touch T2's hand. If T2 is successful in retrieving a 'fat sausage' without being touched, the rhyme continues:
  Four fat sausages frying in the pan,
  (T3's name) ate one, and then there were three.
  If T2 is touched then he/she holds the pan in T1's place, and the original rhyme (five fat sausages) is repeated.

- Continue the rhyme until all the sausages have been captured.

Reflection and reading

- Work with a partner. Can you recall any other action rhyme or action song related to *numbers* or *water*? How old were you when you first learnt it? Write this *action rhyme* down. Teach it to your partner. Circle any words or expressions which recur.
- Work with a new partner. Read the following passage. Working co-operatively with your partner, re-write the passage from the point of view of a teacher who holds an **opposing** opinion on the use of songs/rhymes in the teaching of English.

Using songs and rhymes in the teaching of English to children

Native-speaking children are almost certainly **not** aware of the vast amount of language, rhythm, intonation and stress 'practice' that is embedded within traditional songs and rhymes. In contrast, many language teachers view songs and rhymes mainly for their EFL value in terms of presentation or practice material, and use specific phrases within the rhyme to form the basis for choral and substitution drills. As a consequence the enjoyment children get from acting out or singing a rhyme may take second place. It is certainly possible to demotivate children by turning this form of communication into language structure and vocabulary exercises. Even in the language classroom, the language content of a song or rhyme does not need to be viewed as the main reason for using it.

4.2 Consolidation of techniques: introducing new vocabulary for Treasure Island

MIcro teaching

- Sharing the work among the training group, produce quick, simple drawings on individual sheets of paper of these five vocabulary items related to a 'treasure island': *volcano, bridge, mountain, river, treasure*. These will be used as *flashcard* teaching aids for presenting vocabulary.
- Now follow these instructions:
  1 One member of your training group takes the role of teacher (T), the remainder assume the role of nine-year-old pupils and form groups of five or six.
  2 T uses the five flashcards already prepared and shows them to the whole class.

3 T asks all the 'pupils', in their groups, to choose and draw **one** of these flashcards onto a small blank piece of paper, making sure that each group produces a complete set of five vocabulary pictures. When they have finished, the pupils put their own pictures in their pockets for later.

4 T now chooses at random five pupils (P1–P5) to stand at the front of the class. T gives them the five flashcards (at random), making one pupil responsible for one picture. T names each picture as they are given out. All pupils listen only. T divides the remaining pupils into five groups (G1–G5).

5 T names the flashcards. P1–P5 hold up the appropriate pictures. They don't speak. The remaining pupils observe only.

6 P1–P5 exchange flashcards. T names the items again. P1–P5 hold up the appropriate flashcard when they hear their word. The remaining pupils observe only. They don't speak at this stage.

7 T instructs P1–P5 to stand next to G1–G5 (e.g. P1 stands with G1, P2 with G2, etc.). T encourages P1–P5 to teach (as best they can) **their** group the word they are holding.

8 T then names the pictures. Groups raise their hands and wave when they hear their word. They don't speak at this stage.

9 T asks P1–P5 to move to a new group (e.g. P1 moves to G2, P2 moves to G3, etc.). T encourages P1–P5 to teach their new group the word they are holding.

10 T names the pictures. When they hear their words, the groups do a simple mime/gesture to represent meaning or action associated with the picture. They don't speak at this stage.

11 Collect in the pictures from P1–P5.

Either, if there is space:
- T asks all the pupils to stand in random positions in a circle. T asks them to take out the pictures they drew at the beginning.
- T then names (confirms) each of the pictures. Pupils hold up their picture when they hear their word.
- T now asks the pupils to form *island sets*, i.e. they must re-form into groups so that each group holds a complete set of five different vocabulary pictures. T moves into the background as this activity gathers momentum, encouraging the pupils to call out the names of their items during this activity and to help each other with the words they are unsure of.

Or, if pupils need to remain seated:
- T asks them to take out the pictures they drew at the beginning. T then names (confirms) each of the pictures. Pupils hold up their picture when they hear their word.
- T encourages the pupils to keep exchanging pictures (for about two minutes), and help each other to identify and name each of the five picture items.

Note: With a small group ...

In a small training class, 'groups' may consist of one or two *pupils*.

If there are fewer than twelve teachers in the training class, adapt the procedure from step 8 as follows:

8 P1–P5 place their flashcards on the floor.

9 All participants stand beside the flashcard of their choice.

10 T names each of the items. Ps *wave* when they hear their word.

11 T instructs all participants to move/stand beside a new flashcard of their choice. T names each of the items. Ps do an action/gesture when they hear their word.

The remaining procedure follows that of the above.

Feedback/discussion on the task

- Work in groups of five or six. Discuss the teaching procedure that you have just followed. Confirm that all the teachers in your group are familiar with the steps involved.

- A similar technique was practised in the last unit. Can you improve, develop or adapt it in any way, e.g. by using the OHP/board to present the vocabulary: drawing an island onto a transparency/the board, then adding the vocabulary, one item at a time.

- Discuss with your group other possible techniques for introducing vocabulary, e.g.

  translation

  look, listen and point, listen and repeat

  look, listen, draw, listen and repeat, copy or write

  copy from the board, listen and repeat

  question and answer, e.g. *What's this? It's a ...* (pairwork)

- Decide:
  - whether you think all these techniques are appropriate to children;
  - which of these techniques, if any, are appropriate to 'mixed ability' classes;
  - which of all these techniques takes the least time;
  - how important saving time is;
  - if teaching time = learning time.

4.3 Total 'island' response activity

Starting point

- Work in a group of five or six. Listen to your trainer, then read the following *total island response* text.

  You are looking for treasure on Treasure Island. You walk and you walk and you walk. You come to a bridge. Walk across the bridge. You come to a wide river. Swim across the river. You come to a high

mountain. Climb the mountain. You come to a volcano. Run round
the volcano. You see an enormous lion. Shoot at the lion. (You missed,
of course.) You come to a dark cave. You tip-toe into the cave. You
find a spot marked X. Pick up a shovel and dig. You find a large box.
Open it up. What's inside?
Experience has shown that the above text is too long and too complicated to use as a TPR activity with children in their first year of English.
Shooting at a lion may also be considered as a very negative concept to
reinforce with children. Your task is therefore to:

- simplify the text so that **you** would be happy to use it with a group
  of twenty ten-year-old children;
- practise using your simplified text within your group.
- When you have finished, follow your trainer's instructions.

Challenge

- Now work in a *base* group of six. The challenge for each base group is
  to produce a *How to do TPR* instruction sheet to suit a class of twenty
  eight/nine-year-old children.
- In each *base* group appoint:
  - T1 who will read and produce an *Introduction to TPR* (page 52);
  - T2 who will read, try out and produce teaching notes for
    Procedure 1 (page 53);
  - T3 who will read, try out and produce teaching notes for
    Procedure 2 (page 53);
  - T4 who will read, try out and produce teaching notes for
    Procedure 3 (page 54);
  - T5 who will read, try out and produce teaching notes for
    Procedure 4 (page 54);
  - T6 who will read, try out and produce teaching notes for
    Procedure 5, and also summarise the section on *Management of
    classroom space for TPR* (page 55).
- The whole training group then reorganises into six *expert* groups:
  Group 1 is the *Introduction to TPR* group and consists of the T1 mem-
  bers from each *base* group.
  Group 2 is the *Procedure 1* group and consists of the T2 members
  from each *base* group.
  Group 3 is the *Procedure 2* group and consists of the T3 members
  from each *base* group, and so on.
- Expert groups now read, discuss and practise the procedures where
  appropriate, and write.
- When finished, Ts return to their *base* groups, share notes, think of
  their own teaching situations, improve or adapt the procedures as necessary, and produce a large (A1) visual aid of a *How to do TPR*
  instruction sheet. Include notes that you think may be necessary in
  order to adapt TPR to an older audience, e.g. eleven year olds.

TPR/Action games

INTRODUCTION

TPR activities, or *action games* are based on a short sequence of instructions or descriptions. The content of this sequence may be specifically designed to relate directly to the language or theme of the practical work the children will complete in a unit. In this respect, they may be labelled according to the topic, for example: *total potato response, total spider response, total island response, total 'present simple' response*, etc.

The initial purpose of an action game within a teaching unit is as a pre-teaching, or *access* tool. Pupils respond to a sequence of instructions, questions or descriptions without speaking. They gain confidence and active understanding of key elements of the language they need for ensuing practical work without the stress of having to produce this language correctly at too early a stage. As the unit progresses, the action game script is reviewed in a number of ways that provide the necessary variety to maintain the children's interest. For example, instead of merely *acting out* the instructions, pupils can be asked to:

- draw (literally or symbolically) the actions/instructions on a partner's back or hand with a finger;
- draw (literally or symbolically) the actions/instructions on a sheet of paper, then describe their drawings;
- act as a 'mirror' with a partner, and, while one child acts out the instructions, the other 'mirrors' these actions exactly;
- act as a 'puppet' with a partner, who moves the 'puppet' according to the instructions of the action game;
- make simple paper or sock puppets and move these according to the instructions of the action game.

The action game can thus be developed into a language teaching text in its own right. The pupils can be encouraged to teach this text to their classmates (and possibly to their parents). Finally, the pupils may be encouraged to use the action game script as a basis for further language work, including written work. Such action games can be recorded on a cassette, in which case this recording could contain special sound effects which put across the *feeling* of the language.

Action games can be used throughout a language course, and not only with beginners. Typically, an action game is introduced in Lesson 1 of a unit – and practises key language for the unit. In Lesson 2, if used at the beginning of the lesson, the action game may function additionally as a *group-formation activity*. In all events pupils are given further practice of the language involved and are encouraged to give some of the action instructions themselves. In Lesson 3, the action game may again also function as a *group-formation activity*. At this stage, the pupils are encouraged to give more/all of the action instructions themselves. With older pupils, the action game may be further developed in Lessons 4 and 5. In this case, pupils may produce a written script for the action game, or an alternative script, and go on to use this script for additional language work.

PROCEDURES

The basic teaching procedures and learning progression involved are outlined below. They assume that the *action game* script is also recorded on a cassette. If this is not so, the teacher needs to say the action game script him/herself.

Procedure 1 – Lesson 1
1 Explain, with the aid of gestures (and a quick drawing on the board or a sheet of paper, if this helps your explanation) what you are going to do.
2 Play the script and demonstrate the actions. The pupils listen and watch only (no speaking). Use lots of exaggerated gestures to encourage involvement and understanding from the pupils.
3 Play the script and demonstrate the actions. Encourage the pupils to do the actions with you. The pupils don't speak.
4 Play the script again. Encourage the pupils to do the actions by themselves. They don't need to speak.

Procedure 2 – Lesson 2
1 Organise the pupils in a large circle, all facing the same direction, e.g. clockwise.
   • Pupils touch, with a finger, the back of the person standing on their left in the circle. (It may be easier to ask them first to put their hands on the shoulders of the pupil on their left in order to produce the correct distance between each of them.)
   • Play the script. Pupils draw or represent, using a finger, the actions/scene within the script as it is played – on the *back* of the pupil standing in front of them in the circle.
   • Pupils in the circle now turn 180 degrees to face the other way. Play the script again.
2 Organise the class into groups of three or four. Ask groups to recall as many of the words and phrases as they can. Don't expect the pupils to recall everything or to be accurate at this stage. (The main aim here is the *sharing* of information by the pupils.) **Don't correct errors.** Encourage the pupils to do the best they can. After the pupils have tried, play the action game lines again to the whole class. They listen.
3 The children then give you the action instructions. You do the actions.

Procedure 3 – Lesson 3

1 Organise the class into pairs. P1 in each pair is the *actor*. P2 is the *mirror*. You play or say the complete action game script. P1 does the appropriate actions. P2 in each pair copies P1's actions exactly. Ensure that all movements are slow and deliberate. Pairs change roles and repeat this step.

2 Divide the class into groups of three or four. Choose one leader per group. Play or say (softly) the action game script. Leaders repeat with or after you. Don't correct errors at this stage. The remaining pupils in the groups do the actions.

3 Change leaders. This time the groups repeat the activity without your prompts. You go around the groups, helping if necessary. Whenever feasible, say the **complete** script while the pupils are listening. Then let them try. Encourage student-to-student correction rather than allowing the pupils merely to repeat line by line after you. Also, encourage the pupils to experiment with the language and to substitute/add language or actions of their own.

4 At the end of the activity, choose one group to give the instructions. You do the actions. If appropriate, make deliberate mistakes and encourage the class to correct you.

Procedure 4 – Lesson 4 (pupils aged nine and over)

1 Play the action lines/script. The pupils listen only.

2 Write the key words from the script for the action game on the board in *sets*, in random word order, e.g.

walk	across	Treasure Island
swim	over	river
climb	up	mountain
run		volcano
open		treasure chest
		bridge
What's inside?	the	

3 Ask P1 and P2 to come to the board. You play or say the first two sentences of the script one by one. As you do this, encourage P1 and P2 to touch the appropriate words on the board. Ask two new pupils to come to the board and you play the next two sentences of the script. They touch the appropriate words. Continue in this way to the end of the script.

4 Organise the class into groups of four. Appoint a secretary (P1) for each group. Group members share ideas and P1 writes out the script for his/her group. Go round and help where needed.

5 When they have finished, encourage the groups to use their written script in the following manner. There are three roles within each group:
P1 in each group is the *prompter/checker* and holds the written script.

P2 in each group is the *teacher* and gives the action game instructions. P2 must not look at the written script while he or she is speaking. P1 (the checker) may help (verbally or with gesture) or correct P2 at the end of each sentence, but P1 must not show P2 the script.
P3 and P4 are the *actors* and do the actions.
You go around and check that groups understand the mechanics of the activity. When they have finished, the pupils repeat the activity, changing roles within their groups as follows:
The *checker* becomes the new *teacher*.
The *teacher* becomes a new *actor*.
One of the *actors* (P3 or P4) becomes the new *prompter/checker*.
Continue the activity until all the pupils have had a chance to be a *teacher*.
6 Finally, collect in the written scripts and keep them for the next lesson.

Procedure 5 – Lesson 5 (pupils aged nine and over):
1 Organise the class into groups of four. Appoint a leader (P1) for each group. Give each leader a copy of the action game script that the pupils wrote in the last lesson.
2 The leaders read the script to their group. The group does the actions.
3 Change leaders and repeat the activity.
4 Change leaders. Give each pupil (except the leaders) a sheet of paper. The leaders dictate the action game script to the children in their group. When finished, each leader checks and corrects his/her group's dictations. You go round and help where necessary.

MANAGEMENT OF CLASSROOM SPACE FOR ACTION GAMES

Class size and classroom layout are important factors for an action game. However, under normal circumstances, an action game can be adapted to suit most classroom environments:
If the desks and chairs need to (and can) be moved, the first step of the action game can be a series of instructions for moving furniture absolutely silently. (If appropriate, encourage the pupils to give these.)
In a more traditional classroom setting, and with very large classes, it may be more convenient to:
– create a demonstration space in the classroom. In this case, ask teams to demonstrate, and get the remainder of the class to comment on performance; or:
– ask the children to make simple paper *cut-outs* (or puppets) or drawings to represent the main character(s) or items/locations in the action game text. These can be moved on their desk tops as the action game instructions are given.

4.4 Treasure Island 'EFL techniques' a forfeit game

The following is an *EFL forfeit key* for an 'island' board game for **teachers** of English.

- Work in a group of five or six. Work through the list taking turns around your group to **do** each forfeit. Make sure you enact the forfeit where appropriate.

Forfeits

Ask a *yes/no* question about the treasure.

Draw a happy (island) face on the board, or on a friend's back, with your finger.

Mime burying the treasure.

Make up and chant a four-line island rap rhyme.

Check if your partner can say *island* correctly.

Stand up, rub your stomach, say *Yo, ho, ho, for a bottle of rum* and sit down.

Think of an island word. Draw it.

Stand opposite a partner. You are your partner's mirror. Your partner must eat a large oyster, slowly and with feeling. Mirror your partner's actions exactly.

Ask an 'open question' about the treasure island.

Dictate instructions on how to find the treasure.

Make up a difficult 'island sentence'. Say it. Make a mistake in it. Ask one of your group to correct you.

Dictate the shape of the island to your group. They follow your instructions and draw it.

Make up an island tongue twister. (Don't say it aloud.) Whisper it to the person sitting next to you. Ask him/her to pass it on (whisper it) to the next person in the group.

Write a quick recipe for a delicious island drink or dish. Cut up and jumble the sentences. Hand them to your group to sort into the correct order.

Make up a four-line island dialogue.

Play *There's a ... on my island* with the rest of your group. Example:
On my island there is a mountain.
On my island there is a mountain and a volcano.
On my island there is a mountain, a volcano and a ...

Teach three island adjectives to your group.

Draw an island item on your partner's back with your finger.

Write an island sentence on the board, then write a simple substitution drill exercise on the board around this sentence.

Play a quick island team game (such as *Touch the word on the board* or *Draw the word on the board*).

Play island *Simon says*.

When you have tried all the forfeits:

Identify which of the forfeits was the most/least enjoyable or difficult.

Identify and list the practical teaching (EFL) techniques that are illustrated in the forfeits listed in this game and:

- circle the ones you often use in your own teaching;
- highlight any that you are unsure of;
- add others that **you** use to the list.

Discuss with others in your group how many of these techniques you would use in any one forty-minute lesson. Are any of them **not** appropriate to teaching children?

4.5 Practical task: designing a 'Treasure Island' board game for an EFL classroom

Planning and preparation

- Work in a group of five or six. Appoint an *editor* (TE) for your group. You are now going to make a *Treasure Island board game* for children aged eight to eleven.
- Make a rough plan of the game on a sheet of A4 paper. Consider the design of the game, the rules and simplicity/interest of playing it. Also consider the *language focus* you intend the game to generate or consolidate. There may be more than one language focus, e.g.

  Vocabulary for the game: *Treasure Island words, numbers, colours,* etc.

  The language of playing the game: *your turn, my turn, numbers 1–6,* etc.

  The language on the 'forfeit cards': *say your name, spell a Treasure Island word, ask a question about the island, ask what is inside the treasure chest,* etc.

  Note: You may wish to produce **two** sets of forfeit cards, one set focusing on, e.g. the affirmative form of a specific language point, the other set on the negative or interrogative.
- In addition, consider the language you expect the children to recognise (i.e. input from the teacher or game) as well as the language you expect the children to produce by the end of the activity.

Action

- When you are ready, on a sheet of A3 or A2 paper/card, construct a *Treasure Island board game* with up to 36 squares. Square 36 contains the treasure. Include structures such as a bridge, mountains, trees, etc.

Make a die and counters for the game.

Part 1

Write a set of rules for the game.

Write teaching notes for the use of the game by teachers.

Allocate *forfeits* to about ten or twelve of the playing squares. These can be written on 'forfeit cards' which your group may make.

● When you are ready, play the game you have made. Make improvements as necessary.

   Note: TE must make sure that **all** members of the group take part. In addition, TE must ensure that early finishers within the group are given a new task. Passive observers are not allowed!

● When you have completed your game, move on to another game constructed by another group in your room. T1 from your group stays behind to welcome and instruct incoming players to your game.

Follow up: the importance of a language focus

● First read the following example lesson notes. They relate to the next step in a teaching situation where children have just finished playing a *Treasure Island* board game:

Treasure Island lesson notes: language work on can't .../have to

1 Presenting the structures *can't .../have to ....*

● Draw a large map of a Treasure Island on the board.

● Review the key *Treasure Island* words: ask children to draw in the various obstacles, such as *volcano, mountain , river*, etc. on the map.

● Point to the first obstacle. Use lots of mime and gesture. Say:
   What's this? A volcano. I can't go through it. I can't go under it. I can't go over it. I have to run round it.

● Continue in the same manner with the other obstacles. Encourage the pupils to participate with you:
   What's this? A river. I can't go round it. I can't go under it. I can't go over it. I have to swim across it.
   What's this? A mountain. I can't go round it. I can't go under it. I can't go through it. I have to climb over it.

● When finished, choose a pupil (P1) to take your role. P1 points to an obstacle and says *What's this?* You and the class complete the statement, e.g. *A volcano. I can't go through it. I can't go under it. I can't go over it. I have to run round it.*

● Arrange the class into groups of four or five. Groups look at their board game. Appoint a leader for each group. The leaders point to obstacles on the board and ask the prompt question *What's this?* The remainder of the group complete the statement as practised above. You go round and help with the language where necessary.

● Finally, encourage groups or individual pupils to demonstrate to the rest of the class what they can say. Do not correct errors at this stage.

2 **Consolidation of structures: use of action rhyme** *We're all going on a treasure hunt*

- Organise the class into a semicircle if possible. Sit at the front of the class and use this rhyme. Make sure you use lots of gestures and mime as you tell the rhyme:
  We're all going on a treasure hunt. I'm not scared. I've got my guns by my side, bullets too. Oh-oh. What's that? A river. I can't go round it. I can't go under it. I can't go over it. I have to swim across it.
  We're all going on a treasure hunt. I'm not scared. I've got my guns by my side, bullets too. Oh-oh. What's that? A volcano. I can't go through it. I can't go under it. I can't go over it. I have to run round it.
  We're all going on a treasure hunt. I'm not scared. I've got my guns by my side, bullets too. Oh-oh. What's that? A mountain. I can't go round it. I can't go under it. I can't go through it. I have to climb over it.
  We're all going on a treasure hunt. I'm not scared. I've got my guns by my side, bullets too. Oh-oh. What's that? A dark cave. I can't go round it. I can't go under it. I can't go over it. I have to tip-toe into it.
  We're all going on a treasure hunt. I'm not scared. I've got my guns by my side, bullets too. Oh-oh. What's THIS? Two big eyes ... One wide mouth ... lots of sharp teeth ... lots of sharp claws ... Help, it's a lion! Help!
  Tip-toe out of the cave ... climb over the mountain ... run round the volcano ... swim across the river ... Phew. Home safe ... We're all going on **another** *treasure hunt.*

3 **Consolidation step**

Re-tell the rhyme. Make deliberate mistakes. Encourage the pupils to correct you, e.g. *We're all going on a treasure hunt. I'm not* **cold***. I've got my* **gums** *by my side,* **tickets** *too. Oh-oh. What's this? A* **liver***. I can't go round it. I can't go under it. I can't go over it. I have to* **jump** *across it ....,* etc.

4 **Reading and writing practice**

- Hand the pupils a copy of the rhyme. Write up the following statements on the board for the children to copy into their exercise books:

volcano	can't go through it	have to climb over it
mountain	can't go over it	have to swim across it
river	can't go under it	have to tip-toe into into it
cave	can't go over it	have to run round it

- The children draw lines to link the most appropriate statements.
- Finally, organise the children in pairs. Write an example sentence, with gaps, on the board:
  What's this. A volcano. I _____ go _____ it. I _____ ___ under ___ . I _____ ___ _____ it. I _____ ___ run round it.
  Ask pupils to come to the board and complete it. Now encourage the children to share knowledge and help each other to write complete sentences about the remaining obstacles.

- Now, read the following comment on the above lesson notes:
  As you can see from the above, the language focus does not arise **directly** from the language generated by the *Treasure Island board game*. It is developed from an *associated* task.

Experience in dealing with anxious parents and 'traditional' language teachers has shown us that it is extremely important that there is a predicted and planned language focus/teaching point, and that this focus fits into what is commonly regarded as a traditional EFL language syllabus. Moreover, teachers who use an activity-based approach, but neglect to integrate overtly the teaching of a specific language point as a necessary stage in a lesson plan, may soon receive complaints that pupils are 'having a good time', but 'what has that got to do with learning English?' To avoid this, it is essential for teachers to be able to show concrete evidence to anxious parents that specific **language work** is taking place as a result of the practical task.

● As a final task, assume you have about 15–20 minutes within a language lesson with ten-year-old children for specific language work associated with the board game. In the light of the above lesson notes and comment, with your group, decide on a **specific** language focus that you could introduce in a follow-up activity that links to the theme/topic of the *Treasure Island board game*. Write an outline of the procedure(s)/techniques you would use for this language work.

4.6 Teaching techniques: are they from EFL or primary education, or ...?

Starting points

● The following notes were taken at a seminar concerning *teaching techniques*. Work co-operatively with a partner and:
 – write the complete passage, putting the six sections in the sequence you feel is most appropriate (there is no **one** correct answer);
 – discuss any techniques you use in your teaching that you feel the author of the notes below would favour.
● Compare your conclusions and passage with other pairs in your training group.

TEACHING TECHNIQUES

– Techniques should be regarded as a set of flexible and adjustable tools that teachers carry into a lesson.
– The overall attitude and approach to teaching should dictate the use of techniques and not the reverse.
– The mastery of one or more particular techniques will not change a dull teacher into one who motivates his or her class.
– Recipes that fit the teaching of a specific structure, function or theme may work well in a workshop seminar in London, Tokyo or Singapore, especially if demonstrated by the author of the recipe,

but may not suit teachers working with a class of thirty active children in Southern Spain, Greece or Italy.
- The collection of these tools relates to actual classroom experience and the sharing of this experience among practising teachers.
- Techniques do not belong exclusively to EFL or primary education, or any other educational/training field.

Discussion: the top ten techniques

• The chart on pages 62–63 contains a list of *techniques, activities* and *recipes* that have been extracted from current EFL training courses. The table also provides incomplete information with respect to the use of these techniques in EFL, mainstream primary education and in other training fields. Work with a partner and, where feasible, complete the chart. When you have finished, compare your chart with those of other pairs in your training group. Make a *top 10 or top 20 chart* of techniques, activities and recipes for your training group. Discuss how useful such a list is.

4.7 Round-up activity: review the chant *We're all going on a treasure hunt*

Work in groups of six or seven, or as a whole training group. Take turns to take the leading role, and say the action rhyme *We're all going on a treasure hunt* as a group. Use the script on page 59.

The 'top 30' techniques and recipes	Examples of use in EFL	Examples from mainstream primary education	Examples from other fields
Choral drills	Repeating words and sentences, pronunciation practice	Maths tables, rhymes	Military training
Pairwork/group work	Question and answer practice, class surveys		Management training
Roleplay		Drama work focusing on social and creative development of the child	Therapy, leadership training
Oral dictation	Testing of acquired knowledge of a text, testing listening skills		Note taking
Picture dictation		Developing spatial awareness and linguistic accuracy	Free-time activity
Read, look up and say, check	Language consolidation, self assessment		Preparing a speech
Pelmanism/matching games		Developing early reading/writing skills	Free-time activity
Bingo games	Vocabulary review game		Social game
TPR		Developing skills for following instructions	Recipes for cooking, driving instruction
Translating	Introducing language/ language awareness		Business and politics
Chinese whispers		Listening skills	Relaying messages
Mime and gesture	Presentation technique		Therapy, acting
Chaining or combining sentences		Developing speaking/writing skills	Writing from notes

Listen and repeat	Pronunciation practice	Military training
Puzzles, crosswords, charades, etc.	Consolidation, socialisation	Free-time activities
Questionnaires	Language form practice, question and answer	Market research
Class and team games: *I spy, spelling bee*, etc.	Consolidation activities, socialisation	Time fillers on long journeys, particularly for children
Substitution tables (spoken and written)	Language form practice	——
Comprehension questions (spoken and written)	Evaluation/testing	Quiz shows
Storytelling	Presentation of language	Personal reading, social interaction
Listen and draw	Pre-writing activity	Recording information
Information-gap activities	Communicative practice	Social interaction
Imagine it, draw it, describe it	Creative art, drama and writing	Creative work, fiction writing
Cuisenaire rods/*Silent way* techniques	Correction of errors, presentation of language	——
Finger correction	Correction	——
Jumbled-up sentences	Reading comprehension	Free-time activity
Yes/no games	Consolidation, socialisation	Quiz game
Minimal pair pronunciation exercises	Pronunciation practice	Comedy sketches
Chants/rhymes for vocabulary, stress and intonation	Language development	Mother and child interaction
Written gap-filling exercises	Assessment	——

5 A balanced teaching diet

5.1 Starting points

Group-formation activities

A) SAFETY BALANCE

Work in groups of three as follows:
- T1 stands between T2 and T3.
- T1 turns to face T2, and has his/her back to T3.
- T1 closes his/her eyes and keeps them closed.
- T1 allows him/herself to fall gently forwards towards T2. T2 gently stops T1 from falling by supporting him/her with both hands, then gently pushes T1 towards T3.
- T1 allows him/herself to fall gently backwards towards T3. T3 gently stops T1 from falling by supporting him/her with both hands, then gently pushes T1 towards T2.
- Continue this for about thirty seconds, then change roles. Repeat the activity until all teachers have had a chance to *balance* to and fro.

B) SEE-SAW MARJORIE DAW

Sit in two parallel lines, on the floor. Turn to face a partner. Stretch your legs out so that your feet are touching your partner's feet. Stretch your arms out and grip your partner's hands. Rock and balance back and forward in harmony with others in your line, singing as you do so:
See-saw, Marjorie Daw. Johnny shall have a new master.
He shall get a penny a day to make him go a bit faster.
Note: *Daw* is pronounced /dɔː/

Sorting activity

- Copy the headings in this chart onto a piece of paper.

Stimulates or excites pupils	Quietens pupils	Encourages spoken communication	Discourages spoken communication	Encourages social interaction	Discourages social interaction	Dynamic activity	Passive activity

- Work with a partner. Look at the list of EFL activities and lesson stages below. Sort them under the headings in the chart. You may include any of them under more than one heading.

action games (TPR)	listening to instructions .
pairwork	groupwork
cutting, colouring and sticking	silent or co-operative reading
individual or co-operative writing	testing
setting homework	team games
roleplay	listening and repeating
listening and responding	chanting or singing
dancing	miming
relaxation	question and answer practice
practical work	puzzles and board games
copying	describing
listening to a story	filling in blanks
sequencing sentences or pictures	dictation

- When you have finished, join with another pair of teachers. Compare your decisions. Finally, share your decisions with the whole training group and write up a *consensus* table on the board.

5.2 Background reading challenge

- Work in a *base* group of three. The challenge for each base group is to produce *A balanced teaching diet* information sheet.
- In each base group appoint:
    - T1 who will read and summarise the *Introduction* of the reading and *Section A*;
    - T2 who will read and summarise *Section B*;
    - T3 who will read and summarise *Sections C, D, E and F*.
- In each case, summaries should include **own** points of view.
- The whole training group now reorganises into three *expert* groups:
  Group 1 is the *Introduction* and *Section A* group and consists of the T1 members from each base group.
  Group 2 is the *Section B* group and consists of the T2 members from each base group.
  Group 3 is the *Sections C–F* group and consists of the T3 members from each base group.
  The expert groups can divide into smaller groups if they are very large.
- Expert groups now read, discuss and summarise their sections.
- When finished, Ts return to their base groups, share notes, and produce a large (A1) visual aid of *A balanced teaching diet.*
- Early finishers may draw the page layout for the *Pupil's Book* content of Coursebook B, the *Teacher's Notes* for which are on pages 71–72.

A balanced teaching diet

Introduction

In the teaching of English to younger learners, the importance of providing a change of pace and a balanced variety of activities within any given lesson is often highlighted. This, without doubt, has priority in terms of the lesson-to-lesson practical needs of the children and the teacher. However, it is extremely important to strike a healthy balance between **all** of the issues that exist in the teaching situation. Such a balance must be flexible and dynamic, since the factors involved change from lesson to lesson, day to day, class to class. The chart below outlines some of the issues the teacher has to consider when making decisions about balance, and these points are discussed in more detail in the ensuing paragraphs.

Issues raised in terms of primary education	Practical issues raised within the language teaching classroom
A English is not an isolated educational issue. The child has *whole needs* in terms of learning. It is important to acquire language across the curriculum.	An imposed language curriculum places demands and time constraints on children and teachers.
B Children need a change of pace and a flexible variety of activities within any one lesson.	Activities are usually prescribed by a coursebook, and the preparation time available to the teacher is limited.
C Most authentic communication requires the teacher to adapt classroom space and to spend time on classroom organisation.	There are practical restrictions on the ability to change existing classroom space and organisation.
D When developing their understanding of language, children need a lot of opportunity for review, recycling and consolidation of language, ideally through a variety of cross-curricular contexts.	There is a need to complete a prescribed course within a prescribed number of lessons.
E A child needs to assimilate new learning at his/her own pace.	Most coursebooks present a fixed language learning content to be achieved within a fixed time frame by the whole class. There is also usually great pressure from parents and school administration for concrete (spoken) evidence of learning.
F It is very important to recognise the value of errors and risk taking in the process of learning a language.	The need for accuracy of performance in a language is driven by the academic pressure and future examinations that will exist in the secondary school.

A   Teaching a second language is not an isolated educational issue.

Within mainstream education in L1, importance is normally given to the development of language (L1) across the curriculum. Each curriculum subject generates language which is specific to particular topics and which also adds to the richness of an individual child's language expertise and potential. Here are some examples from different subject areas:

	Children at pre-reading and writing stage of development	Children developing reading and writing skills	Encouraging children to use alternative and accurate description
mathematics	$4 \times 2 = 8$ (written by the teacher) or *4 times 2 = eight* (written by the teacher)	*Four multiplied by two equals eight.*	*If you multiply four by two, you get eight.*
science	*This is a picture of a butterfly.* (written by the teacher)	*A butterfly is an insect. It has six legs and wings.*	*A butterfly is an insect. Insects have three body parts. The parts are called the head, the thorax and the body. Insects have two eyes and six legs. They don't have a skeleton. Many insects can fly.*
	The life cycle of a butterfly. (written by the teacher)	*The life cycle of a butterfly: The egg turns into a caterpillar. The caterpillar gets fat. It turns into a butterfly.*	*Butterflies lay eggs. The eggs grow into caterpillars. The caterpillars eat lots of food. When they are big they make a cocoon. They grow into a butterfly inside the cocoon.*
history	*This is a picture of a kitchen in 1893.* (written by the teacher)	*Kitchens 100 years ago and now. These things are different: the cooker, the sink, the fire.*	*In 1893 people cooked on an open cooker. They washed their clothes on a scrubbing board. They didn't have electricity. They didn't have washing machines and TV. Life was very different.*
	This is a picture of a kitchen in 1993. (written by the teacher)	*These things are the same: the table, the chairs, the plates.*	*In 1993 people cook on electric cookers. They wash their clothes in a washing machine. They watch TV. Life is much easier because …*

In the foreign language situation there is much controversy as to the value of teaching parts of the curriculum **in** a foreign language (L2). There are concerns about the ability of children to cope with both new content and new language at the same time. Extensive bilingual experiments in Canada suggest that children can and do cope, whereas experiences of teaching English through some of the curriculum in Europe have raised doubts. Moreover, where education authorities have decided to introduce L2 as a separate subject into the primary curriculum, there is an obvious question of which part of the curriculum to squeeze out of the timetable to make room for it.

One compromise has been to select part of a lesson, or topic which is normally taught in L1 within the mainstream curriculum, and to teach this **in** English. Since this kind of experience cannot compare with full time bilingual education, the initial expectation and focus has been on encouraging younger learners to understand and respond to English and to do practical work in an English-speaking environment, and not necessarily to speak extensively in English. This *speaking* stage might normally occur when the children have had enough experience and reinforcement to make a focus on spoken language meaningful.

One advantage of this type of compromise is that it provides a rich and authentic language input/language environment, and can be integrated within an existing full primary school timetable. One disadvantage is that it may be difficult for an individual teacher (or educational body) to decide which part of the curriculum to teach in English, and to identify, in traditional terms, the exact language structures and functions that are being learnt.

The balance, therefore, lies between the decision whether to regard English as a *tool* of communication, and to encourage children to *experience* English within a cross-curricular context, or whether to regard English as a separate curriculum subject, the nuts and bolts of which are taught (and tested) outside the authentic curriculum content.

B   A child needs a change of pace and a flexible variety of activities within a lesson.

It is easier for a busy teacher to follow a coursebook where the majority of units and lessons have been predetermined and pre-timed. This instant type of lesson plan saves a lot of preparation time, but carries the danger of encouraging a mechanical learning situation. For example, a language-based teaching sequence for children would frequently follow this order:

Presentation
Children are shown examples of the target language in a dialogue.

Practice
1 Children repeat the model dialogue after the tape/teacher.
2 Children carry out question and answer practice in pairs on specific language items extracted from the dialogue.

Production

1 Children act out the dialogue in pairs in front of the class.
2 Children do written exercises to reinforce the language forms.

Here and there, such lesson plans may suggest stimulating games and activities as 'cherries on the cake', for example in 'extension' or 'resource file' activities. However, in real terms, there may be little time left in an already full *language* lesson for the children actually to taste the cherries. Moreover, there is often the temptation to use these games and activities as time-fillers or as a special treat for good behaviour.

Providing a variety of motivating activities (and changes of pace) within a lesson should not be seen as a bonus or as a final stage to a lesson, but as essential for the children's learning situation. Since many coursebooks do not take this aspect into consideration, teachers need, at the very least, to look at the activities and activity sequence within a particular coursebook unit, and to adapt these to provide a balance in terms of pace and variety.

However, the provision of *variety* should also take *authenticity* of content into consideration. In the following example lesson plans, Coursebook A illustrates an example of a language-based EFL concept of variety, change of pace and lesson balance. The lesson plan for Coursebook B reflects the type of balance that is often encouraged within contemporary primary practice in mainstream education.

COURSEBOOK A – TEACHER'S BOOK UNIT 4: LESSON PLAN

(Pupils' Book Unit is on page 70.)

1 Teach the vocabulary
- Teach the colours and the items of children's clothing.

2 Teach the dialogue
- The children cover the text and look at the pictures. Play the cassette. The children listen and point to the right pictures.
- Play the cassette for Picture 1. The children listen and repeat. Continue in this manner for the rest of the dialogue.
- Ask the children to uncover the text and read the dialogue. Play the cassette. The children read silently with the cassette.
- Question and answer practice on the dialogue: first, you ask the questions, and choose children to answer; then put the children into pairs. Pairs practise the questions and answers.
- Roleplay. Choose children to act out the dialogue in front of the rest of the class. Help them with the language by playing the cassette if necessary.
- Finally, ask the children to copy the dialogue into their books.

3 Teach the action game
- Action game. Give the children these instructions:
  Stand up. Go to the door. Open the door. Shut the door. Sit down. Put your hand up. Put your hand down.

Demonstrate the actions with two or three children. When they can follow your instructions, repeat with other children.

4 Teach the song: *My dress is green*

My dress is green, green. Yes, my dress is green. Green is good. Green is good.
My shirt is blue, blue. Yes, my shirt is blue. Blue is good. Blue is good.
My shoes are black, black. Yes, my shoes are black. Black is good. Black is good.

- Play the cassette. The children listen and touch or point to the colours and clothes in the song.
- Play the song line by line. The children repeat after the cassette.
- Play the cassette again. The children sing along. Make sure they point to, or touch the correct colours and clothes as they sing.
- Finally, ask the children to touch an item of their own clothes and add to the song as appropriate.

Extension activities

Refer to the resource file:
- Play twister or bingo with the colours.
- Make a collection of *green* items.

COURSEBOOK A – PUPIL'S BOOK A UNIT 4

Cathy's dress is green

Mummy. Where is my green dress, please?

I'm sorry, Cathy. It's dirty. Wear your red skirt and your white blouse.

Oh, no. I don't like my red skirt. I want my green dress …

COURSEBOOK B – TEACHER'S BOOK UNIT 4: LESSON PLAN

Theme – colours and the colour green

1 Group-dynamics activity (action game): *growing from a seed to a plant.*
Use the following text, which is recorded on the cassette:
You're a tiny, tiny, seed. Curl up really small. Start to grow. Now, uncurl, really slowly. Now slowly stand up. Stretch your arms up. Slowly. Stretch higher and higher and higher. Now stretch wider, and wider and wider ... and relax.

- You say the script and demonstrate the actions. The pupils listen and watch only (no speaking). Use lots of exaggerated gestures to encourage involvement and understanding from the pupils.
- You play the cassette or say the script. Encourage the pupils to do the actions with you. The pupils don't speak.
- Play the cassette again. Encourage the pupils to do the actions by themselves. Encourage them to express freely the movement of the seed growing to a tall plant. They don't need to speak.

2 Presentation of colour vocabulary
Use colour flashcards, or coloured items, such as crayons, as teaching aids.

- Hand the items/flashcards to the children. Say the colour of each item as you do so.
- You name the colours. The pupils hold up or point to the appropriate flashcard/item. They don't speak. The pupils exchange flashcards and repeat this step.
- Instruct the pupils to place their flashcards or coloured items in various locations around the classroom. Tell all the pupils to stand in groups near specific colours. You then name the colours. Groups touch their colour when they hear their word. They don't speak.
- Ask the pupils to move to a new colour of their choice and repeat the activity.
- Ask the pupils to stand in a circle. You choose one colour. You walk up to P1 and name the colour. After you say the name of your colour, P1 says the name of his/her colour. You both then exchange flashcards/coloured items with each other. Repeat this step several times with different pupils.
- Stop the activity. You name each of the colours. The pupils hold their flashcards/items above their heads when they hear their word.
- As a finale, all the pupils shout (or whisper) the names of their colours in unison.

3 Activity: focusing on the colour *green*; sorting green items
- Organise the children into pairs or groups. Allow them five minutes and ask them to draw items that are green. Go round and help the children to label these items while they are working. When finished, put three headings on the board:
  These things are always green
  These things are usually green
  These things are sometimes green
  If necessary, explain the headings by drawing/eliciting one (or more) item for each heading.
- Ask children to come to the front, and to draw their items under the correct heading.

4 Language focus

At the end of this stage, as a language focus, encourage the children to describe the items they have sorted.

- Give a language model for them to listen to:
  T: *These things are always green: green paint, 'go' lights, pine trees.*
  These things are usually green: leaves, grass, ... etc.
- Organise the children into groups. The children help each other within their groups and practise this description. Go round and help them while they are working.
- Encourage individual children to describe their green items to the whole class.
- With the help of the children, write several of these descriptions on the board. The children work in their groups. They help each other to write a similar description for their own *green* items. Go round and help where necessary.
- For homework, ask the children to bring in *green items* for a *green corner* for the next lesson.

5 'Colours' bingo

Play bingo with the colours introduced at the beginning of the lesson.

- Ask all the pupils to draw four small squares in their exercise books. Display a variety of coloured crayons, pencils, felt tips, etc. Ask them to colour the squares they have drawn with any four colours of their choice from the colours you have displayed.
- Play bingo. Put the coloured items you displayed into a bag or box. When the pupils are ready, P1 picks out an item from the bag, and you call the colour out to the class. The winner is the first pupil to have all four of his/her colours called out. If you play more than one game, the first pupil to match his/her colours becomes the caller for a repeat game, and you become one of the bingo players.

6 Song: Ten green bottles

Finish the class with the action song *Ten green bottles:*
Ten green bottles, hanging on the wall,
Ten green bottles, hanging on the wall,
If one green bottle accidently falls.
There'll be nine green bottles hanging on the wall,
Nine green bottles hanging on the wall, ... etc.

- Play the cassette. Demonstrate the action of the bottles falling, and the number of bottles as the song progresses.
- Play the song line by line. The children demonstrate the action, and participate in the song as best they can.
- Play the cassette again. The children sing along as best they can. Make sure they demonstrate the action as they sing.

In the above examples, Coursebook A encourages the teacher to focus on the value of the language in the dialogue. The action game functions as a recreation activity, but seems to bear no relation to the language in the dialogue, or its theme, or the rest of the unit. Similarly, the song seems to have been added with language consolidation in mind, but at the expense of authenticity.

Furthermore, the resource file activities may well be impossible to use, due to the difficulty of fitting them into the class time available – and the pressure to complete the next page in the book.

Although it is possible to describe this type of lesson as *balanced,* since it does contain a variety of passive and more active activities, it seems that the balance is mainly artificial. It is achieved with little thought of continuity in terms of valid content for the children. Similarly, the unit could be described as *activity-based*, since there are indeed suggestions for activities such as *collecting green items.* Such activities, however, are not at the centre of the unit, nor will the achievement of the language aims depend on them.

In contrast, the lesson plan from Coursebook B seems to attempt to integrate the need for pace and variety with the overall *cross-curricular* objectives of the topic *green*:

The *group-dynamics activity* uses the growing of a seed into a plant. As well as encouraging *creative movement*, the content provides a link to the potential growing of (green) grass or mustard seeds as a later activity in the unit, or part of a larger L1 topic.

The main activity of drawing and sorting *green* items provides a cognitive challenge for most nine year olds, which is quite achievable at beginner level in terms of language. In language terms, it reinforces the concept of *always, usually, sometimes.*

The bingo game recycles the colours.

The song is another authentic link in the *green* chain.

In summary, a lesson should not only provide a balance of active and passive activities, it should also provide as balanced – and authentic – a content diet as is feasible within any particular teaching situation. The job of the teacher is to consider ways of providing this balance where it does not occur within a prescribed coursebook.

C   *Most authentic communication requires the teacher to
    adapt classroom space.*

There are major advantages to planning the most effective use of the classroom space available. These might include:
- facilitating authentic communication;
- providing a functional layout for practical work;
- facilitating social interaction;
- facilitating pupil-to-pupil help and support;
- encouraging a special atmosphere for the language class;
- raising motivation through the provision of a new space to work in;
- encouraging pupil motivation through involving them in the
  decision-making process for changes in classroom space.

However, changing and reorganising classroom space requires both time and energy. Teachers often give one or more of the following reasons for **not** moving desks and chairs:

The desks and chairs are in rows. They must be returned to their original position at the end of the lesson.

The floor is solid and transmits the sound of desks and chairs being moved or scraped to other classes, much to the annoyance of the teachers concerned.

The English teacher only teaches in the classroom three periods a week, for forty minutes in each period.

The classroom is used full time by the regular class teacher, who is very hostile to any classroom reorganisation.

Since both the teacher and the children are sharing the classroom space, it makes sense to explain to the pupils the reasons why any particular classroom layout should be changed or created. Involving pupils in the decision-making process provides high motivation for its execution. It also serves as a learning tool for the development of the children's spatial awareness. Through sharing the decision-making process, children can be encouraged and motivated to:

- reorganise the desks and chairs quickly and silently;
- respond without fuss to minimal prompts such as *Organise your desks and chairs for working in groups of five;*
- set out and return desks and chairs at the beginning and end of a lesson without teacher supervision.

On balance, time spent on classroom organisation, and spent on involving the children in the decision-making process, can more than compensate for the *convenience* of leaving things as they are.

D   *A child needs a lot of opportunity for review, recycling and consolidation of language.*

The pressure to complete a coursebook within a prescribed amount of time is common in the teaching situation. This pressure can provoke the teacher to make greater and greater demands on the children. This in turn will cause a greater and greater percentage of the children to fail, or to regard English as a chore. Indeed, quite often the stated objectives of the new National Curricula for English in the primary school across Europe and Asia are more modest than those of many current coursebooks.

Since coursebooks may be used within a school for several years, and are expensive acquisitions, teachers naturally want to make the best use of them. However, a coursebook that presents language in a structured and sequential manner assumes that once successfully tested, pupils are ready to learn more. It also implies that all pupils:

- learn at the same pace and in the same manner;
- are motivated to learn by the same content;
- will retain knowledge equally;
- will be able to transfer knowledge of language in one context to

another, and will therefore be able to use it to complete successive units.

Most practising teachers realise that such assumptions are not normally valid. The reality of the situation suggests that teaching may not equal learning, and that learning may be taking place, even though at any moment during a course children may be unable to repeat a complete sentence or pass a formal test.

Moreover, many teachers feel that children:
- should be allowed to assimilate language into the world as they know it, as well as through coursebook experiences and exercises;
- should be encouraged to develop their own learning strategies.

It therefore follows that a balance must be achieved between the aims of a coursebook and the needs of the children.

Coursebooks may certainly provide a strong framework and guidelines for learning content, but teachers should provide the flexibility for including review, recycling and consolidation activities if and when the need arises – and in contexts that children can relate to.

E A child needs to assimilate language at his or her own pace.

There is much external pressure on the children to produce language as quickly as possible, perhaps before they are ready to do so.
- Most coursebooks present a fixed language learning content to be achieved within a fixed time frame by the whole class.
- Teachers may feel threatened and insecure if the children in their class cannot display concrete evidence of being able to *speak* English.
- Parents may expect too much too soon in terms of results from their children. In other words, they want to hear their children speak English. This type of parent is perhaps also likely to make the most noise if such results are not achieved.

However, *repeating language formulae* or *responding mechanically to language stimuli* does not necessarily mean that language acquisition is taking place. Moreover, children may switch from an apparent unwillingness or inability to speak in English to a series of highly communicative utterances – if and when the appropriate interest/motivation is provided, and when they are *confident* enough to do so. Furthermore, not all parents want pressure applied to their children. A considerable percentage say that they are happy for their children to be *exposed* to English in a positive and supportive manner.

However, whatever their attitude, parents should be seen as partners in the learning process for their children. Support and involvement of the parents is essential to the success and ongoing motivation of the children in the class. Positive support can usually be

achieved through, at the very least, keeping parents informed of classroom activities, e.g. asking parents to:
- look at, comment on and sign completed work brought home by their child;
- share a story, a song or an exercise in English at home with their child;
- visit the classroom at any time to share in the fun and learning.

This will tend to minimise anxiety, misunderstanding and potential hostility. Such involvement will help to allow the children more space to assimilate language at their own pace. It will also foster the development of a healthy and balanced parent-teacher-child relationship.

F   *It is very important to recognise the value of errors and risk-taking in the process of learning of a language.*

Much of the history of EFL has been concerned with the need for language accuracy, i.e. language the pupils use that is mainly for display, to be assessed in terms of its accuracy of form by the teacher. This contrasts with language *fluency*, where language is being used for a purpose or as a means to an end, where the pupil is focusing on the outcome of the task, rather than the form which is being used. This has led to most teachers focusing mainly on the accurate production of linguistic patterns as opposed to encouraging pupils to express their personalities in the foreign language. If they are non-native speakers, this may be reflected in their insecurity about their own language skills. Consequently, they may over-compensate in terms of how they regard the importance of accuracy in language production.

In addition, the desire for accuracy may be driven by the future need to pass formal examinations. It may not arise from an objective evaluation of the importance of accuracy in early stages of children's acquisition of English. Experience in the classroom soon shows the great importance of allowing errors and risk-taking in the language learning process.

The language classroom usually requires children to produce spoken English at a very early stage. They may be asked to speak, in front of a competitive peer group, words, phrases, whole sentences that they are unsure of. This uncertainty may be related to a variety of language areas such as pronunciation, meaning, usage, intonation, stress and rhythm, etc. Mistakes and errors could therefore be regarded as the norm, as a positive part of the learning process, not the exception. Over-zealous correction of such errors by the teacher at too early a stage may encourage:
- reluctance to speak for fear of making a mistake;
- reluctance to take risks or experiment with language;

- fear of punishment;
- loss of self-image in front of peers and teacher;
- reliance on the teacher to provide the correct model;
- division of the class into those that *can* and those that *can't*;
- fear or dislike of learning English.

There are certainly times within a lesson when correct language models need to be given to a class, or to an individual, but it is not always necessary for the teacher to hear and comment on the result (or repetition). Pupils can be allowed the opportunity to try language out with others in the class in a non-threatening situation, such as by rehearsal within a group. The skill of the teacher is to achieve a balance between the importance of eventual accuracy against the value of encouraging the children to share their strengths and weaknesses with their peers. It is also important for teachers to show their class that they value a successful communicative event as well as an accurate and complete sentence.

Feedback

Follow your trainer's instructions.

5.3 Practical tasks and teaching plans

Starting points

- Work in a team of five or six and draw a cross-curricular *topic web* for the theme of *bridges and balances*. Highlight the part(s) of the web that you think you may complete in English. When you have finished, display and compare your topic web with those of other groups. (If you need help, refer to page 238 of the Resource file.)
- You are going to set up, work in and write teaching plans for one activity area or corner in your training classroom related to this theme of *bridges and balances*. Choose from:
  - a science corner for making a balance/scales for *weighing*;
  - a *bridge* reading corner for telling the story of *Billy Goats Gruff* (see page 268);
  - a *Billy Goats Gruff* roleplay area for a 'shadow puppet' performance;
  - a construction corner for the construction of a bridge.

Practical work

- As a first step, choose which area your group wants to work in (if feasible, ensure that all four activity areas are covered within the training group), and decide the materials and equipment you need. If these materials are not readily available, bring them to your next training session, and continue this activity at that time.

- When the materials have been collected, spend about 45 minutes working within your activity area. Discuss the practical work, and carry it out, e.g.
  - in the science area, make a *beam balance* and carry out *weighing activities*;
  - in the reading area, illustrate the *Billy Goats Gruff* story, then take turns to give an active reading of it to the rest of your group. If feasible, find and display other stories/rhymes/songs related to bridges;
  - in the roleplay area, make 'shadow puppets' using mini cut-outs of the characters (from card) attached to cocktail sticks, projecting them on an OHP; write a dialogue, then act it out;
  - in the construction area, plan and make a bridge. Test it for strength.

Creating a teaching plan for a practical task

- Each group then produces a teaching plan for using the practical task in a specified **language** class with younger learners. The main points to consider include:
  - the importance of creating a *balance* within your teaching plan;
  - the *language focus* that can be developed from the practical task, and how this may be achieved;
  - the organisation of the children, the space in the classroom and the time involved;
  - ensuring the teaching plan suits **your** teaching situation.
- Copy your teaching plan for other teachers in your training group, and spend time with them discussing how it might work in their teaching situation.

Reflection and feedback

Discuss the activity, following your trainer's instructions.

5.4 Practical task: making a 'lift the flap book' – Where's the troll?

Note: This activity assumes that the *Billy Goats Gruff* story has been read.

- You are going to produce a book to read to a group of seven-year-old children. Work in groups of five or six. Each teacher needs one sheet of A4 paper to draw on, and an additional half of an A4 sheet for the flap.
- Decide on:
  - six (illustratable) *Where's the troll?* questions, e.g.
    Is the troll under the log?
    Is the troll in the tree?
    Is the troll in the cave?
  - five *no* responses, e.g.
    No. *A snake is under the log.*
    No. *A giant spider is in the tree.*
    No. *A bear is in the cave.*
  - one *yes* response, e.g.
    Yes, the troll is under the bridge.
- Decide *who* will produce which page within your group. Prepare the pages, e.g.

- On the top half of the sheet draw a large log. Write the question *Is the troll under the log?* at the top of the picture.
- On the bottom half of the sheet draw a snake under the log.

- On the top of the *flap*, draw a large question mark (?).
- On the underside of the flap write *No. A snake is under the log.*
- Attach the flap so that it covers the snake under the log. The '?' is face up when the flap is closed.

● When the book is complete, bind it using staples or string. Discuss, first with your group, then with the whole training group, how this type of activity can be used:
  - in the language classroom;
  - to motivate children to *write* in English;
  - to encourage older children to write and read for younger children.

● Also discuss:
  - how this type of writing activity differs from typical writing activities in EFL coursebooks that you are familiar with;
  - at what age/stage you feel writing should be introduced into a language course.

5.5 Round-up activities

A) LONDON BRIDGE

● Work in a large group of about eight. Write the third verse for this rhyme, find a tune for it and sing it to the rest of the training group:
London bridge is falling down, falling down, falling down.
London bridge is falling down, my fair lady.

Build it up with bricks and stones, bricks and stones, bricks and stones.
Build it up with bricks and stones, my fair lady.

B) BRIDGE RACE

● Follow your trainer's instructions.

6 Storytelling, comprehension, errors and correction

6.1 Starting points

Group-dynamics activity (action game)

Growing from a seed to a plant.
Follow your trainer's instructions to play an action game. Use the script on page 193 if necessary.

Producing your own action game

Work in groups of four or five. You are going to use the story *Jack and the Beanstalk* (see page 267) as a central theme for this unit. The action game script you have just used introduces and provides a link with the themes of *growing* and *height*. Discuss the task with your group, and write an alternative short action game script that matches or integrates with *Jack and the Beanstalk*. Assume you are writing for eight/nine-year-old children who have had one year of English.
- Try out your action game, then compare it with those written by other groups.

6.2 Storytelling and comprehension

Introduction

Sit with a partner and share the reading of the following text. From your own experience/beliefs, discuss additions, changes or provisos to the text that you would like to make.

Storytelling and reading

Reading is much more than finding out what happens next in a story, or being able to answer comprehension questions related to a piece of text. From the age of three or four years old, children are developing their identity as *readers*, and it is vitally important that we, as teachers and parents, support this development. In terms of this support, the following statements about reading should be carefully considered:

- Reading is a quest for meaning which requires children to be active participants in the construction of meaning.
- Readers learn about reading **by** reading. Children become readers by being fully involved in books, in comics and magazines, in text on a computer screen, with texts of **all** kinds – and by getting joy and satisfaction from reading.
- Both independent and shared reading are vital for the development of children as readers.
- Children need to be exposed to many kinds of writing. However, an active involvement with literature is essential. Literature has a social and emotional value that is a vital part of its role in the development of children's language and literacy.

In practical classroom terms, therefore, what are we doing to support and encourage children as *readers*? What, if anything, should we change? Could we do it better?

Reading comprehension

As language teachers, we often regard the teaching of reading to imply a variety of comprehension activities, most of which:
- require one predetermined response;
- focus on word or structure content of a small section of the text;
- require the children to work out the 'answer' individually;
- depend on the skill of the children to carry out a word/text prediction, search or recall;
- *check* comprehension, rather than *teach* it.

Yet the above activities do not seem to encourage children to make a contribution as a *creative* individual to the reading of, or listening to a story. Such activities often discourage children from sharing their responses with others in the class. Indeed, many children learn the *skill* of how to find the answer the *teacher wants* without the need to understand or become involved with the text. In other words, while reading comprehension tasks may develop an ability to analyse text for a test, they may actively **discourage** children from becoming *readers* of English.

Consider, for example, the following opening paragraph of the story of *Jack and the Beanstalk*:

Once upon a time there was a boy called Jack. He lived with his mother in a little house. They were very, very poor. They had one old cow and two old hens.

When teachers are invited to suggest questions they would ask their pupils about this text, the following are often mentioned:
What is (was) the boy's name?

Who does (did) Jack live with?
Are (were) they rich or poor?
What animals do (did) they have?
Does (did) Jack have two cows and three hens? etc.

The above questions seem to reflect the way we, as students, were taught reading, and therefore the way we may teach reading. However, such questions assume that children are empty vessels who bring nothing of themselves to a story. Moreover, imagine how we would feel if we were asked by a potential reader of our favourite book questions such as:
What are the names of the people in your favourite book?
Were they rich or poor?
What possessions do they have?
Do they have one car or two cars?, etc.

Constructive and creative comprehension

When children read or listen to a story, in terms of comprehension/ response, we can say that there are four main types of mental processes involved:
Picturing and imaging. Children create a mental picture of what they are reading or listening to.
Predicting and recalling. Children imagine or predict what is going to happen next, or relate what has happened previously to what is taking place.
Identification and personalising. Children identify with, or relate to, the characters and situations in the story according to their own personal experiences.
Making value judgements. Children apply their own values to those encountered in the story.
The results of each of these four processes are unique to the individual child. Therefore, if children are encouraged to express their ideas in these areas, a creative *partnership* between the child and the story can be developed. In this case, the child's response:
- is not pre-determined, and demonstrates individual interpretation. It is not a simple repetition or direct extraction from the text;
- relates to the *whole* story, and not only to discrete words or small sections;
- may involve the use of alternative means of communication to speech and writing, such as drawing, construction or mime;
- can be discussed, shared and developed with other children in the class.

Referring once more to the extract from *Jack and the Beanstalk,* consider the children's response to the following questions:
How old is Jack? How tall is he? What colour hair/eyes does he have?

Jack and his mother are poor. Draw a plan of their house. Describe it.
What do you think they eat for breakfast/lunch/dinner?
Who feeds the animals? What do Jack's animals eat every day?

The above type of question stimulates a *creative and constructive partnership* between the text and the children. Moreover, with respect to the language classroom, such questions invite responses which have a clearly defined language focus, and which are accessible (through drawing, key word answer, etc.) to beginner level children, as well as the more experienced pupil. Perhaps, most important of all, they take the children back as **readers** into the whole story without the need to focus mechanically on specific parts of the text.

Storytelling – Jack and the Beanstalk

- Sit in a semicircle with the rest of your training group. Make yourself comfortable. Your trainer will read you the story of *Jack and the Beanstalk*.
- Next, work with a partner. Read this list of comprehension questions. Sort them into two categories:

Questions which have only one 'right' answer.	**Questions which encourage the listener/reader to 'construct' his/her own meaning from the text.**

1 Was Jack rich or poor?
2 Draw and describe Jack's house.
3 What colour was Jack's cow?
4 How many beans did Jack get?
5 How tall was the giant? What size shoes did he wear?
6 What did Jack do when he heard the giant coming?
7 How much does one golden egg weigh? How much money is it worth?
8 How did Jack escape from the giant? What happened to the giant?
9 What did Jack's mother buy with one golden egg?
10 What did the giant say when he chased Jack?
11 Jack and his mother lived happ ....
12 You have a hen that lays golden eggs. What would you do?

Feedback

- With your partner:
  1 Agree which of the above questions you usually associate with reading/listening comprehension in TEFL. Discuss the possible teaching aims of questions 1, 4, 6, 8, 10 and 11.
  2 Discuss the possible teaching aims of questions 2, 3, 5, 7, 9 and 12,

and whether these aims are achievable in the *language* classroom with children.

3 Write similar questions for the *Billy Goats Gruff* story (page 268) and *Incy Wincy Spider* (page 147).

- Share your questions and your viewpoints with other pairs in the training group, e.g.

Can you think of ways of improving/changing the comprehension questions **you** usually ask in your teaching?

If available, look at an EFL reading text for children. Can you improve the comprehension questions listed in the text?

Summary

As teachers of English, it is our responsibility to prepare our pupils for the analytical reading comprehension questions they will be asked throughout their years as students of English.

As teachers of children, it is also our responsibility to show our pupils that we value them as *readers*. In this respect, it is vital to offer a balance of reading activities, some of which encourage a creative and constructive partnership with the text, and involve the experience and interests of the individual child.

And finally, as literate adults, we should always keep in mind that we never stop learning to read.

For further background information on reading (and writing) refer to the Resource file, Section C, pages 246-56.

6.3 Practical tasks

- Work in a team of five or six. Draw a cross-curricular topic web for the theme of *growing*. Highlight the part(s) of the web that you think you may complete in English. (If you need help, refer to page 239 of the Resource file.) When you have finished, display and compare your topic web with those of other groups.
- Stay in your team. You are going to set up, work in and write teaching plans for **one** activity area or corner in your training classroom related to the theme of *growing and height*. Choose from the chart on the next page, or use it as a guide.

Subject area/activity	Equipment needed includes
Physical education (PE): you will be working outside on running, stretching and timing activities	Tape measure, stop-watch, string
An art and craft area: you will be making a beanstalk, and leaf collage	Leaves, paints, aprons, glue, Sellotape, sheets of white and coloured paper, string
A puppet/roleplay area: you will be making puppets from paper plates, and re-enacting *Jack and the Beanstalk*	Paper plates, rods/sticks, Sellotape, crayons, felt tip pens, scissors
A science corner: you will be growing a variety of seeds and recording your results	Jars, seeds, soil, water, filter paper
A technology corner: you will be collecting/making *giant* objects and devising ways to wrap/contain them	*Giant* objects, (wrapping) paper, card, Sellotape, glue, stapler, ruler/tape measure
A maths corner: you will be measuring (estimating) the height of trees and tall buildings	Rulers, graph paper, tape measures, string, etc.

- As a first step, choose the area your group wants to work in (if feasible, ensure that four of the six activity areas suggested above are covered within the training group), and decide on the equipment you need.
- When the materials have been collected, spend about 45 minutes working within your activity area. As in Unit 5 (page 79), discuss the practical work, and carry it out.
- When you have finished, produce a teaching outline that incorporates the practical task you have completed. Write your outline for a specific **language** class (in terms of age and language ability) with younger learners. The main points to consider include the following:

1 The *language focus* that can be developed from the practical task (see examples below), and how this may be achieved.

   Example language focus for areas:
   a) Maths area: _____ is _____ metres high or _____ is taller than _____.
   b) PE area: *I can run* _____ *metres in* _____ *seconds. I can reach* _____ *metres.*
   c) Puppet area dialogue:
   Mum: *Sell the cow, Jack.*
   Jack: *OK, Mum.*
   Old man: *Take these five magic beans.*
   Jack: *Thank you. Take the cow.*
   Mum: *Five beans! You stupid boy.*
   Jack: *Ouch!!!*

d) Art and craft: *How many leaves are there? What colours are they? Which is the biggest leaf? Which is the smallest leaf? How high is the beanstalk?*

2 The stages within the teaching outline:
Example stages from an activity-based teaching outline:
group-formation activity
teaching new words
action game incorporating the new words
review *Jack and the Beanstalk*: storytelling
practical task
language focus
review game
round-up activity

3 The time involved, e.g. can your teaching outline be completed in one, two, three or four(+) fifty-minute lessons?
  • Also consider:
    – the importance of creating a balance of activities within your teaching outline;
    – the organisation of the children and the space in the classroom;
    – the relevance of the outline to **your** teaching situation.
  • Copy your teaching outline for other teachers in your training group, and spend time with them discussing how it might work in **their** teaching situation.

6.4 An 'errors and correction' beanstalk

• Stay in your group. You are going to make an *'errors beanstalk'*.

Introduction

For a/the language focus you chose in the activity above:
– discuss, predict and list the likely *errors* that **your** pupils (i.e. young learners of English) might make;
– say *how/if* you will correct these errors.
• Consider if young learners are likely to:
  – make more/fewer errors than adults;
  – require a different approach to correction than adult learners.

Action

• Make the 'stem' for the *beanstalk* using string, wool or twisted paper. Use green paper and cut out leaves of various sizes.
• Write the *errors* you have listed on each of the leaves. Use the size of

the leaf to indicate the importance of the error. Write the most important/serious errors on the biggest leaves. Write minor errors on the smallest leaves. Attach the leaves to the beanstalk.

- While you are working, your trainer will prepare a similar beanstalk. The leaves on his/her beanstalk deal with the following issues:
  if to correct
  why to correct
  when to correct
  what to correct
  how to correct
  who should do the correcting
- When you are ready, follow your trainer's instructions.

6.5 Errors and correction: how it feels to correct and be corrected

How it feels as a learner

- Your trainer (or, if feasible, one of your training group) will say a sentence in L3 (a new language). Take turns to repeat after the trainer and to say this sentence in front of the rest of the group. Your trainer will correct you.
- Your trainer will say another sentence. Repeat the sentence in chorus with the rest of your training group. Your trainer may then choose you to repeat the sentence on your own in front of the rest of the group.
- Stand with a partner. Your trainer will say another sentence. Take turns with your partner to say this sentence to each other. Help and support and correct your partner if necessary.
- Stand in a group of four or five. Work as a team with your group. Your trainer is going to say another sentence in L3, which you will need to produce accurately. Before this happens, discuss and plan your learning/error correction strategies with your team. Inform your trainer of your strategy so that he/she may present the sentence in the appropriate manner.

How you feel as a teacher

- Work in a group of four or five.
  Underline the correction techniques (below) that you associate with your teaching.
  Extend the list with other correction techniques that you are familiar with.
  Discuss the techniques **you** find most effective and give your reasons.
  Correction techniques
  Repeat individually after me.

Everybody repeat after me. (in a choral drill)
*I'll write the word/phrase on the board, then say it and ask everybody
to repeat after me.*
Listen to me but don't repeat. (I'll ask you again later.)
*Listen to me then rehearse with a partner or group. (I'll listen to you
later.)*
*Watch the way I move my mouth and where I put my tongue. You try
it.*
A phonetic correction approach, using a chart or fingers.
No immediate correction given. (*I'll repeat/teach the correct form to
the class at an appropriate time later in the lesson.*)

Feedback

Individual children respond differently to correction by a teacher.
Examine this list of stages in a teaching unit:
group-dynamics activity
presentation of new vocabulary
action game
presentation of a new structure or function
pairwork on a two/four-line dialogue
groupwork on a two/four-line dialogue
practical work
roleplay
guided language practice stage
communicative practice stage
language games
extension (free practice) stage

For each of the above stages, discuss with your group which correction
techniques might bring about the following responses/reactions in young
learners:
a sense of failure
a sense of achievement and value
'risk-taking' and experimentation with new language
use of 'safe and simple' language
silence/lack of response
uncertainty as to whether he/she is correct
confidence
dependency on the teacher
mispronunciation
improvement of pronunciation
fluency
accuracy
hesitation
self-correction

- When you have finished, share your comments with the rest of your training group.

6.6 Round-up activity: chant – *Fee, fi, fo, fum*

- Read the chant from *Jack and the Beanstalk* again:
  Fee, fi, fo, fum,
  I smell the blood of an Englishman.
  Be he alive or be he dead,
  I'll grind his bones to make my bread.
  Note: The pronunciation of *Fee, fi, fo, fum* is /fiːfaɪfəʊfʌm/
- Work in a group of up to six. Decide on a suitable rhythm and stress for this chant. When ready, make space for your group. Say the chant loudly (as a giant) while walking around this space. Use exaggerated facial and body expressions to put across the *feeling* of the chant as you move.

7 Classroom management and organisation

7.1 Starting points

'Bear' group formation

A) ROUND AND ROUND ...

Stand in a circle and take the right hand of the person standing on your left. Draw and enact with your finger the following *bear rhyme* on the palm of your partner's hand. (The phrase *tiddledee* /tɪdliːdiː/ *under there* is enacted by trying to tickle under your partner's arm.)
Round and round the island, like a teddy bear,
One step, two steps, a tiddledee under there.

B) THIS LITTLE BEAR ...

Work with a partner. Enact the following *bear rhyme*.

T1 in each pair holds his/her partner's (T2's) left hand. For each line in the rhyme, T1 holds, pulls and wiggles one different finger (= *little bear*) of T2's left hand.

For 'WEEEEEE' *and ran all the way home* T1 *runs* his/her fingers up T2's arm, ending with a tickle under T2's arm!
This little bear went to Treasure Island,
This little bear stayed at home,
This little bear had honey,
This little bear had none,
This little bear said 'WEEEEEE' and ran all the way home.

C) THE BEAR IS IN HIS DEN

- Work in teams of six or seven. T1 is the bear. The remaining Ts:
  - form a small circle around the bear;
  - hold hands and walk clockwise around the bear singing Verse 1;
  - reverse direction for Verse 2, and circle the bear anticlockwise while singing the verse. (T1 growls during this verse.)
- For Verse 3, Ts stand in a circle around the bear, *stroking* the bear gently as they sing the verse.
  1 The bear is in his den, the bear is in his den.
  Eee ay addio the bear is in his den.

2 *The bear starts to growl. Grrr. The bear starts to growl. Grrr.*
   Eee ay addio the bear starts to growl.
3 *We all stroke the bear. We all stroke the bear.*
   Eee ay addio we all stroke the bear.
Note: *Eee ay addio* is pronounced /iːaɪædɪəʊ/.

7.2 Seating arrangements in the classroom

Looking at your training space

- As a starting activity for this topic, work collaboratively with three others. Use a sheet of graph paper or make a copy of page 269 (to represent your training classroom) and page 270 (to represent your classroom furniture). Cut out the shapes of classroom furniture, adding to them if necessary. Arrange this furniture in various ways, e.g.
    - to create a working space for physical activities and roleplay;
    - to create working surfaces for groups of six to work together on a craft activity;
    - to create a comfortable space for a storytelling activity;
    - to rearrange the furnishing to fit in twenty per cent more (or less) furniture.

  Compare your solutions with those of other groups in the room. Are you happy with the present layout of your training room? If not, change it.

Looking at your teaching space

- Work with a partner or small group. Look at the following seating arrangements and list of teaching statements/purposes.
- Under each seating arrangement, write four or five statements/purposes from the list that best match the seating arrangement. (Some statements obviously apply to more than one seating arrangement. However, for the purpose of this activity you may only use each statement **once**.)

Seating arrangements

Class in rows. Teacher at front of class.

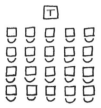

Class in a horseshoe/U-shape, seats behind the desks. Teacher at the front centre of the U.

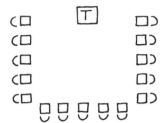

Class in a horseshoe/U-shape, desks against the wall, seats in the space created by moving the desks against the wall. Teacher at the front centre of the U, or mobile.

Class in circle or diamond shape. Teacher in the circle/diamond.

Class in groups of five or six. Groups in space in the classroom. Teacher mobile or at a selected place in the room.

Class in pairs. Teacher mobile or at a selected place in the room.

Teaching purpose/lesson phase

Facilitates large/whole group discussion

Allows for several different activities to take place at the same time

Encourages interaction between children

Facilitates child-initiated dialogue practice

Creates the impression of the teacher as an equal in the group

Facilitates roleplay and game playing

Facilitates introduction of new material

Makes it easy to attract all the children's attention

Encourages peer teaching and sharing of information

Encourages social interaction among the children

Encourages P–P interaction within language practice activities

Facilitates P–P communication in a whole-class discussion/activity

Useful for formal testing

Useful when all the children are doing the same thing at the same time

Facilitates a wide range of communicative activities

Facilitates the playing of communicative games

Facilitates the handling of children who finish early or allows for remedial work within the class

Facilitates the planning and practice of roleplays

Provides an informal setting for feedback on an activity or task

Useful for choral work

Facilitates the use of self-access materials

Facilitates the demonstration of new visual aids, such as flashcards

- Finally, explain to your partner/group which classroom seating arrangement **you** use most or least often.

7.3 Classroom management: storytelling as a starting point

- Work in groups of six or seven. One of the group takes the role of *teacher* (T). The remainder take the role of seven- to nine-year-old pupils (Ps).
- T gives an active reading of the story (script below), encouraging the Ps to participate. This can be done by asking Ps to take the roles of the main characters **and** their possessions, e.g. 'Daddy Bear' is also assigned the roles of Daddy Bear's bowl, chair and bed. 'Mummy Bear' and 'Baby Bear' are assigned similar roles. This will encourage lots of fun and active participation throughout the storytelling.
- Change the storyteller and repeat this step.

Goldilocks and the Three Bears
Once upon a time there were three bears: Daddy Bear, Mummy Bear and Baby Bear. The bears lived in a big wooden house in the middle

of a big forest. One day Daddy Bear made the breakfast. He made lots and lots of hot, delicious porridge. He poured the porridge into three bowls: a little bowl for Baby Bear, a medium-sized bowl for Mummy Bear and a big bowl for Daddy Bear.

The three bears sat at the table. 'Ouch,' said Baby Bear, 'My porridge is too hot.' 'Ouch,' said Mummy Bear, 'My porridge is too hot.' 'Ouch,' said Daddy Bear, 'My porridge is too hot. Let's go for a walk. We can eat our porridge later.' So the three bears put on their hats and coats and they went for a walk.

Five minutes later a girl called Goldilocks went to the bears' house. She knocked on the front door. Rat-a-tat-tat. No one answered. Goldilocks looked through the windows. She saw three bowls of hot, delicious porridge. She was very hungry. She opened the door and went in. Goldilocks went to the table. She picked up Daddy Bear's bowl and tasted the porridge. Ouch. Too hot. Then she picked up Mummy Bear's bowl and tasted the porridge. Yukk. Too sweet. Then she picked up Baby Bear's bowl and tasted the porridge. Yumm. Just right. And Goldilocks ate Baby Bear's porridge. Yumm.

Now, Goldilocks looked around. She saw three chairs: Daddy Bear's chair, Mummy Bear's chair and Baby Bear's chair. She sat on Daddy Bear's chair. Ouch. Too hard. Then she sat on Mummy Bear's chair. Oooof. Too soft. Then she sat on Baby Bear's chair. She broke it. Oh dear! Then Goldilocks went upstairs. She saw three beds: Daddy Bear's bed, Mummy Bear's bed and Baby Bear's bed. She jumped on Daddy Bear's bed. Ouch. Too hard. Then she jumped on Mummy Bear's bed. Oooof. Too soft. Then she jumped on Baby Bear's bed. Aaah. Just right. And Goldilocks lay down on Baby Bear's bed. She went to sleep.

Five minutes later the bears came home. They were very hungry. They sat at the table. Daddy Bear looked at his porridge. 'Someone's been eating my porridge,' he said. Mummy Bear looked at her porridge. 'Someone's been eating **my** porridge,' she said. Baby Bear looked at his porridge. 'Someone's been eating **my** porridge,' he said, 'And it's all gone!' Baby Bear started to cry. 'It's all gone. It's all gone.'

The three bears looked around. 'Someone's been sitting on my chair,' said Daddy Bear. 'Someone's been sitting on **my** chair,' said Mummy Bear. 'Someone's been sitting on **my** chair,' said Baby Bear, 'And it's broken.' Baby Bear started to cry. 'It's broken. It's broken.' The three bears went upstairs. 'Someone's been lying on my bed,' said Daddy Bear. 'Someone's been lying on **my** bed,' said Mummy Bear. 'Someone's been lying on **my** bed,' said Baby Bear, 'And here she is, fast asleep.'

Goldilocks woke up with a jump. She opened her eyes. She saw three bears. They GROWLED. Goldilocks jumped off the bed. She ran downstairs. She ran to the front door. She opened the door and ran into the forest. And Goldilocks ran away. She never came back again. And the three bears? What do you think?

- When ready, work in a team of five or six. Draw a cross-curricular topic web for the theme of *Goldilocks and the Three Bears*. Highlight the part(s) of the web that you think you may complete in English. (If you need help, refer to page 240 in the Resource file.) When you have finished, display and compare your topic web with those of other groups.

7.4 Organisation of the teaching space in your classroom

- Use sheets of graph paper or make seven copies of page 269 (classroom grid) and an additional copy of page 270 (classroom furniture). Cut out the furniture items and add to them as necessary, in order to be able to experiment more easily with different layouts.
- Work with a partner. Design alternative classroom layouts for twenty or thirty children (according to your usual class size) for the following activities related to *Goldilocks and the Three Bears*:
  storytelling
  practical work, working in groups of four or five
  pair practice for language points
  choral drill practice
  learning a new chant or song
- Join up with another pair of teachers:
  Share ideas and agree on appropriate layouts.
  Discuss practical ways of making **your** classroom organisation more effective for the work **you** do with your pupils.
  Glue the classroom furniture onto the grids to show your finally agreed layouts for the above activities. Share your group's ideas with those of other groups.
- Stay in your teams. You are going to set up, work in and write a teaching outline for one activity area or *work station* in your training classroom related to the theme of *Goldilocks and the Three Bears*. Choose from or use the following as a guide:
  A *listening or storytelling area:* Work as a team and illustrate the story on eight or nine OHP transparencies. Write the key lines under each illustration. Use these illustrations, and take turns to give an active reading of it to the rest of the group in the reading corner.
  A *writing area:* Write an illustrated letter of apology from Goldilocks to Baby Bear, a newspaper article for the *Bear Times*, or Baby Bear's diary entry for the event and the next day.
  A *construction area:* Plan and make furniture for the bears' home or make a bed to fit Baby Bear.
  A *home area:* Plan and make bear food. Write recipes for the food you make.

As a starting guide, consider the following materials/equipment in your plans:

For storytelling

carpet squares, cushions, pillows, shoe boxes, glue, Sellotape, soft material, scraps of wool, paper bags (for paper bag puppets) and other realia linked to the *Goldilocks and the Three Bears* story, copies of *Goldilocks and the Three Bears* books

For writing

pens, pencils, felt tips, brushes, OHP transparencies and pens, paper of various types, colours and sizes

For construction

shoe boxes, other boxes or cartons, scraps of string, wool, scissors, glue, Sellotape, Blu-tack, pieces of cloth of various colours, straws, small rods

For the home corner

recipes for porridge and rice pudding, ingredients for porridge/bear food, ingredients for honey sandwiches, bowls, spoons, paper plates, knives, forks

- As a first step, choose the work station your group wants to work in (if feasible, ensure that more than one of the activity areas suggested above are covered within the training group), and decide on the equipment you need.

- When the materials have been collected, spend about 45 minutes within your activity area. As in the previous two units, discuss the practical work, and carry it out.

- As in Stage 3 of Unit 6 (page 85), each group then produces a teaching outline for using the practical task in a specified **language** class with younger learners. As before, the main points to consider include:
  - the organisation of the children, the space in the classroom and the time involved;
  - the importance of creating a balance within your teaching outline;
  - ensuring the teaching outline suits **your** teaching situation;
  - the language focus that can be developed from the practical task, and how this may be achieved.

Note: In any given practical task, it is likely that 15–25% of the children:
- may find it too easy and will finish early;
- may find it too difficult, and give up early.

Any teaching plan should therefore have provisions for these children. For the talented children, the following might be considered:

self-access corner

additional tasks

own tasks (negotiated beforehand)

And for the less able children:

individual attention

team work, sharing work with more able team members

own tasks or targets (negotiated beforehand).

7.5 Management of time

Introduction

- Work individually. Write your own responses to the following points and questions:
  1 What makes the greatest demand on your time? Is it possible to get rid of, or share (with parents, other teachers, children) some of this demand?
  2 What puts you under pressure with respect to time? Is there any practical way of relieving this pressure or improving the situation?
  3 Do you invite other adults or older students/teenagers to help you? If so, do they know what is expected of them?
  4 Do you have regular meetings with other teachers, or with teachers from other schools to share ideas and problems?
  5 Does your school organisation support your classroom organisation? Are there ways in which they could support you further?
- Estimate how you spend your class, and class related time. How much time in each lesson is *effective learning* time? If feasible and appropriate, keep a diary and record how your time is spent. Record this information on a pie chart or similar. Compare it with that of other teachers. Share ideas on how to improve your use of time.

Your suggestions

- Next, work with a partner. Share ideas, look at and, where possible, complete the *suggestions* columns in the following chart. You may also add other *time eaters* that you feel are important.

Time eaters	Best suggestion for saving time	Other suggestions for saving time
Registration	Children take the register	Self registration
Late arrivals	Have a 'late arrivals' desk	
Classroom reorganisation	Train children to do this	
Too many new words to teach		
Taking out and putting away materials		
Preparing materials for practical work		
Preparing teaching aids		
A few low-ability children in the class		
Missing items or materials		

Time eaters	Best suggestion for saving time	Other suggestions for saving time
Review and consolidation		
Tests and marking them		
Copying/writing		
Correcting homework		
Lots of cutting and sticking		
Complex practical tasks		

7.6 Management of children

Reading and writing task

- Work in a group of five or six. Complete the following challenge:
  Read and share comments on the following passage.
  Make some flashcards for 'important classroom/training room rules'.
  Make a large, (humorously) illustrated visual aid called 'Management of children'.

Introduction to managing children

Teachers who have extensive previous experience working with adults or teenagers may lack the years of training, both practical and theoretical, that the primary teacher will have gained through formal study and classroom practice. Those who are working with younger learners for the first time need much support and guidance with respect to managing children. There is a fear of *losing control*. There is uncertainty with respect to how to handle difficult pupils, who, for example, may be disruptive or over-active. Certainly, many of the techniques and attitudes associated with traditional EFL methodology for adults and young adults may not be relevant to misbehaviour on the part of the younger learner – or to the motivation of bored children. Managing children requires the teacher to look at the learning needs of children, and to make sure that these needs are put first.

Priorities

As mentioned in the reading task in Unit 2 of this book, a key priority for teachers is to establish a good relationship with children, and to encourage them to do the same with their classmates. Children who are treated negatively tend to adopt negative behaviour. Similarly, those who are treated positively tend to become positive. Many problems of misbehaviour arise through children seeking attention. Such attention-seeking may be the result of a lack of love at home, insecurity, a sense of worthlessness – rather than a feeling of superiority or over-confidence.

Guidelines to classroom control

The chart below illustrates some of the general issues involved in the day-to-day management of children.

Example factors you can control or improve	Example factors you can't control
Classroom space	The weather
Space for display	Natural abilities or disabilities
Lesson content	The children's previous experience
Lesson pace	Classroom size and furniture
Variety of content	Outside noise
Motivation of the class	The children's home environment
Rules for behaviour	An imposed coursebook
Involving children in decision-making processes	
Fairness in class	
Mutual respect	
Group dynamics/relationships within the class	

While the above chart outlines some of the global factors involved in day-to-day classroom management, inexperienced teachers often ask for solutions to more immediate classroom issues related to the management of children (i.e. classroom control) within a lesson. The following is a list of ideas:

A) GETTING THE CHILDREN'S ATTENTION

- Establish an *attention-getting code*, e.g. when you raise your right hand, or clap, or sound a horn, everyone must stop what they are doing and look at you. Do not speak until there is silence.
- Give a short series of action game (or *Simon says*) type instructions, e.g. *Everyone touch your left knee with your right hand. Good. Now close your right eye and stand on your left leg.*
- Cough or fold your arms and give a *heavy look* at the class.
- Walk up to a noisy child or group and start talking quietly to them.

B) MAINTAINING A FAIRLY LOW NOISE LEVEL

- Make *silence* flashcards. These can contain a picture, the word *Silence* or both picture and word. Such cards can be used by the teacher, or by children when they want to speak, or they feel the noise level is too high.
- Always speak **quietly**. Do not raise your voice above the noise in order to get quiet in the room. Instead, make eye contact with noise offenders, or call their names in a normal voice. Children will hear their names even in a noisy room.
- Culture permitting, place a hand gently on a child's head or shoulder.

C) CALMING A CLASS DOWN

- Do a relaxation activity. You may play *relaxation music* such as Baroque music (build up a favourite relaxation music collection) during these activities, e.g.
  Children sit with eyes closed and relax, then tense, then relax each part of the body that you name.
  Give instructions for deep breathing.
  Play the *melting snowman* game. The children imagine they are a freezing snowman in the sun. They gradually melt (relax) as they get warm.
- Use a calming gesture (both hands and arms). Wait till the class is quiet, then do a relaxation activity.
- Have a *time-out* cushion, or chair. Any child may be sent to, or may go to, this chair to take *time out* for one minute. While on the chair, he/she is not allowed to communicate or take part in other class activities. The teacher may also sit on this chair to calm down. (**Note:** This is **not** a punishment chair.)
- Stop the activity, and introduce a new activity that provides a change of pace or focus.
- Ask for complete quiet for two minutes. Get the children to *draw* the sounds they can hear. After the period of silence, they may then explain the sounds they have drawn to a partner.

D) DEVELOPING RESPONSIBLE BEHAVIOUR

- Negotiate with the children and write an agreed *behaviour contract* for the whole class. Include **yourself** in this contract. You may re-negotiate specific terms with individual children if you feel this is productive.
- Notice when the children are being good. Support a disruptive child by praising even the most minor of good actions. Build up a list of positive statements about such children, rather than focusing on their negative behaviour.

- Produce illustrated (and humorous) *classroom rules*, created and drawn by the children themselves. Display them in the class. Point or refer specific children to them when the need arises. Renew them at regular intervals with new posters or signs.

However, the provision of an *ideas list* on how to manage children is only a small part of an effective solution. Experience working in the teaching situation has demonstrated that good classroom management/control is developed through a *process*, and not by merely following a *recipe list*. This process includes elements such as:
- the sharing of management ideas with other teachers;
- criticial discussion with other teachers;
- support and feedback on classroom performance;
- team teaching;
- trying new management approaches and assessing them;
- involving the children in key issues that affect their learning.

Your teaching

- As a next step, work with four or five other teachers. Read the following list of phrases:
  encouraging good class relationships
  punishment of a child for bad behaviour
  firm, kind and supportive
  unfair
  sending out of class
  positive comments
  working co-operatively in teams
  ridicule of a naughty child
  'time-out' chair
  mixed-ability groups
  sharing decision-making with children
  awarding prizes for good behaviour
  tests followed by a grading list
  strict
  whole-class punishment
  notice the child being good
  negative comments
  displaying and valuing children's work
  written tasks for misbehaviour
  streaming
  a *behaviour contract*
  desks in rows
- Decide which of these phrases you associate with **your** teaching. Share ideas with your group. Add other key words or phrases to this list.
- Delete the words and phrases you wish to remove from your management of children.

Observation and feedback

Where feasible, visit teachers in class, or watch videos of classroom practice. Note points of class and child management and organisation. After your first observation, discuss with other members of your training group and design/develop an *observation sheet* that highlights key classroom and children management issues that you feel are important to observe and comment on. You can refer to the example observation sheet on pages 272-3, but adapt it as necessary to suit your situation.

7.7 Round-up activity: bear rhymes and games

● Work in one of three teams:

Team A
Choose a leader (T1) for each verse. T1 leads the rest of the team in the reading and acting out of *The Bear Hunt*.

The Bear Hunt
We're all going on a bear hunt. I'm not scared. I've got my torch in my hand, penknife too. Oh-oh. What's that? Long grass. I can't go round it. I can't go under it. I can't go over it. I have to run through it. Swish, swish, swish, swish.

We're all going on a bear hunt. I'm not scared. I've got my torch in my hand, penknife too. Oh-oh. What's that? Deep mud. I can't go round it. I can't go under it. I can't go over it. I have to walk through it.

We're all going on a bear hunt. I'm not scared. I've got my torch in my hand, penknife too. Oh-oh. What's that? A river. I can't go round it. I can't go under it. I can't go over it. I have to swim across it.

We're all going on a bear hunt. I'm not scared. I've got my torch in my hand, penknife too. Oh-oh. What's that? A high mountain. I can't go through it. I can't go under it. I can't go round it. I have to climb over it. Up, up, up, up ...

We're all going on a bear hunt. I'm not scared. I've got my torch in my hand, penknife too. Oh-oh. What's that? A dark cave. I can't go over it. I can't go under it. I can't go round it. I have to tip-toe into it. Creep, creep, creep, creep.

*We're all going on a bear hunt. I'm not scared. I've got my torch in my hand, penknife too. Oh-oh. What's that? Big wet nose. Big round eyes. Long soft fur. Long sharp teeth. Long sharp claws. Help ... it's a bear! Out of the cave. Over the mountain. Across the river. Through the mud. Through the long grass ... We're all going on **another** bear hunt ...*

Team B
Read this chant, then create a tune and sing it:
Milky porridge hot.
Milky porridge cold.
Milky porridge in the pot, nine days old.
I like it hot.
You like it cold.
S/he (Maria, Mario, etc.) likes it in the pot, nine days old.

Team C
Play and say *The bear is sleeping.*
It's winter. The bear is sleeping. The bear is snoring. The snow is softly falling, falling. The little animals are eating, eating ...
It's spring. Now the sun is shining. The snow is melting. Splish, Splosh. Slowly, slowly the bear is ... waking ... UP!
T1 is the bear. The bear curls up tightly and pretends to be asleep. The remainder of the group are little animals that search for food around, and as close to the bear as they dare – sometimes gently touching the bear. The little animals say the rhyme as they move around the bear.
The bear slowly stretches according to the content of each line in the rhyme. The bear (not the little animals) suddenly says the last word *UP* in the rhyme and tries to catch one or more of the little animals as he/she says the word.
Repeat the activity several times with new bears and new little animals.

- When you have finished, demonstrate and teach your rhyme/song/game to the other two teams.

8 Visual and other teaching aids

8.1 Starting points

A) THE WITCH IS IN HER CAVE

(A Hallowe'en version of *The bear is in his den.*)
- Work in groups of about eight. Choose one of your group to be the *cat*, one to be the *wolf*, and one to be the *witch*. The remaining teachers stand in a circle around the *cat, wolf* and *witch*, link arms and walk round them as they chant:
  The witch is in her cave. The witch is in her cave. Eee ay addio. The witch is in her cave.
  The witch casts a spell. The witch casts a spell. Eee ay addio. The witch casts a spell.
  The wolf starts to howl. The wolf starts to howl. Eee ay addio. The wolf starts to howl.
  The cat starts to meow. The cat starts to meow. Eee ay addio. The cat starts to meow.
  We all pat the cat. We all pat the cat. Eee ay addio. We all pat the cat.
  Note: *Meow* is pronounced /miːaʊ/.
- The witch, wolf and cat make appropriate actions and sounds as the chant progresses. All the participants **gently** pat the cat during the last verse. Change roles and repeat the game.

B) WITCH MODELS

Work in a group of three. T1 is the *sculptor*, T2 is the *Wicked Witch* and T3 is the *clay.*

Sculptor Clay   Witch

Follow these 'modelling' instructions:
- *Clay* stands opposite *sculptor*, facing him/her.
- *Witch* stands behind *clay* and faces *sculptor*.
- *Clay* has his/her back to *witch* and is not allowed to see him/her.
- *Witch* strikes an interesting pose. *Sculptor* has one minute to 'model' (hands-on) the *clay* to copy the pose of the *witch*. When finished, *clay* turns round slowly to check the accuracy of the *sculptor*'s modelling.
- Change roles twice and repeat the activity.

8.2 Reading task 1: visual aids

Work with a partner. Read the following extract. List any ways of using visual aids described in the text that you are familiar with.

Speaking English with pictures
We live in a world dominated by visual messages. Young children learn much about the written word long before they have formal reading and writing activities at school. Information in the form of words and picture clues are displayed in most public places, in the home, and on television, and children soon realise that there is a close association between visual information and the spoken word.

Children therefore grow up expecting their world to be visual. They are accustomed to receiving constant visual support where communication is concerned. It is no coincidence that most popular stories for young children are beautifully illustrated. Indeed, part of the process of learning to read involves using these visual clues to support the written form. It follows that illustrations and the use of visual aids are extremely important in the teaching of a *second* language to younger learners. For example, teachers can use visual aids to:
- support understanding when the children are listening;
- put across the meaning of vocabulary;
- prompt and support reading;
- provide a topic or visual focus to prompt speaking or writing;
- provide a visual link between L1 and English;
- provide support and motivation for early reading and writing in English;
- provide ways around communication barriers.

In the classroom, the most immediate and accessible of visual aids are probably:
the teacher
the children
the board
classroom displays
pictures, flashcards, real items
videos

It is therefore possible for teachers who always wear the same clothes, stand in the same place in the class, talk in the same manner to become as uninteresting as the classroom furniture, assuming that this furniture also remains in the same position for every class. Similarly, an old, dog-eared and yellowing *Map of the English Speaking World*, stategically placed well above the children's eye level, does not provide a sparkling resource for language work ...

- Now work with a partner and do these tasks:
List other ways you may use visuals (not mentioned in the text).
Compare what you have written with other pairs within the group.
Decide on two practical ways of using visuals that will improve the visual impact of **your** classroom.
Finally, take a few moments to look at your trainer, your training environment and visual content around the room. On a separate piece of paper, write one positive and one negative statement about each – in terms of visual presentation only. Fold this paper and put it in a pocket. You may share this information with others in your training group.

8.3 Planning for Hallowe'en

- Work in a team of five or six. On a large sheet of paper, draw a cross-curricular topic web for the theme of *Hallowe'en/festivals*. Highlight the part(s) of the web that you think you may complete in English. When you have finished, display and compare your topic web with those of other groups. If necessary, refer to page 241 of the Resource file for guidance.
- You are going to prepare a series of visual and other teaching aids for the topic of Hallowe'en or a similar festival. There are excellent reference texts available that contain practical ideas on how to produce visual aids e.g. *Pictures for Language Learning* (Andrew Wright, CUP) and *Language in Colour* (Moira Andrew, Bel Air Publications). Although such advice is outside the scope of this book, it is very likely that at least one of your training group has the expertise to support you if you lack the initial *artistic* confidence. In all events, you do not have to be an expert artist to produce practical visual/teaching aids. The confidence and skill to produce visual/teaching aids develops from practice and experience of producing them yourself.
- Stay in your team. For the topic of *Hallowe'en:*
Copy onto an OHP transparency (or a large sheet of paper) the *visual aids cauldron* below.

Brainstorm ideas with your team. Beside each animal around the cauldron, list ideas for *visual/teaching aids* that would support the *learning areas* the animals represent. (Some visual/teaching aids can be used
for more than one category. In this case, discuss with your group how
you would adapt the use of these aids for each relevant category.) You
may also add other animals of your own.

● When you have finished, display and compare your ideas with the
other teams. List them on the board. Sort the ideas into categories such
as *easy to make/find, difficult to make/find* or *teacher must make/find,
parents might make/find*, and *pupils can make/find*.

8.4 Practical tasks

Making a witch *concertina book*

● Work in a team of five or six. Using the outline below as a guide, your
challenge is to make a *witch concertina book* (see illustration below)
to read to an eight-year-old audience. Assign the following roles
within your team:

T1 takes the role of *editor*. The editor has overall responsibility for the
final book.

T2 takes the role of *designer*. The designer has overall responsibility
for the layout of the book.

T3 takes the role of *artist*. The artist co-ordinates with the editor and
designer and has overall responsibility for the illustrations.

Remaining teachers are *authors*. The authors co-ordinate with the editor and designer and have overall responsibility for the text.

All teachers in the team support each other irrespective of role.

Outline for a witch story
- Willamena the Witch lives in black house with black cat called Cookie. *Everything* in the house is black.
- W keeps on tripping over cat. One day she gets angry and changes the cat's colour to green.
- Everything is fine until cat falls asleep in the green grass. W falls over cat and falls into a very prickly rose bush/thistles.
- W is furious and changes cat into all colours of the rainbow.
- W can see the cat wherever he is. The cat is very sad because he looks very silly. Cat hides in the top of a tall tree and is too ashamed to come down.
- W loves her cat very much and feels sorry for him.
- W has a brilliant idea ...

- Discuss and plan the story, deciding on size of paper (folded A4, A3, A2 or A1 – the larger the better); number of pages, etc. Make a dummy book to check it functions correctly as a book. Decide on any special effects, such as *flaps* and *pop-ups*.

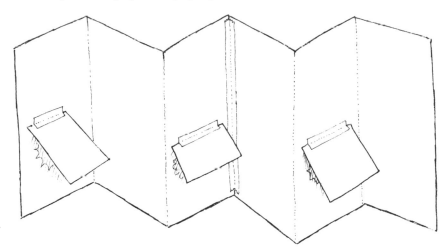

- Share the work out equally. Set a time frame for the work.
- Artist and authors work to designer's/editor's specifications. Editor and designer help/support whenever possible.
  Note: To avoid mistakes, it is wiser to work on separate sheets of paper, then glue them onto the concertina book rather than working directly into the book.
- When you have finished, read and show your finished book to the rest of the training group. Discuss how you might use and develop a similar project in **your** language class.
- Finally, if available, compare your finished books with *Winnie the Witch* (Korky Paul and Valerie Thomas, OUP, 1987).

Part 1

Producing teaching/visual aids for Hallowe'en/festivals

A) PREPARATION

- Assume a language class of twenty ten/eleven-year-old children. Think of the four most useful *teaching/visual aids* that will encourage and help children to *speak* (in English) within the topic of *Hallowe'en* or *festivals*. You have five minutes. Work individually and write your ideas on four separate slips of paper. Write **very briefly** how each teaching aid will help/how you will use the teaching aid. When you have finished, display your slips of paper alongside the rest of your group's suggestions on a long table.
- Stand up. Select the **four** most useful ideas that are on display (they need not be the ones you have written).
- Work with a partner. Share the ideas you have collected. You have five minutes to discuss and select the **four** most useful out of the eight you have collected between you.
- With your partner, join another pair of teachers. Share the ideas you have decided on. You have five minutes to discuss and select the **four** most useful out of the eight you now have in your group.
- With your group, join another group of four teachers. Share the ideas you have decided on. You have up to ten minutes to discuss and select the **four** most useful out of the eight you now have in your group. When you have finished, report your final selection to the whole training group. Choose two teachers: one to write the final selections on the board, the other to copy them onto a sheet of A4 paper, and to photocopy it for the rest of the group.

B) PRODUCTION

- Now work in a *base* team of four. The challenge for each base team is to produce the four *teaching aids* that were decided upon above.
- In each base team appoint:
  - T1 who will work on Teaching Aid 1;
  - T2 who will work on Teaching Aid 2;
  - T3 who will work on Teaching Aid 3;
  - T4 who will work on Teaching Aid 4.
- The whole training group now reorganises into four *expert* teams:
  Team 1 is the Teaching Aid 1 team and consists of the T1 members from each base team.
  Team 2 is the Teaching Aid 2 team and consists of the T2 members from each base team, and so on.
- Expert teams now discuss and produce the teaching aids, and, where appropriate, teaching notes to accompany the teaching aids.
- When they have finished, Ts return to their base teams and prepare a display of their *teaching aids/teaching notes* for the rest of the training group.

C) DISPLAY AND FEEDBACK

Make a display of all the visual products of your team work. Discuss the activities/processes you have just completed, and their value to **your** teaching situation.

8.5   Reading task 2: video

Preparation

- Work within a team of six and discuss any children's EFL videos you have experience of using.
- When you have finished, work with a partner within your team. Share the reading of the following (incomplete) passage. Complete it by adding one or two paragraphs.
- Read the completed passage to others in your team, and comment on its implications.

EFL Videos for children – use or misuse of resources?

Much can be gained (and money saved) through the regular watching of videos or TV programmes that have been produced for English-speaking children. Such TV materials are usually rich in terms of interest to children. They provide a wealth of language input in a highly supportive visual context. They may also contain much cultural information. However, children viewing video in this manner cannot be expected to reproduce the language they hear, or answer specific comprehension questions on the content. In this respect, personal experience has shown that children may watch television in a new foreign language for hours, seemingly understanding what is happening, yet unable to translate or use any specific words on request. At some point, connections seem to be made between the language input from the TV and the foreign language in the outside world. In other words, use of video or TV in this way does not *teach* language, but it most certainly *supports its acquisition*.

With respect to using video in the language classroom with children, the following points need therefore to be considered:
Is the material authentic? In other words, would a native-speaking child want to watch it?

Is the material didactic? Such material may seem attractive to a teacher, but video can be a very expensive – and passive – medium for the presentation of the present tense, or guided practice of the verb *to be*.

Is the content interesting? Will the children want to watch the video again and again? If left alone, children would usually watch a

video once through without stopping the tape. When they have finished, they might normally look for another video.
Do the children have self-access to video material? Can they take it home? Viewing need not be an in-class activity ...

Action

Now work with your team and produce a promotional pamphlet or sheet for a (good) commercial EFL video for children. The video may be real or fictional. As in section 4 of this unit, assume roles (editor, designer, etc.) within your team at the beginning of the task and work co-operatively.

Feedback

Display and explain your pamphlet to other teams in your training group. If available, compare the pamphlets that accompany commercial videos with those you have prepared.

Note: Most children's EFL videos have been designed with the teaching of specific language points in mind. These materials provide extensive teaching notes. If you are interested in such videos, these materials should be evaluated by your training group. By way of comparison, non-EFL videos for younger children (if available), e.g. *Postman Pat – Pat's difficult day*, or other children's videos for native speakers, should also be viewed and evaluated.

8.6 Round-up activity: spell competition

Work with a partner. Work together and produce an *illustrated spell* for Hallowe'en. When you have finished, sit in a large circle with the others in your training group. Cast your spell on the group. When everyone has had a turn, vote on the best spell.

9   Content and curriculum

9.1   Starting points

House/castle group-formation activities

A) THIS IS THE HOUSE

This is the house. This is the door.
These are the walls, and this is the floor.
This is the kitchen, and this is a chair.
What's at the table? Help, it's a bear!

- Work in a group of at least five. T1 (*the bear*) stands aside from the group and says the above chant. The remaining Ts must join hands, arms, etc. to make the shape of the items in the rhyme. When the rhyme reaches the word *bear* the *actors*, shouting *Help, it's a bear!*, must try to reach one of the walls in the class before the bear (T1) catches them.
- Change roles and repeat this activity several times.

B) I'M THE KING (QUEEN) OF THE CASTLE

- Stand in circles of five. Place a chair in the centre of the circle. T1 is king/queen and stands on the chair.
- Remaining Ts circle T1. T1 chants:
  I'm the king/queen of the castle.
  Carry me like a parcel.
- Ts then lift and gently carry T1 to a safe spot in the room, while chanting *You're the king/queen of the castle. We're carrying you like a parcel.*

C) SING A SONG OF SIXPENCE

Work in a team of six. Create a tune for the rhyme below and sing it to the rest of the training group.

Sing a song of sixpence, a pocket full of rice,
Four-and-twenty blackbirds baked in two pies.
When the pies were opened, the birds began to sing,
Wasn't that a yummy meal to set before the king?

The king was in his bedroom, counting out his money,
The queen was in the kitchen, eating bread and honey,
The prince was in the garden, hanging out the clothes,
When down came a blackbird and pecked off his nose.

Sing a song of sixpence topic web

- Work in a team of five or six and draw a cross-curricular topic web with the theme of *Sing a song of sixpence* at the centre.
- Highlight the part(s) of the web that you think you may complete in English. State the possibilities for the *language focus* that could be developed within this web, and discuss how this/these might be integrated into a first-year language curriculum for nine/ten-year-old children.
- When you have finished, display and compare your topic web with those of other groups.
- Now follow your trainer's instructions to compare language presented in an activity-based curriculum with that presented in a language-based curriculum.

9.2   The House that Jack Built

The rhyme

Work in teams of five or six. Follow your trainer's instructions for this activity.

Reading and illustrating task

- Work individually and read the following paragraph:

The learning-training-teaching process may be likened to a house. There are foundations and supporting walls – certain concepts, attitudes, approaches that underpin the learning situation and support the teacher. The bricks function as techniques, strategies and skills. Some arrangements may lead to row upon row of semi-detached houses that all look the same. Others may lead to an originality that may only suit the few. Similarly, the furniture and decoration of the house could be likened to the teaching content. The type and arrangement of such *furniture* and *decor* will vary according to the personality of the inhabitants (i.e. teacher and children) and to the type of house (i.e. school and classroom). Moreover, traditional/contemporary teaching content and methodology seems to come in and out of fashion in a very similar manner to traditional and contemporary decor.

- Work co-operatively with a partner. Make a large (at least A1) size poster or display of *The House that Jack Built*. Inside (or on the outside of) the house, list the key words/statements that represent your/your partner's teaching approach, attitudes, techniques, strategies, skills, etc.

Producing a 'curriculum wall' for your training course

- Work in groups of four or five. Share information and:
- write an outline or curriculum of the *training course content* you have studied so far;
- design a large imaginative wall, made of large bricks. In each brick, write in the key words or key phrases from this course that were – and are – important to you as a teacher of children.
- When you have finished, display your wall for other groups to read. Read those produced by the rest of the groups.

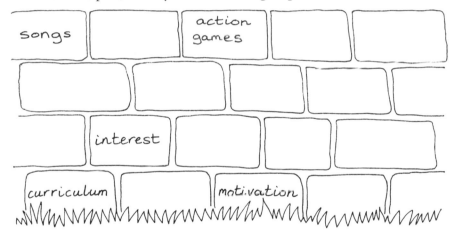

9.3 The content and curriculum of a children's EFL coursebook

- Work with a new team of five or six. Choose two contemporary coursebooks for teaching English to children. Look at the stated curriculum for Year 1 of each coursebook. Copy and complete Table 1 below using the curriculum content of Coursebook 1. Where there are gaps in the table (i.e. not in the coursebook curriculum), suggest and write relevant and suitable activities (title of activity only) of your own.

Part 1

Table 1 **Coursebook curriculum content**

Unit	Examples of language input from the teacher	Language output expected from the children			Action game language	Suggested practical work
		Structures	Functions	Vocabulary		
1						
2						
3						
4						
5						
6						
7						
8						

- When you have finished, compare your completed table with that of the curriculum in the coursebook. Discuss the reasons for, and implications of the differences.
- Work and share ideas with your group. Copy and complete Table 2 below (at least five units, more if you have time), and develop your ideal curriculum for Year 1 of a children's EFL coursebook. If you need a guide, first complete the *Structure, Function* and *Vocabulary* columns with the language curriculum provided by Year 1 of Coursebook 2.

Table 2 **Ideal curriculum content**

Unit	Examples of language input from the teacher	Suggested practical work	Action game language	Potential language output from the children		
				Structures	Functions	Vocabulary
1						
2						
3						
4						
5						

- When you are ready, join with another group of teachers. Share the curriculum you have decided on. You have about twenty minutes to discuss and select the *most promising ideas* for a curriculum within your new group. When you have finished, report this *final* curriculum to the whole group. Choose two teachers: one to write the final selections on the board, the other to copy them onto A4 paper and to photocopy the curricula for the rest of the group.

9.4 Games children play

Preparation

Work in teams of six. Discuss the role of play/games in the curriculum, taking the following ten points into consideration:
1 Play has a key role in the learning process for children.
2 Play is a source of motivation, interest and enjoyment.
3 Parents may become anxious if children say they have 'played' in the language lesson.
4 Teachers may reject coursebooks which place a high priority on 'play'.
5 For children, inside and outside the classroom, playing is a source of language, and a context for language use.
6 The content of play/games should be linked to the overall theme/topic of the lesson.
7 Games/play are an essential part of a curriculum, not a time filler or reward.
8 Games/play should encourage group support and not merely competition between children and groups.
9 Children should be encouraged to decide/bring/choose the games they want to play in English.
10 The play/game I enjoyed playing when I was a child was _____ . It is/isn't possible to use this game in my language teaching.

Action

Work in a team of at least six. You have up to thirty minutes to share with each other:
– your favourite games as children;
– games you have used successfully in the language class with children.

Feedback

Share the games you have played in your team with the rest of the training group. Discuss how you might integrate/adapt these games into the curriculum you have planned in this unit.

9.5 Round-up activity: house/home rhymes and chants

- Look at this example:

Traditional version
There was an old woman who lived in a shoe.
She had so many children she didn't know what to do.
She gave them some gruel without any bread,
Then she whipped them all soundly and sent them to bed.

There was an old woman by Peter Smith, aged 10
There was an old woman who lived in a zoo.
She had seventeen children, pigs and hens too.
She gave them some honey on slices of bread,
Then went to watch TV and stood on her head.

Sing a song of sixpence by Amanda Gee, aged 11
Sing a song of sixpence, a bucket full of ice.
Twenty thousand beetles flying in the skies.
When the ice had melted, the beetles came to look,
Some swam around in circles, others read a book.
The king was in a cocktail bar saying something funny.
The queen was in her favourite shop spending all his money.
The prince was in the bathroom powdering his nose
When in came the beetles and crawled between his toes.
(See pages 113-4 for the traditional version of *Sing a song of sixpence.*)

- Now work in a team of up to six. Read the traditional versions of *Ladybird, ladybird* and *Hickory dickory dock.*

- Change each rhyme so that it is more humorous. Create a tune (traditional, contemporary or house/rap) for your new rhymes and sing them.

Traditional version
Ladybird, ladybird, fly away home.
Your house is on fire and your children have gone.
All except one, and her name is Ann,
And she is safe and hiding under the frying pan.

Traditional version
Hickory dickory dock. The mouse ran up the clock.
The clock struck one. The mouse ran down. Hickory dickory dock.

10 Observation, assessment and records

10.1 Starting points

A) PLEASE MR CROCODILE

This group-formation game may be played outside, or in lots of space within the training room.

- Stand in team lines of six or seven. T1 in each team is *Mr/Mrs Crocodile*. Teams and crocodiles agree on a safe place (e.g. at the back of the room or a nearby tree/post if the game is played outside).
- Draw a chalk line (or use a piece of string) to represent a river. Team lines stand on one side of the 'river', face the crocodile and chant, using lots of gestures: *Please Mr (Mrs) Crocodile, can I cross the water to see your lovely daughter swimming in the water?*
- T1 (Crocodile) surveys the team, chooses a colour or item of clothing that very few of the team are wearing and chants, again using lots of guestures: *Yes, of course you can cross the water to see my lovely daughter swimming in the water, if you are wearing something _____.* (e.g. yellow)
- Ts wearing something yellow may cross the water (the chalk line) safely. Remaining Ts must flee for their lives to the pre-established safe place. The crocodile tries to catch them. The first one caught becomes the new crocodile.

B) WHO IS IT?

- Training group divides into three equal groups (G1, G2, G3).
- All Ts from G2 (i.e. T2 teachers) find a partner from the Ts in G1 (i.e. T1 teachers) and blindfold him/her. Teachers in G3 (i.e. T3 teachers) should remove spectacles, head bands, etc. if worn and stand in a different part of the room from the Ts in G1.
- T2s lead their T1 partners to a T3. T1s gently *feel* the face of the T3.
- When T1s are sure that they will recognise the T3 they are feeling, T2s lead them away. T2s spin T1s around three times. T1s remove blindfold amd must walk over and put their hands on the shoulders of the T3 they believe they have felt.
- Ts change roles and repeat this activity twice.

C) DRAW MY FACE

Follow your trainer's instructions for this game.

10.2 Making a 'wanted poster'

- Work in pairs. Draw a large portrait of your partner, colouring in his/her best features. Use scrap materials to decorate your poster.
- When you have finished, convert this into a 'wanted poster' by writing three *positive* statements about your partner under his/her portrait.
- Finally, display the portraits around your training room.
- Comment on/discuss the use of this activity with the children.

10.3 Assessment

Introduction

- Work with a partner. First, agree on the meaning of and differences (if any) between testing, evaluation and assessment (in an EFL teaching context).
- When you are ready, work in a team of five. Discuss these questions:
  1 How was your work/progress assessed/tested when you were a child?
  2 Which sort of tests did you take as a child?
  3 Do you think your teachers evaluated their work and the course of study you followed in primary school? Do you use similar approaches to testing, assessment and evaluation in your teaching?
  4 How would you like to be assessed (or tested) on your performance during your training course?
- Now agree with your team and list some possible ways of assessing and testing children's work and progress, e.g. formal tests, small group 'conferences', etc. Which of these ways:
  - may be shared with the child?
  - provide(s) accurate information about the child's ability in English?
  - provide(s) necessary information to the teacher for in-school purposes?
  - may be shared with the class, verbally or as a 'performance list'?
  - may motivate/demotivate a weaker learner?
  - require(s) children to work individually?
  - allow(s) children to work co-operatively with others in the class?
  - provide(s) information about what the child **can** do rather than what he/she can't do?
  - may be useful for parents/a child's future teachers?

Reading task

Sit with a new partner and share the reading of the following letter to a regional inspector from a teacher.

18th January, 19...

Dear Madam,

  I am teaching English as a foreign language to eight to ten year olds at one of the primary schools in your inspectoral region. I have recently read your (Ministry) guidelines concerning assessment of the English ability of young learners (aged eight to eleven) in their first and second years of the course. I realise that assessing the language ability in English of eight- to eleven-year-old children is a sensitive issue. I also appreciate that teachers, parents, the school administration and the educational authorities (quite justifiably) want concrete and quick evidence of the skill and knowledge being acquired. However, in your guidelines, you seem to assume that children under the age of eleven have the cognitive skills to analyse language in the absence of the content and context in which it is used. This would seem to be manifestly untrue.

  In my experience, and the experience of my colleagues, children between eight and eleven are most unlikely to be able to separate grammar and function from communication. For example, a child in my class may be able to understand and follow reasonably complex instructions in English for a practical task such as measuring his or her height. He or she may well also be able to reply appropriately and accurately in English to questions about height, using the required structure 'I am …, He is …,' etc. However, this does not mean this child is aware that the verb 'to be' is embedded in this sentence. As a further example, Marie, a nine-year-old girl in one of my classes, failed the formal end-of-year test (recommended by the Ministry) in July. From the test's point of view, she seemed to be a 'near beginner' in English. Marie then spent two months of her summer holidays with a cousin in Liverpool and returned in September, as a fluent communicator in English. However, she still failed the same formal test.

In my opinion (and that of my colleagues), this suggests that the assessment of children acquiring a second language should:
— focus on what children can do, and not on what they can't do;
— be positive and non-competitive;
— allow children the opportunity to work co-operatively with others in the class;
— refer directly to what has been studied, and preferably when it is being studied. It should not relate to transference of what has been studied;
— value the ability of children to understand and respond as well as to speak and to write;
— take into consideration that silence should not be considered as ignorance.

Furthermore, I believe that assessment should not be presented as a one-off chance for success or failure. Children showing a lack of ability in any one assessment task on any given day should be allowed the opportunity to succeed over an extended period of time.

I hope you find my comments constructive, and I look forward to your reply in the near future.

Yours faithfully

Discussion

Now work in groups. Share your comments on the above letter, and on your own personal experience of assessment. Include, for example, the following points in your discussion:

Examples of children (you have known) who reflect or contradict the viewpoints expressed in the reading.

Your own reaction to taking tests/being assessed yourself.

What you think are the best/worst ways you have been tested or assessed.

Whether you like setting, marking and giving children the results of tests.

Ways of testing/assessment that work for **you**.

If you are a parent, how you feel about your children being tested or assessed.

Co-operative writing task

Finally, sit with a partner. Working co-operatively, write the reply you feel the inspector will send.

10.4   Profiling

- Essentially, *profiling* involves the teacher, the child and the parents in an ongoing evaluation and assessment process. Key words and phrases include:
  conferencing with children
  keeping samples of work done in a folder
  discussion with parents
  keeping parents informed about the course and their children's progress
  negotiating with the children about work done, and setting targets
  self and peer evaluation
  passing on of a 'profile folder' to the next teacher
- Discuss with your training group whether you feel such a profiling system, or aspects of it, are relevant to the assessment of a child's ability in English.
- Refer to your own coursework. What, if anything, would you like to be placed in a *profile* of your ability as a teacher/trainee? Which areas would you consider important in terms of assessing your skill:
  - as a teacher of English?
  - as a trainee on the course?
  - as a speaker of English?
- Who would you prefer to carry out your assessment:
  - your trainer?
  - your peers?
  - yourself?

10.5   Classroom assessment and research

Introduction

While to some teachers, classroom observation by the trainer/a peer teacher may be welcome, many feel that this form of assessment of teaching can be very stressful, and may yield invalid or distorted information about the classroom. There are several reasons for this, e.g.
- children may react unpredictably to a stranger in the classroom;
- the teacher may feel threatened by observation by an 'outsider';
- there is a temptation to provide something 'special' for an observer;
- one or two children may play up/have an off-day which may lead to

an exaggerated reaction by the teacher/other children in the presence of an observer.

Therefore, *classroom assessment/research* may be carried out in place of, or in addition to classroom observation. This can be done by the teacher working alone, or as the action of a small team of teachers within one school. Such *classroom research* may be viewed as a *constructive evaluation* of what has been gained, learned and shared during the course.

Procedure

Work with a partner or small team. Read and discuss the following. Decide and commit yourself to **one** aim/objective for classroom research.

A) AIMS/OBJECTIVES

Identify a problem or an area you wish to study. This may be to answer a teaching question, or to see the effect of an activity you have tried during your course, e.g.

Do children learn more effectively through choral repetition?

Do craft activities generate motivation and interest and result in effective learning of a specific language point?

Do children learn vocabulary more effectively from their peers or from the teacher?

B) PLAN/STRATEGIES

Make a written plan with respect to how you intend to carry out your 'research'.

Example considerations:

- how many lessons you will need;
- what classroom management arrangements you will make;
- how you will record/observe the results, etc.

C) ACTION (1)

Put your plans and strategies into action.

D) CHECK/REFLECTION/FEEDBACK

Check the results of c against a and b. If necessary, modify the plans/strategies you originally made.

E) ACTION (2)

What action will you take based on the results of D?
What will be your next step(s)?
What further 'research' do you wish to carry out?

10.6 Round-up activity: assess your skipping and hokey cokey skills

A) I LIKE COFFEE ...

- Work in a small team. Decide on a teaching technique/procedure (and a tune) for introducing the skipping rhyme below to a class of eight- to eleven-year-old EFL learners.
  I like coffee, she likes tea.
  Would you come and skip with me?
  We like ice-cream, they like cakes.
  Can you skip without mistakes?
  One, two, three ... out.
- Share ideas with other groups and reach a consensus teaching procedure. Choose one person in the training group to be the teacher (T). T follows the agreed procedure and teaches the whole group to sing and skip this rhyme.

B) THE HOKEY COKEY

Stand in a large circle with the rest of the training group. Sing and act out the *hokey cokey*:

You put your left arm in, your left arm out. In, out, in, out, you shake it all about. You do the hokey cokey and you turn around. That's what it's all about.

Oh, hokey, cokey cokey. Oh, hokey, cokey cokey. Oh, hokey, cokey cokey. Knees bend, arms raise, rah, rah, rah.

You put your right arm in, your right arm out. In, out, in, out, you shake it all about. You do the hokey cokey and you turn around. That's what it's all about.

Oh, hokey, cokey cokey. Oh, hokey, cokey cokey. Oh, hokey, cokey cokey. Knees bend, arms raise, rah, rah, rah.

You put your left leg in, your left leg out. In, out, in, out, you shake it all about. You do the hokey cokey and you turn around. That's what's it's all about.

Oh, hokey, cokey cokey. Oh, hokey, cokey cokey. Oh, hokey, cokey cokey. Knees bend, arms raise, rah, rah, rah.

You put your right leg in, your right leg out. In, out, in, out, you shake it all about. You do the hokey cokey and you turn around. That's what it's all about.

Oh, hokey, cokey cokey. Oh, hokey, cokey cokey. Oh, hokey, cokey cokey. Knees bend, arms raise, rah, rah, rah.

You put your whole self in, your whole self out. In, out, in, out, you shake it all about. You do the hokey cokey and you turn around. That's what it's all about.

Oh, hokey, cokey cokey. Oh, hokey, cokey cokey. Oh, hokey, cokey cokey. Knees bend, arms raise, rah, rah, rah.

Trainer's guidelines

1   Introduction

The following notes on pages 127 to 134 are intended to act as general guidelines only. They provide some general ideas for conducting the training sessions and for the management of training groups. The rest of this section consists of detailed notes to accompany each activity.

2   Use of a second foreign language (L3)

In most teacher training situations it is useful for the trainees to experience the position of their (prospective) pupils, i.e. to be exposed to an unknown foreign language. There are a few activities in this course which suggest the use of an L3, e.g. Unit 6, page 88. If you know a third language (preferably one your trainees are not familiar with), you will need to prepare a few words and sentences on occasion to demonstrate certain techniques. If you do not know a third language, it might be possible to find a colleague with an unusual second language who will be prepared to assist you.

If you have no access to a third language, you could try to 'invent' a few words/sentences in an imaginary language. However, if none of the above strategies is feasible, the activities can be carried out in English equally as well.

3   Group formation

As mentioned in Unit 2.2, page 21, in any learning situation, where individuals are required to act and interact with others, there are many potential social and emotional constraints and pressures that may interfere with effective learning. The effect of lowering these *learning barriers* makes it easier for learning to take place. It also encourages a wider sharing and exchange of ideas. The content studied becomes of a *higher quality* – as well as of a *greater quantity*.

We have found that training sessions that do not include group-formation activities often develop into a completely different learning atmosphere. They are often less effective in terms of results for the trainees. We have therefore included group-formation suggestions throughout the training notes. The content of the group-formation activities complements the areas of study. (For examples, refer to pages 136, 159, 189, in the Trainer's notes.)

4 Management of classroom/training room space

Arrangement of desks and/or chairs

From your own experience, you will know that classroom layout can easily be taken for granted. Changes in desk and chair formation require time and energy, and there is often resistance and lethargy towards such change. It is important to give the teachers a first-hand opportunity of working within different classroom layouts and classroom space and to make sure that both you and they are satisfied with the layout **before** starting any activity. Moreover, if you realise that the layout of the room is interfering with the smooth running of a particular task that is already under way, it is necessary, and perfectly valid, to stop the activity and rearrange the classroom space. Physical barriers created by a badly organised layout of chairs and desks may cause even the best of activities to fail. For reference, the following illustrations show commonly used training layouts:

In addition to this, many primary school classrooms set up special areas for particular activities. It may be useful to set up and experiment with similar activity areas within your training classroom, e.g.

a reading corner
a writing corner
a shop roleplay area
a home roleplay area
a fast food roleplay area
a measurement area
a travel agent's corner
a topic corner

Display

Encouraging the teachers to display selected pieces of their work, or the results of their activities, will demonstrate that you value the work they produce, and gives ideas for their own classroom. Referring once more to primary practice, examples of display formats include:

wall displays
hall displays
poster presentations/displays
class book (illustrated by the teachers)
activity corners
washing line displays, i.e. hanging illustrations, models, etc. from a line
    of string hanging across a corner of the room.

5   Management of practical tasks

We have found the following techniques and approaches are useful with respect to practical tasks. You may wish to add to this list from your own experience.

Before you start a practical task

1 Plan the practical matters such as group size, room layout, materials and resources needed.
2 Discuss the aims of the task with the teachers.
3 Establish an approximate time framework for the task.
4 Organise the whole training group into small groups. Six is usually a maximum number.
5 Assign roles within each small group, e.g.
    - *tidy monitor* who is responsible for collecting all resources and for cleaning up the work space at the end of the activity;
    - *noise controller* who will control the level of noise within his or her group if you make an appropriate signal;

   – *language teacher* who is responsible for co-ordinating (and raising with you) any issues within his or her group with respect to the teaching implications of the activity.

When the activity is under way

1 If feasible, work on the same task yourself. This will confirm that you attach value to the activity.
2 Be sensitive about interrupting the teachers while they are working. There is a fine line between checking that everything is all right, and informed and appropriate questioning – and interference. If teachers are involved in a task, they may not want to talk to you.
3 Find points to praise, rather than show indifference (or criticism) to work being done.

When the activity has been completed

1 Encourage individuals to share results with, first a partner, then a small group, then the whole group.
2 Encourage the group to evaluate the activity and its usefulness. Ask the group to make suggestions for *next steps*.
3 Comment on the activity from your point of view. However, if you are raising new, critical or contradictory ideas, balance the value of your comments against the importance of developing confidence and an atmosphere of support for the teachers.

As the course progresses, vary the style of feedback and reporting as this demonstrates a range of useful teaching practice.
1 Appoint *reporters*, whose role is to observe and take notes on what is happening, and to communicate this information to other groups and to you. Reporters do not take part in the main activity.
2 Appoint *secretaries* or *scribes* for each small group. After completing the activity, their role is to summarise what their group has produced, and to pass this information to another group, or the whole training group.
3 Appoint *sales representatives* for each small group. Their role is to *sell* the results of their group's work to other groups.
4 You (or a selected trainee) report to the whole group on an individual group's performance.
5 You discuss with the teachers how they wish to conduct the reporting/feedback stage. Abide by their consensus decision.

6 Management of discussion tasks

Types of discussion

From the point of view of this book, we see discussions as either *prescribed, guided* or *open*, and we suggest that you adopt an eclectic approach. The following notes can be used as reference points:

Prescribed
You usually have predetermined ideas concerning the content and outcome of the discussion.
You intervene where appropriate to steer the discussion along the lines you wish.
You summarise the results of the discussion, emphasising those points made which are closest to the conclusions you wish the teachers to reach.

Guided
You give key points, or raise key questions you wish the group to focus their discussion on.
Once the discussion has started, you usually do not intervene, except on points of discussion procedure. However, you may intervene to bring the discussion back on course, especially if the discussion loses direction, and discussion time is running short.
You make sure that all individuals put forward a viewpoint.
At the end of the discussion you encourage selected teachers to summarise the ideas and views put forward.
You comment on the results of the discussion with respect to your own points of view, but do not insist that you are right.

Open
You set, or negotiate the title for the discussion. You also negotiate the discussion format and rules.
Once the discussion has started you do not intervene, except on points of discussion procedure.
At the end of the discussion, you state your own viewpoint with respect to the points raised. You encourage the teachers to evaluate their discussion, and possibly to establish the topic for the next discussion.

Management of group dynamics in discussion tasks

We have already mentioned the use of *reporters* and *secretaries* within a discussion activity. In addition to this, we have found *random restructuring* a particularly useful strategy in terms of:
- sharing information effectively among the whole training group;
- ensuring unwanted 'cliques' do not develop within the training group;
- ensuring 'strong' and 'weak' participants are evenly, but randomly, distributed within discussion tasks over the training period.

The following is an example of random restructuring:

Size of training group	Number of mini-groups required	Example of action needed
25	Five groups of five	1 Count quickly around the training group, assigning a number from 1 to 5 to each participant. (Alternatively, five *colours* or other appropriate vocabulary sets may be used.) 2 Check each participant knows his/her number. 3 Assign five areas (1–5) in the training room where each group may sit. 4 Tell participants to form groups according to their number, i.e. all the number 1s sit together, the number 2s sit together and so on. 5 Set a time limit for the activity/discussion, e.g. ten minutes, and tell the members of each group that they must **all** keep a record of their group's discussion, since they will be required to share this information with a 'new' group (in ten minutes' time). 6 At the specified time, assign a new number (from 1–5) to each participant within their mini-groups. 7 Tell participants to re-group according to their new number, i.e. all the (new) number 1s sit together, the (new) number 2s sit together and so on. 8 Participants (in their new groups) share the points raised in their 'old' groups.
18	Three groups of six	1 Count quickly around the training group, assigning a number from 1 to 3 to each participant. Follow a similar procedure to the one above. 2 At the specified time, assign a new number (from 1–3) to each participant within their mini-groups. In other words **two** members from each 'old' group will be present in each 'new' group.

In the early stages of a training course, it is very beneficial to the overall group dynamics to ask teachers to learn the names of the participants in their 'mini-group' each time random restructuring takes place.

7 Management of time

Time spent on any given activity should be directly related to the experience, needs, and interests of the teachers. Taking new ideas on board takes much time and much consolidation. It also may take time for teachers to feel they have expressed their ideas adequately. It follows that the relevance of any one activity will vary considerably from group to group. In general, therefore, although we have recommended an approximate timing for the completion of specific tasks, we appreciate the need for flexibility in this area.

However, we do recommend that you pay careful attention to the *variety* of activities within a training session. For example, a training sequence should involve passive, semi-passive, active and *adventurous* activities. Similarly, variety implies change of training approach from, e.g. *trainer directed* to *trainee centred* to *trainee autonomous*. Once again, training in this manner reassures the teacher of the importance of variety in their own classroom.

8 Work done at home

If your training course is shorter than the estimated time needed to complete this course, certain strategies can be used to cut down the time needed in the training sessions themselves:
- many of the reading tasks can be done individually at home;
- some of the practical tasks can be done out of 'training time', preferably in pairs/groups, as these are intended to be shared experiences;
- writing tasks can be done individually, and discussed in the training group.

9 Keeping a journal

As mentioned on page 8 of the Introduction, we recommend that trainees keep a journal throughout their training course. This can be used to record notes from reading passages and discussions, particularly ideas that are relevant to the individual's teaching situation. It is also useful for the trainees to keep a record of any new activities they try in their own classes (where applicable) for discussion with other teachers on the course. Finally, the journal can be used to record thoughts about the course itself, which will be of use in feedback/assessment sessions (see below).

10 Management of assessment and evaluation

We have mentioned brief guidelines for the assessment process in Unit 10. However, assessment is an issue which affects the training programme from the beginning.

In terms of assessing the training course itself, regular feedback from the trainees is essential. This can easily be done by asking them to discuss and report on their training course, at regular intervals, possibly in your absence. Alternatively, you may wish feedback from your trainees on certain aspects of the course. In this case, a questionnaire is obviously very effective. Whatever method you choose, we believe that, in the same way as teachers develop as teachers by practising teaching, progress in training comes about through training practice and feedback.

1 Establishing common ground: attitudes and approaches to teaching children

Theme/topic
Spiders and other mini-creatures

Overall aims
This unit examines teaching approaches and attitudes that are relevant to the teaching of English to young learners. It illustrates the manner in which the teaching of EFL to adults has been transferred, in diluted form, to the teaching of children, and offers an opportunity to reflect on alternatives.

Study plan

	Study agenda/activities	Preparation and resources needed	Key points	Approx. timing
1.0	Getting started: group-formation activities	No additional materials needed	Participation in group-formation activities Fostering a supportive atmosphere	15–20 minutes
1.1	Establishing key issues related to the teaching of English to children	No additional materials needed	Raising teachers' awareness of the key issues Encouraging teachers to state their own experience and ideas	45–60 minutes
1.2	Establishing attitudes: What are your views on teaching English?	No additional materials needed	Sharing notes on attitudes to teaching children	15–20+ minutes
1.3	A practical challenge: a spider mobile; making the mobile, reflection on the needs of children	String, Sellotape, elastic bands, crayons, sheets of paper, straws or toothpicks, scraps of materials for additional decoration	The value of practical tasks in the language classroom The needs of children and corresponding action by teachers	60–90 minutes
1.4	Spiders across the curriculum and the needs of children	No additional materials needed	Comparing traditional and activity-based approaches	45–60 minutes

>>→

	Study agenda/activities	Preparation and resources needed	Key points	Approx. timing
1.5	Discussing communication	No additional materials needed	Shared reading task Discussing teaching approaches	30–40 minutes
1.6	Summary	No additional materials needed	Shared reading/writing task	20–30 minutes
1.7	Round up: spider games and rhymes	No additional materials needed	Integrating the theme of the unit with group dynamic tasks	10–20 minutes

1.0 Getting started: group-formation activities

Aims

These activities encourage:
- participation in a variety of group-formation activities;
- a supportive atmosphere within the training group.

Start by outlining the agenda for the first session. Since *spiders* is the first topic in this unit, use the following spider group-formation activities:

A) SPIDER'S WEB

- Divide teachers into groups of four or six. Six is the optimum number. They exchange names. Remaining teachers may act as observers and helpers for each group. Give the following instructions:
  *Take the right hand of someone who is **not** standing immediately next to you.*
  *Take the left hand of someone who is not standing immediately next to you, and who is **not** the person whose hand you are already holding.*
  Unscramble yourselves back into an open circle. You may loosen your grip, but you must not let go of anyone's hands. You have two minutes to complete this task.
  With non-native speakers, appoint a group leader for each group. Copy the above instructions and give them to the leaders. Leaders therefore instruct their groups.

B) SPIDER ALPHABET

- Ts stand in small circles (in groups) of four or five. They exchange names.
- Ts hold hands and take a slow, deep breath.

- Ts let hands go. You call out this sequence of five letters: *H–A–I–R–Y*, one at a time. Ts form the shape of each letter after you say it by linking arms, or hands, etc. with the rest of their group.
- Ask Ts which word they spelt – and how they feel about *hairy spiders*.

C) PLAY 'HAIRY SPIDER'

One word of warning: our experience has shown that over-excitement in this game can lead to injuries. For the sake of safety, place all chairs **against** the wall so that they cannot tip over backwards during the game.

- Ts sit in a circle. Each teacher sits on his or her own chair. Remove any additional chairs. You remain standing to begin with.
- Choose three or four parts of the spider. Assign each teacher the name of one of the parts; one part per teacher. In other words, in a group of fifteen, there may be four teachers who are *legs*, four teachers who are *heads*, four who are *eyes*, and three who are *mouths*.
- Name one of the parts, *legs* for example. All the teachers who are legs must stand up and sit down on a different seat. You must also sit down at this point. In other words, five people (four teachers and the trainer) will try to sit down on four seats. The teacher who doesn't find a seat is the next *caller* of the words.
- The game continues in this way for two or three minutes. If the caller says *hairy spider*, **everyone** must stand up and sit down on a different seat.

D) PLAY 'INCY WINCY SPIDER'

- Say this *Incy* action rhyme to the teachers. Do lots of hand gestures to illustrate the rhyme as you say it. The teachers listen but do not repeat after you.
  Incy Wincy Spider climbed up the spout.
  Down poured the rain and washed poor Incy out.
  Out came the sun, and dried up all the rain.
  Incy Wincy Spider climbed up the spout again.
- Repeat the rhyme. Ts copy your actions, but do not speak.
- Ts stand in a large circle, all facing the same direction, e.g. each facing the back of the person on their left.
- Ts touch, with a finger, the back of the person standing on their left in the circle. (It may be easier to ask them first to put their hands on the shoulders of the person on their left in order to produce the correct distance between each of them.)
- Repeat the rhyme. Ts must draw, using a finger, Incy, the actions and the scene within the rhyme as you say it, on the back of the person standing in front of them in the circle.
- Ts in the circle now turn 180 degrees to face the other way. Repeat the rhyme and Ts now draw on the back of the person on their right.

1.1 Establishing key issues related to the teaching of children

Aims
This activity encourages teachers to:
- state their priorities as trainees;
- consider and discuss what **they** feel are the key issues associated with teaching English to children;
- share views with other trainees.

- Ts follow the detailed instructions in the book. The time restrictions ensure that teacher-teacher discussion is kept at a lively pace during this activity.

1.2 Attitudes: what are your views on teaching English?

Aims
This activity encourages teachers to express opinions as to
- why children learn English;
- why adults learn English;
- why a teacher teaches English to children.

- Ts work in groups of four and follow their instructions. Here are some example responses from teachers to the discussion points in the course notes:
  1 Why do children learn English?
    ○ Curiosity inspired by the media and friends.
    ○ Parental pressure.
    ○ Pleasure of playing with new sounds.
    ○ School pressure.
    ○ Challenge of a new way of speaking.
  2 Why do adults learn English?
    ○ For work.
    ○ For love.
    ○ For a hobby.
    ○ For travel.
    ○ For promotion.
  3 Why do you teach English?
    ○ Decision from above.
    ○ I like English.
    ○ A plus for my career.
    ○ I like children.
    ○ I can get a better school.
    ○ I could use my English.

1.3 A 'practical' challenge: a spider mobile

Aims

This activity encourages the teachers to:
- participate as a group in the carrying out of a practical task;
- raise their awareness of classroom (instruction) language;
- discuss the exploitation of a practical task in terms of its relevance to the child's stage of development and in terms of generating/practising a specific language point in an EFL classroom.

Preparing instructions for the spider mobile

- Ts follow the detailed instructions on page 11. Ensure that they are aware they are writing for an eight-year-old audience. The following is an example of an illustrated set of instructions completed by a group of teachers:

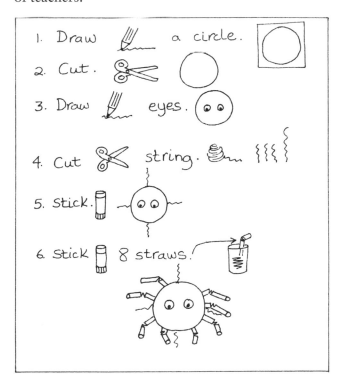

1. Draw ✏ a circle. ◯
2. Cut. ✂ ◯
3. Draw ✏ eyes. (◉ ◉)
4. Cut ✂ string. 🧵 〰〰
5. Stick. 🖊 ~(◉ ◉)~
6. Stick 🖊 8 straws! 🥤

Practical task: making the spider mobile

- Ts work in groups of four or five. Display the results alongside the instructions they have produced.

Discussion

Here are some example responses from teachers to the discussion points in the course notes:

1 How you made the language of instruction clear to an eight-year-old audience:
   - Use of key words.
   - Use of pictures.
   - We need to demonstrate what to do; words are not enough.
   - Translation into L1.

2 How you might exploit these instructions in an EFL classroom:
   - Teach the children to understand the actions such as *cut, stick, colour, draw* and the nouns such as *parts of the body*. They don't need to say these words – they just need to understand them.
   - Teach the children to listen and watch (and read/look at pictures) – not just repeat language.
   - They will soon learn words like *cut, draw*, etc. and *the colours* and *pencil, ruler, rubber, glue, scissors* because they are doing something practical.

3 How you felt as *learners* during the making of the mobile:
   - Very relaxed.
   - It helped me to get to know others in the group.
   - We talked about ourselves, not just the mobile.
   - I felt a bit silly making childish things.
   - I didn't like to be interrupted (by the trainer) while I was making the mobile.

4 How you might exploit the making of a spider mobile as a language teaching activity in an EFL classroom:
   - Teach parts of the body, adjectives *long, thin*, practise *has got ...* (*has got eight legs, has got a hairy body*), numbers 1–8.
   - It takes a long time to do this activity. There isn't enough time.
   - We have to teach a coursebook.
   - Difficult to organise. We need a lot of equipment.
   - It takes more time to organise but children will remember better because they are involved.
   - We could organise language practice, e.g. focusing on *has got ...* or *parts of the body* **after** the task has been completed.

5 How you might adapt this activity to suit an eleven-year-old audience rather than a class of eight year olds:
   - Ask children to sort small creatures by the number of legs they have got. With a more advanced class, you could then focus on *more than (eight legs), fewer than (eight legs), the same number as ...*, as a language point.
   - The activity suits the whole age range. We enjoyed it as adults.

○ Make a more complex mobile with several spiders. You could introduce the structure *How many (legs/spiders, etc.) are there?*

○ Compare the model to the real thing. Ask the children to observe spiders closely. As a language point you could focus on *same/different* and *comparisons*.

Finally, ask teachers to reflect on their **own** learning experience as children:

– what they remember from their own primary school teachers;
– what motivated them to learn when they were children;
– what demotivated them from learning.

1.4 Spiders across the curriculum and the needs of children

A cross-curricular analysis

Aims

This activity encourages the teachers to:

– develop a cross-curricular topic web that focuses on 'the spider' (and other mini-creatures);
– discuss the potential language points that can be generated by a range of cross-curricular tasks;
– compare the kinds of activities that may take place in a primary classroom with those that usually take place in an EFL classroom.

● Ts complete the cross-curricular chart in the course notes. Example responses include:

Curricular area	Example activity	Example language focus
Art and craft	Making a spider mobile Making glue and salt webs	Parts of the body: *A spider has ...* Colours and shapes
Music	A tune for a spider rhyme	Singing the rhyme
Science	Close observation of spiders Sorting mini-creatures by the number of legs	Present simple: *Spiders eat/don't* *eat ...* Numbers, parts of the body, *has/doesn't have*
Maths	Working with the number 8	*Numbers, multiply, add, subtract, divide*
Geography	*Habitats, where spiders come from*	*Countries, nationalities, comes from*
Drama and movement	*Moving like spiders*	*Adverbs: slowly, quickly, carefully, lightly, heavily*
Hygiene	*Diseases spread by mini- creatures*	*Wash your hands, cover the food,* etc.

- Encourage Ts to discuss the integration of cross-curricular tasks into their own language teaching, e.g.
  - to list the advantages and disadvantages of introducing cross-curricular tasks in a language lesson;
  - to say if language practice is best carried out before or after a practical task has been completed, or whilst it is being completed;
  - to list the practical limitations, e.g. in terms of time, classroom space, existing coursebook;
  - to say if 'other teacher' co-operation is necessary/can be easily obtained;
  - to say if children will learn *language* more effectively.

A 'needs' spidergram: reflection and feedback

Aims
This activity encourages the teachers to:
- discuss the needs of children in a learning situation;
- discuss how a teacher can take these needs into consideration within the EFL classroom.

- Ts work in pairs/groups on the needs/action spidergrams, then discuss results with their partners/group, and whole training group. In terms of organisation of this activity, ensure that within the pairs/groups, the participants who have worked on the 'action taken by the teacher' spidergram respond point by point to the issues raised by the 'needs of children' participants.

The following are examples of completed spidergrams:

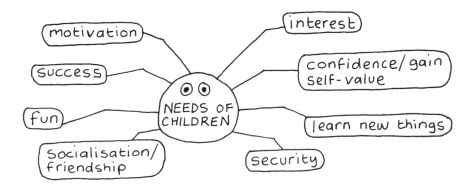

142

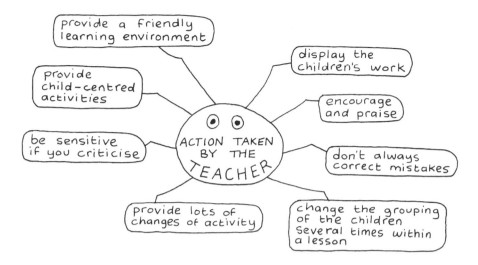

- Ask Ts to consider:
  - what happens where factors such as *motivation, interest, success,* etc. are **not** taken into consideration by the teacher;
  - how/if EFL coursebooks for children integrate these factors into teaching materials.

1.5 Discussing *communication*

Aims

This activity asks teachers to discuss:
- the meaning of *authentic communication*;
- the importance of authentic communication in the EFL classroom;
- teaching approaches and strategies that encourage authentic communication in the classroom.

It also encourages teachers to share previous classroom experience with their colleagues.

Discussion

- Start this activity by asking Ts to give examples of *authentic* and *non-authentic* communication, e.g.

authentic	non-authentic
What animal is this?	Is this a book?
What colour are your sister's eyes	What colour is this pen?
Is there a desk in **your** room at home?	Is there a desk in the classroom?

Ask them to complete the mind map and to consider the importance of factors such as *context, audience* and *purpose* in communication. Also ask Ts to discuss:
- the differences in authentic communication between adults as opposed to between children;
- how an adult/child might deal with (and react to) a particular *non-authentic* communication practice in the EFL classroom.

- Ts then do the step word game, which will form the basis of the discussion and chart completion stage of the session.
- The training group produces a consensus table. Here are some example responses from teachers:

Factors, approaches, strategies and attitudes that encourage authentic communication	Factors, approaches, strategies and attitudes that discourage authentic communication
challenging activities, activities with a clearly defined purpose, activities where there is a genuine need to exchange/find out new information, flexible layout of classroom, flexible curriculum, time to prepare for classes, lively coursebook, supportive director of school, supportive parents	choral drills, prescribed activities, children in rows, all children working on the same task, dull coursebook, too many children, prescribed language curriculum, no time to prepare, fear of making too much noise

Reading task: 'Teaching approaches'

- Ts work in *base* and *expert* groups. Experience has shown that it is desirable to establish a time-schedule for the reading and discussion before starting the activity. Write on the board:
  - the time for initial discussion and preparation in the base group;
  - the time allocated for discussion in the expert group;
  - the time allocated for feedback in the base group;
  - the time allocated for whole-group feedback.

Note that the jigsaw organisation of groups in this activity provides many opportunities for Ts to share previous experience with colleagues. At the end of the activity, discuss both the general issues raised by the reading, and the jigsaw method used.

1.6 Summary

Aim
Teachers apply their new knowledge and experiences to complete a text.

- Ts work with partners and complete the shared reading and writing task in the book. To start this activity, draw two quick *webs* on the board:

In web 1 place a language point at the centre and eight traditional EFL language tasks around it, e.g.

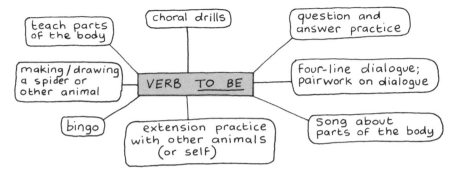

In web 2 place the word *spider* at the centre and develop a cross-curricular web around it, e.g.

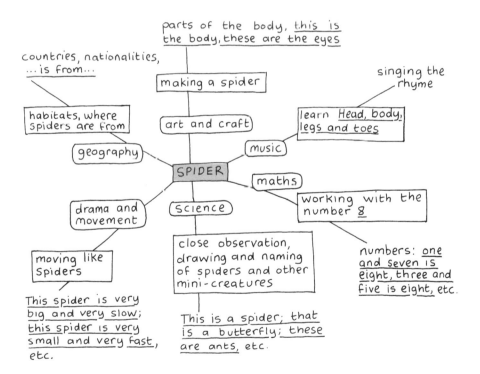

- Ask the training group to say whether they think practical tasks should be generated by a language-based syllabus or whether language aims should be generated by an activity- (or topic-) based syllabus. Do Ts feel that the starting point affects the motivation/ interest of children?
- Display the results of the writing activity on a notice board so that participants have the opportunity to compare their views with those of the rest of the group.

1.7 Round-up: spider games and rhymes

A) LITTLE MISS MUFFET

- Say and act out the rhyme. Ts watch and listen:
  Little Miss Muffet sat on a bucket,
  Eating a chocolate ice-cream.
  Along came a spider and sat down beside her,
  And made poor Miss Muffet scream.
- Ts listen in groups of four or five. Repeat the rhyme. Ts do the actions. They don't speak.
- Repeat the rhyme. T1 and T2 in each group take the roles of *spider* and *Miss Muffet*. Remaining Ts say the rhyme with you.
- Ts change roles and repeat this step.

B) ONE LITTLE ELEPHANT WENT OUT TO PLAY

- Ask two Ts to form a web with hands and legs, e.g.

Choose T1 to be the elephant. Say the first verse of the rhyme. Ensure T1 *plays* in/out/over/under/around the web. The remaining teachers watch and listen.
One little elephant went out to play,
In a spider's web one day.
She had such ENORMOUS fun,
She asked for another elephant to come.

- For Verse 2, add another teacher to the web. T1 chooses T2 to be an additional elephant. Ensure T1 and T2 *play* in/out/over/under/ around the web. The remaining teachers watch and listen.
  Two little elephants went out to play,
  In a spider's web one day.
  They had such ENORMOUS fun,
  They asked for two more elephants to come.
  Four little elephants went out to play …
- The number of elephants doubles with each verse, so, for Verse 3, ask T1 and T2 to choose two more Ts to be elephants. You add another teacher to the web.
- Play the game until all the teachers are involved. Join in the last verse yourself:
  … little elephants went out to play,
  In a spider's web one day.
  They had such ENORMOUS fun,
  They asked for (their teacher trainer) to come …

C) INCY WINCY SPIDER

- Finally, review the *Incy* action rhyme:
  Incy Wincy Spider climbed up the spout.
  Down poured the rain and washed poor Incy out.
  Out came the sun, and dried up all the rain.
  Incy Wincy spider climbed up the spout again.
- Ts work in pairs. T1 in each pair is the *actor*, T2 a *mirror*. Repeat the rhyme. T2 must copy T1's actions exactly. Ts change roles and repeat this step.

Optional

If time is available, Ts sit down in groups of four. Groups produce an illustrated *mini-book* of the rhyme:
Each teacher in the group of four receives a sheet of A4 paper. In each group, T1 is responsible for writing and illustrating line 1 of the rhyme, T2 for line 2, etc.
Re-tell the rhyme. Each group completes its *Incy* mini-book. Display the finished books.

147

2 Starting points: starting lessons in a language course

Theme/topic
Circus

Overall aims
This unit deals with the issue of the first steps of the first English class for young learners. It offers teachers the opportunity to examine several alternative aspects and approaches to the beginning of a language course.

Study plan

	Study agenda/ activities	Preparation and resources needed	Key points	Approx. timing
2.1	Examining alternative ways of starting the first lesson	Bean bag(s) or a ball	Trying out alternative starting activities for the first lessons Learn how to say *Hello, my name is ... I'm a teacher* in L3	20–30 minutes
2.2	Introduction to group-formation activities	No additional materials needed	The importance of starting a lesson with group-dynamics activities	15–20+ minutes
2.3	Practical task: the first page, the first lessons	*For reference purposes:* a range of children's EFL books *For a clown mask:* sheets of card, crayons or felt-tips, Sellotape, scissors, glue, string or elastic *For puppet making:* old socks/paper bags, scrap materials, glue, crayons	Comparing language-based with activity-based approaches Using masks and puppets	60–90 minutes

	Study agenda/ activities	Preparation and resources needed	Key points	Approx. timing
2.4	Circus across the curriculum: feedback/ discussion on teaching approaches	No additional materials needed	Sharing notes with colleagues	15–20 minutes
2.5	Concluding activities: group-dynamics activity	No additional materials needed	Creating a positive group feeling at the end of the study session	10–15 minutes
2.6	Reading assignment	No additional materials needed	Background information on activity-based learning	30–40 minutes (outside assignment)

2.1 Alternative ways of starting a language course

Aims

This activity provides and encourages:
- the pooling of ideas on the expectations of teachers, children and parents for the first English class;
- a comparison of traditional and contemporary approaches to beginning the first lessons in a language course;
- a hands-on experience as a *pupil* starting the first lesson.

Introduction: expectations for the first English class

- Ts sit in groups of three, share ideas, and complete the chart. Encourage Ts to find ways of matching (if feasible) and contrasting the expectations of parents, teachers and children.
- Ts discuss their completed table in groups of six, then report to whole group.

Here are some examples of teachers' responses:

Expectations for the first English class

Teacher	Parents	Children
To set rules To start straight away in English To teach them a few basic words and sentences To start the first lesson in the book	To speak some English To get 'exposure' to English To say something in English	To speak English To have fun To be able to understand songs in English

- Ts (in groups of six) now discuss the issues raised in the course notes, under the table. Allow up to ten minutes for discussion. Tell the members of each group that they must **all** keep a record of their group's discussion, since they will be required to share this information with a 'new' group (in ten minutes' time).
- After ten minutes, re-group the teachers as follows:
  Count quickly around each group of six, assigning a number from 1 to 3 to each participant. Where there are more or fewer than six in a group continue the number count (up to 3) on to the next group.
  Check each participant knows his/her number.
  Assign three areas (1–3) in the training room, where each group may sit.
  Tell participants to form groups according to their number, i.e. all the number 1s sit together, the number 2s sit together and so on.
  Ts share the main points from their 'old' group discussion with their 'new' group.

Here are some example responses from teachers to the discussion points in the course notes:

1 How might you feel if half the class cannot **say** anything at the end of Lesson 1, or, at the start of Lesson 2, seem to have forgotten everything they could say in Lesson 1?
   ○ Very disappointed. It is my job to get them to speak English.
   ○ I should look at other aspects of the lesson, such as how well the children get on with me and with each other – and the layout of the classroom.
   ○ Repeating does not mean the children understand or have learnt the language. I should check understanding of most things over the first few lessons.

2 What is your course of action if in the first lesson some children will not repeat words you want them to, or speak only in L1?
   ○ Encourage the children to work with different partners and to speak to each other, rather than me.
   ○ Allow them more time to feel comfortable in the class and allow them to use any language they want to in the beginning.
   ○ Use puppets.
   ○ Repeat or echo what they say in L1 in English.
   ○ Get more confident pupils to act as teachers in pairwork.
   ○ Use choral repetition.

3 What is your course of action if some children misbehave during the first class?
   ○ Explain the rules of the class and the purpose of each activity.
   ○ Talk to the parents – or send them a note.
   ○ Speak to the children after the class.
   ○ Tell the children they won't get through exams.

4 What is your course of action if some children do not participate during the first class?
   ○ Make sure they work with different partners during the lesson.
   ○ No action. Give them time to settle in.
   ○ Put them in pairs and show them the activity.
   ○ Get the whole class to repeat.

Starting a language course

- Start this activity by asking Ts to list and compare the ways they start their language course. Display this list.
- Next, present three different ways of starting Lesson 1 in a language course:

Way (A)
Ts sit in rows or in a semicircle. They take turns to stand up and introduce themselves to the rest of their group in English or L3. If Ts cannot use L3, teach an L3 sentence you have prepared. (See page 127.) Adopt as traditional a role as possible, e.g. correcting teachers while, or immediately after they speak, insisting that all teachers take turns to introduce themselves to the whole group.

Way (B)
Ts stand or sit in a circle. Introduce yourself in L3. Throw a bean bag or a ball to T1. T1 introduces him/herself in L3, and throws the bag/ball to T2, who must then introduce him/herself in English/L3. The ball goes round and across the circle in this way until everyone has given their names.
   If Ts cannot use L3, teach the L3 sentence you have prepared. By way of comparison with Way (A) do not correct any errors that Ts make.

Way (C)
Ts stand in a large *circus ring*:
T1 starts the game by saying his/her name and adding a gesture, such as a curtsey/arm movement.
The whole group repeats the gesture and T1's name.
T2 (standing next to T1) says his/her name and adds a different gesture.
The whole group repeats T1's name and gesture, then T2's name and gesture.
T3 (standing next to T2) says his/her name and adds a different gesture.
The whole group repeats T1's name and gesture, then T2's name and gesture, then T3's name and gesture.
Continue around the *circus ring* until each teacher in the group has said his/her name and given a gesture.

Note: If there are more than twelve teachers in your training group, organise them into equal circles (up to) twelve.

- After completing the three activities, Ts comment on how they felt both as a *new learner* and as a *teacher* during each of the activities. Use the questions below to encourage discussion.

Here are some example responses by teachers:

1 Which activity created the most/least stress for you and the group?
   ○ The name + action game was really funny. We also learned everyone's names.
   ○ Repeating in front of the others was very stressful.
   ○ The bean bag game was a lot of fun. It could get out of control though.

2 Which activity enabled you to get to know others in the group most effectively?
   ○ The name + action game. The actions helped fix the name.
   ○ Passing the bean bag. I had to listen very carefully.

3 Which activity encouraged the most participation from all the group?
   ○ The name + action game. It was very funny. We all took part all of the time.
   ○ Saying our names one by one was very boring and slow.

4 Which activity takes up too much valuable class time?
   ○ The name + action game because I had to wait for everyone to have their turn, but it was the most fun.
   ○ Saying our names one by one to the teacher took a lot of time and was very boring and stressful.
   ○ The bean bag seemed the most practical activity and it was the fastest.

2.2 Group formation and the learning community

Aims
This activity provides:
- explanation of the meaning of *group formation*;
- further hands-on experience of *group formation*.

- Ts read the background information then work in pairs and convince their partners of the value of group-formation activities.
- When they have finished, organise the following group-formation activities:

A) CIRCUS ALPHABET

- Ts stand in small circles (in groups) of four or five.

- Ts hold hands and take a slow, deep breath.
- Ts let hands go. Call out this sequence of six letters: *C–I–R–C–U–S*, one at a time. Ts form the shape of each letter after you say it by linking arms or hands, etc. with the rest of their group.
- Ask Ts if they can name the word they have spelt.

B) CIRCUS 'TELEPHONE MIMES'

- Ts stand in (equal) lines of up to seven. Lines face the back wall of the room (and away from you). T1, the teacher in each line closest to the front wall (and to you), turns to face you. The remaining teachers must not turn round. Allow no talking until the end of the game.
- You demonstrate a short *circus* mime to the T1 teachers. Each T1 then taps T2 (the next in line) on the shoulder. T2 turns to face T1. The remaining Ts must not turn round. T1 'passes on' your mime to T2.
- Each T2 then taps T3 (the next in line) on the shoulder. T3 turns to face T2. The remaining Ts must not turn round. T2 'passes on' the mime to T3. Continue the game in this way until the last teacher in each line, who repeats the mime for the whole group, and says what they think it is.
- Each line then gets together and individual Ts explain the mime they were trying to 'pass on'.

C) 'CLOWNS'

- All Ts stand in a circle. Choose T1 to be the clown. The clown does a *clown* action and says *Clown, clown, clown, clown* very quickly.
- The teacher on the *left* of the clown must put his/her *right* hand on her head and raise his/her (imaginary) *clown's hat*.
- The teacher standing on the *right* of the clown must put his/her *left* hand on her head and raise his/her (imaginary) *clown's hat*.
- The clown checks this is correct. The clown then throws an imaginary *custard pie* at another teacher (T2), saying T2's name as the pie is thrown. T2 is now the new clown.
- The new clown repeats the actions and words of the old clown. The teachers standing on the left and right of T2 have to put the correct hand on their heads immediately, and raise their clown's hats.
- Play the game for one or two minutes at a fast pace.

As a final reflection activity Ts discuss which of the group-formation activities they find appropriate or not to their own class and personalities.

2.3 Practical task: the first page, the first lessons

Aims

This activity encourages a comparison of different first pages in children's EFL coursebooks, and the various ways coursebooks start a language course with children. It also asks teachers to reflect on the way **they** start (would like to start) their first lesson in a course.

The first page in the coursebook

- Ts work in groups of four or five and follow the instructions in the course notes.
- First, within their groups, Ts agree on and complete a simple dialogue for the five cartoon frames in the book.
- Next, each T makes a clown's mask or simple *stick puppet*. Ts use their masks to practise, within their group, the dialogue they have written on the cartoon frames.
- Next, display the masks/puppets. Ask Ts to write dialogue bubbles and attach them to the display around the masks/puppets:

- Finally, Ts mention the language teaching books for children they associate with various types of activity in the first lesson. They then discuss how **they** would start their first lesson.

The first lessons

In groups of four, Ts discuss and circle the activities listed that they think are the most appropriate as **early stages** in a language course. In terms of organisation for this activity:

- Go quickly around the whole training group, assigning four 'circus jobs', one to each participant, e.g. *clown, acrobat, juggler, strongman/woman.*

- Check each participant knows his/her job.
- Assign four areas (one each for the *clowns, acrobats, jugglers, strong-men/women*) in the training room where each group may sit.
- Tell participants to form groups according to their job, i.e. all the clowns sit together, the acrobats sit together and so on.
- Set a time limit for the discussion, e.g. ten minutes, and tell the members of each group that they must **all** keep a record of their group's discussion, since they will be required to share this information with a 'new' group.
- At the specified time, assign a new job (e.g. *clown, acrobat, juggler, strongman/woman*) to each participant within their mini-groups.
- Tell participants to re-group according to their new job, i.e. all the (new) clowns sit together, the (new) acrobats sit together, and so on.
- Participants (in their new groups) share the points raised in their 'old' groups.

Example points to consider:
- Ask Ts to explain why they have rejected specific activities and why they favour others as starters. Create a 'top five' list.
- Since most children in a class may already know each other, ask Ts if they feel that *Hello, my name is* ... should form the core of a first lesson of a language course. Similarly, identifying known objects (e.g. *This is a book*) would seem to present little intellectual challenge to normal eight- to-ten year olds. Can Ts suggest alternatives?
- In a primary school situation, many children get to know each other through doing things together, and through studying together. Do Ts feel this has any practical carry-over in the EFL classroom? In other words, should first lessons present a *practical task* challenge as well as (or instead of) a *language* challenge?

For the next activity, if feasible, provide a range of potential puppet-making materials.
- Re-group the Ts as above into new groups of four. Ts make a list of different kinds of puppets that children might make in the classroom. They choose one type of puppet material and make a *circus set*. Display the finished puppets and organise the room so that Ts can practise a range of 'starting' activities with their puppets.
- Re-group the Ts as above into new groups of five. Ts discuss how they could further develop the use of these puppets with young beginners in the language classroom.
  Examples:
  roleplay
  presenters of new language
  taking the identity of characters in a coursebook

2.4 Follow-up: circus across the curriculum

Aims

This activity encourages Ts to:
- expand a topic across the curriculum;
- suggest a language focus for a variety of cross-curricular tasks;
- examine the feasibility of doing cross-curricular tasks in L1 and L2.

- Ts discuss in groups of five or six how they might develop the theme of *circus* across the curriculum in L1 (i.e. the children's native language). Draw the following topic web on the board (or dictate) as an example:

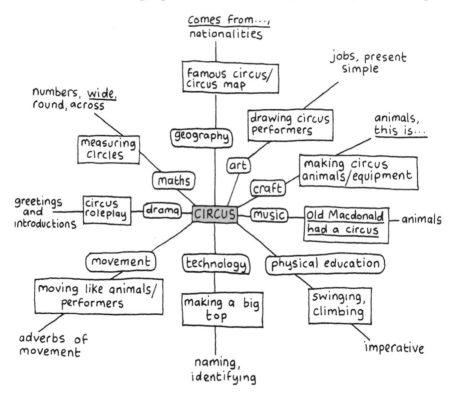

- Ensure that Ts include the point of age/ability range in their discussions. For example, how may a task be developed to challenge a bright eleven year old, or simplified to suit a less able eight year old?
- In addition, ask Ts to comment on those activities in coursebooks they are familiar with which develop the use of language as a *tool* of communication, and those which focus on practising the language *form*, irrespective of *content* value.
- The final activity in this section asks Ts to choose one language focus from their table where puppets could be used to practise/develop a

short dialogue. The aim of this last phase is to ensure that Ts realise the importance of keeping a clear language focus 'in mind', even during an activity stage of a lesson. In this way, even more traditionally oriented EFL teachers (and parents) can feel satisfied that *language* learning is taking place and is being monitored.

If time is available, encourage selected pairs of teachers to demonstrate their dialogue to the whole group with their (finger) puppets.

2.5 Concluding activities

Aims
This activity encourages Ts to:
– use songs in the language classroom;
– view songs as a *springboard* for language work.

● Ts work in groups of five or six and follow the instructions in the book. Ask Ts to give opinions on the use of songs in the language classroom.

2.6 Reading assignment

Aims
This activity provides extensive background information on *an activity-based approach*.

● Ts may complete the reading outside the training room. Ensure Ts respond to the preparation questions in the book prior to the reading.
● As an alternative, Ts work in *base* and *expert* groups as in the activity on page 14 in Unit 1. In this case, the reading within each base group can be divided as follows:
T1 – reads up to *An example framework for teaching in English*.
T2 – reads up to *Group support*.
T3 – reads from *Group support* to the end.
Each base group finally pieces together all the information in their own words. This can be displayed on a poster and presented to the whole training group under your direction.

3 Building up a teaching sequence

Theme/topic
Potatoes

Overall aims
This unit illustrates the value of linking the activities within a teaching unit to one specific topic or theme.

Study plan

	Study agenda/ activities	Preparation and resources needed	Key points	Approx. timing
3.1	Starting points: *potato* group-dynamics activities	One potato per teacher	Hands-on experience of topic-based group-dynamics activities The value of a *theme-based* unit	up to 20 minutes
3.2	Introducing new vocabulary	Sheets of A4 paper, crayons or felt tips	Presentation techniques for teaching new words to children	up to 40 minutes
3.3	Participating in a total 'potato' response activity	No additional materials needed	The concept of *topic-based TPR*	20–30 minutes
3.4	Telling the 'Giant Potato' story	Transparencies or A4 sheets of paper	Storytelling in the teaching of children	40–60 minutes
3.5	Reading task: potato puppets	No additional materials needed	Use of puppets in the teaching of children Linking all activities (including language focus) to a theme/topic	40–60 minutes
3.6	Playing bingo: using key 'potato' vocabulary	No additional materials needed	Topic-based word games	up to 20 minutes
3.7	Concluding/ group-dynamics activity using *potato chants*	No additional materials needed	Topic-based group dynamics activities	10–15 minutes

	Study agenda/ activities	Preparation and resources needed	Key points	Approx. timing
3.8	Summary: reflection on the sequencing of the stages in an activity-based lesson	No additional materials needed	Suggesting or discussing alternatives to the teaching sequence in the book	up to 20 minutes

3.1 Starting points

Aims

This activity encourages:
- participation in a variety of *theme-based* group-formation activities;
- the development of theme-based formation activities.

A) PLAY POTATO ALPHABET

- Ts stand in small circles (in groups) of four or five.
- Ts hold hands and take a slow, deep breath.
- Ts let hands go. You call out this sequence of five letters: *C–H–I–P–S*, one at a time. Ts form the shape of each letter after you say it by linking arms, or hands, etc. with the rest of their group.
- Ask Ts which word they have spelt.

B) PLAY HOT POTATO

- Form large circles of six to ten teachers. (You may need to do this activity outside.) T1 receives a *hot potato*. For this you can use a real potato (cold!), a bean bag, a ball, etc.
- T1 walks around the outside of the circle with the 'potato', and suddenly gives the potato to T2, who is standing in the circle. T1 shouts *hot potato*, and begins to run around the outside of the circle while the teachers in the circle pass the potato from one to the other, saying *It's hot. It's very hot.* As they do so, T1 should run around and reach the original starting position (T2) before the teachers can pass the potato right around the circle and back to T2. If T1 succeeds, the teacher holding the potato when T1 reaches the starting position is the new *hot potato* holder for a repeat game. Anyone dropping the potato automatically becomes the new *hot potato* holder.

C) PLAY PASS THE POTATO

- Ts stand in equal team lines of about six to ten teachers. T1 at the front of each line holds a large potato in the bend of his/her elbow or between the *insides* of his/her wrists.

- Say *Pass the potato*. Each team must pass their potato back to the last team member and then back to T1 at the front, without using their hands. Dropped potatoes must be returned to the starting point.

D) PLAY VEGETABLE SOUP

Note: Experience has shown that over-excitement during this game can lead to injuries. For the sake of safety, place all chairs **against** the wall so that they cannot tip over backwards during the game.

- Ts sit in a circle. Each T sits on his/her own chair. Remove any additional chairs.
- Choose any three or four vegetables (depending on the size of your training group). Assign each T the name of a vegetable: one vegetable per T. In other words, in a group of fifteen, there may be four teachers who are *potatoes*, four teachers who are *tomatoes*, four who are *carrots*, and three who are *spinach*. Now follow the instructions for *Hairy spider* on page 137.

Follow-up/discussion

At the end of these *formation* games, Ts sit in teams of five or six. Teams follow the instructions concerning the discussion in the course notes. In terms of support for teachers in this discussion, it is useful to write a partially completed topic web on the board. This can be produced from the topic web on page 236 of the Resource file. Use different colours to distinguish between *cross-curricular* tasks and *language* focus/teaching point.

Make sure that groups exchange ideas at the end of their small group discussion and that the topic web is completed on the board.

Ts reflect carefully on which cross-curricular activities can/cannot be carried out feasibly within a language lesson in the teaching situations they are familiar with.

Notes on points you may wish to raise:
Many practical tasks can only be done within the regular school timetable. There may be no resources available in the language lesson.

○ It is not difficult to organise a language class for most simple activities. For example, to make potato puppets, only a little preparation is needed in terms of bringing in potatoes and materials for the puppets – and children can be motivated to help you to do this. You need to take care of the safety aspect.

Ts consider the differences (if any) between developing a language focus as a result of completing a practical activity and doing a practical activity as an 'extension task' once a language point has been taught.

○ It is a question of purpose and motivation. Children may not see any purpose in learning the present simple just because it is the next page in a coursebook. However, if they need to (and want to) describe the animals in a potato zoo they have created, there is both purpose and motivation to the learning.

○ Children may learn the present simple in a coursebook context and make no connection with its use in **their** terms. In other words, until children can see how a particular language point affects their world, the learning of a structure may be purely by rote, and be easily forgotten. It makes sense to provide the purpose (e.g. a practical task) first and then the tools for describing it (e.g. the present simple tense).

3.2 Introducing new vocabulary

Aims
This activity practises pupil-centred techniques for teaching vocabulary.

Micro teaching

● You may need to demonstrate this teaching procedure to the whole group. In this case, choose a set of four common classroom objects as vocabulary items for the demonstration. Encourage a *co-operative* development of the procedure for presenting vocabulary, the Ts referring to the procedure in the book while you demonstrate.

● When ready, Ts work in groups of six or seven. They follow their instructions for *micro teaching*. If there are L3 speakers in the training group, encourage them to use L3 and act as *teachers* in the micro-groups.

Feedback/discussion

Ts refer to their instructions in groups of five or six and discuss the *micro-teaching* activity. Here are some example responses from teachers to the discussion points:

1 Could you use this technique for presenting other sets of vocabulary?
   ○ Yes, any set of vocabulary that can be easily drawn onto A4 paper, or can be brought into the classroom as real objects.

2 What types of vocabulary could **not** be easily presented in this way?
   ○ Words that are not nouns or adjectives.

3 What are the limitations or restrictions of this technique with young beginners in the language classroom?
   ○ Time may be a restriction.
   ○ Parents may not understand the relevance of this activity to learning language.

○ It could be difficult to organise.
○ No restrictions.

For example, how would you adapt this technique for teaching groups of 15 or 35 pupils?
○ It's difficult to use in large classes.
○ Organise the pupils into groups and rearrange the desks and chairs.

4 Would this technique be suitable for mixed-ability classes?
○ Very suitable because it encourages all the children to help each other. There is no pressure on the weaker pupils; they can achieve at their own level.

5 Would this technique need to be adapted for older children, say eleven year olds?
○ There is no problem here. Teenagers might be a little self-conscious about the gestures, but they would depend on the teacher to make them feel comfortable.

6 How would you imagine the classroom layout for introducing vocabulary in this way?
○ Tables in groups.
○ Put the chairs into circles of six or seven.
○ Keep the classroom as it is.
○ Divide the classroom into teaching zones, each containing one or two rows of desks and chairs (and children). *Label* the zones with numbers or colours, and appoint pupils as *monitors* in charge of each zone.

3.3 Total 'potato' response activity/action games

Aims
This activity provides:
– an introduction to *TPR*;
– an example of 'theme-based' TPR content.

Introduction

As an introduction to *TPR*, Ts play *Simon says* or sing *This is the way ...* (See Resource file, pages 262 and 261.)

Practice

● Next, for the *TPR practice*, Ts stand in groups of five or six. Each group stands in a circle. Appoint a leader (T1) for each group. T1 stands in the centre of his/her group circle. There are four steps to this activity:

1 **Explanation/introduction:** Tell the teachers they are going to do a *TPR* task. Confirm that the language involved is relevant to the story you will be telling as the next step in the training session.

2 **Presentation:** Read out the text below once through without stopping, demonstrating the actions with gesture and mime as you say the text. Teachers watch and listen only. They don't speak.
    Text: Dig a big hole. Take a potato. Plant it. Water it. The sun shines. Then the rain pours down. Pours down. The potato starts to grow. It grows higher and higher and higher. The leaves start to grow. They grow wider and wider and wider. The wind starts to blow. It blows harder and harder and harder and ... stops. Relax.

3 **Controlled practice 1:** Say the text once more, demonstrating the associated actions as you speak. Stop after each sentence. T1 of each group repeats the sentence and/or does the actions, the rest of the teachers do the actions without speaking.

4 **Controlled practice 2:** Say the text once without demonstrating the associated actions as you speak. Stop after each sentence. T1 of each group repeats the sentence and/or does the actions, the rest of the teachers do the actions without speaking.

● At the end of the activity, Ts refer to their instructions in groups of five or six and discuss it. Here are some example responses from teachers to the discussion points:

1 How many teaching steps were there in this activity? What were they?
    ○ Four teaching steps:

	Trainer	Trainees
a	Introduced and explained the task, organised the space and trainees.	Listened, watched and responded.
b	Demonstrated the task, spoke and did the associated actions and gestures.	Listened and watched only.
c	Demonstrated the task again, spoke and did the associated actions and gestures.	T1 in each group repeated the actions and gestures, and some of the verbal instructions (as best they could); the remaining trainees did the actions.
d	Spoke without doing the associated actions and gestures.	T1 in each group did the actions and gestures, and said the verbal instructions (as best they could); the remaining trainees did the actions.

2 What, if any, is the relationship between the content of this text and the vocabulary you have worked with in the previous tasks?
    ○ All the activities are related to potatoes and growing.

3 This activity precedes a storytelling. Assuming that the content of this TPR activity is relevant to the story, what do you think the content or theme of the story will be?
   ○ Possibly *Jack and the Beanstalk*.
   ○ A story about plants and growing bigger and bigger.

4 Could this activity threaten the *status* of the teacher?
   ○ Teachers need to be lively and enthusiastic. They mustn't be afraid of acting in front of the children.

5 How much classroom space is needed for this activity? Could it be adapted to suit large classes and/or classrooms where movement of the pupils is very difficult to organise?
   ○ The children could do this activity sitting down in their seats.
   ○ It would work in large classes. Children could use puppets or their hands and arms for the actions.

6 In this activity, the trainer used a *team leader* for each group. If you did this same activity with children, would you use *team leaders*? If so, would their role differ?
   ○ Team leaders could help to manage large groups; the roles would be about the same.
   ○ It's a good idea to give responsibility to the pupils.

3.4 The 'giant potato story'

Aim

This activity provides an introduction to *active* storytelling.

Introduction

Ts work in pairs. They follow the instructions.

Active storytelling

● Organise Ts into *family groups* of five or six (T1–T5) for the story-telling.
● Within each group, assign T1–T5 the roles of *Mr Fry, Mrs Fry, Peter Fry, Barbara Fry*. The remaining Ts in each group are other children or *the pets*.
● Confirm that Ts know their roles, e.g. say:
  Hands up, Mr Fry. Hands up, Mr Fry's wife. Hands up, Mr Fry's son, Peter. Hands up, Mrs Fry's daughter. Hands up, Barbara Fry's pet cat, Pepper. Hands up, Peter Fry's father, etc.
● Families sit in small, open semicircles, with *Mr Fry* at one end, *Mrs Fry* next to *Mr Fry*, *Peter* next to *Mrs Fry*, *Barbara* next to *Peter*, and the remaining *children* or *pets* next to *Barbara*.

• Tell the story, using lots of gestures and action during the storytelling. Encourage T1–T5 in each group to assume their roles and actively participate during the storytelling. In addition, every time you mention the word *potato* (**not** *potatoes*), Ts must make an 'enormous potato' gesture. If you wish to make this more complicated, substitute the words *strange vegetable* for *potato* in lines 9 and 30. Ts must not make the 'enormous potato' gesture here.

The giant potato story
Once upon a time there was a man called Mr Fry. He loved potatoes. He ate potatoes for breakfast. He ate potatoes for lunch. He ate potatoes for afternoon tea and he ate potatoes for dinner.

One day Mr Fry got a parcel. It was from his brother, in Peru. Inside the parcel there was a very strange potato. It was very small. It was very round. It was very yellow. There was a note in the parcel. It said: 'Plant this potato in a very big hole in your garden. Don't, repeat, **don't** water it.' Mr Fry was very excited. He went into his garden. He dug a very big hole. He planted the potato. The sun was shining. It was very hot. So Mr Fry picked up a watering can and watered the potato. Suddenly, there was a flash of lightning and it started to rain. The rain poured down. Poured down. And the potato started to grow. It grew bigger and bigger and bigger. And the leaves started to grow. They grew wider and wider and wider. Mr Fry looked at the enormous plant. He was very hungry. He thought 'enormous plant = enormous potato'. So he held the top of the plant and he pulled harder and harder and harder, but nothing happened.

So he called his wife, Mrs Fry, to help. Mr Fry held the plant. Mrs Fry held Mr Fry. They pulled harder and harder and harder, but nothing happened.

So Mrs Fry called her son, Peter, to help. Mr Fry held the plant. Mrs Fry held Mr Fry. Peter held Mrs Fry. They pulled harder and harder and harder, but nothing happened.

So Peter called his sister, Barbara, to help. Mr Fry held the plant. Mrs Fry held Mr Fry. Peter held Mrs Fry. Barbara held Peter. They pulled harder and harder and harder, but nothing happened.

So Barbara called the pets to help. Mr Fry held the plant. Mrs Fry held Mr Fry. Peter held Mrs Fry. Barbara held Peter. The pets held Barbara. They pulled harder and harder and harder, and they pulled harder and harder, and HARDER, and suddenly, out came the potato. It was ENORMOUS. It was the biggest potato they had ever seen.

'I'm hungry,' said Mr Fry. 'What's for dinner?' 'Potatoes,' said Peter and Barbara …

Note: If teachers in your training group may be offended at taking the roles of pets, change the story to include extra children, or aunts/uncles, etc.

Follow-up

- After the storytelling stage, Ts follow their instructions to reproduce an illustrated version of the story on OHP transparencies or paper.
- As an optional activity, encourage Ts to make small cut-outs of the Fry family and use these as *mini-shadow puppets* on the OHP for re-telling the story.
- Next, Ts discuss the issues listed in the course notes. Here are example responses from teachers for the last two points in the discussion task: What would the possible next steps be in the teaching sequence?
  - ○ Potato printing – teaching colours and shapes.
  - ○ Further language practice of the comparatives, starting from *bigger, harder, higher*.
  - ○ Further language practice of members of the family.
  - ○ Roleplay of the story.

  What are the practical uses of this activity in the primary classroom as part of an L1 topic on vegetables or potatoes?
  - ○ Definitely possible to integrate into project work done in L1.
  - ○ Difficult, because we only teach the children for English two hours a week … need to co-ordinate with the children's full-time class teacher.
  - ○ We don't usually do project work.
  - ○ We think we should integrate this kind of learning into the regular curriculum.

- Finally, using the chart in the book as a guide, Ts produce a cross-curricular topic web, with *potato* at the centre. Encourage Ts to use their own ideas rather than merely to copy the ones in the table, and to produce an attractively illustrated poster. Display the posters.

3.5 Reading task: potato puppets

Aims
This activity demonstrates:
- the use of puppets in the teaching of children;
- the *linking* of activities (including language focus) to a theme/topic.

- Ts work in teams of five or six, complete the reading task, then follow the discussion instructions. Here are some example responses from teachers to the discussion points:
1 What are the ways of creating a stage for puppet activities?
  - ○ A table or desk, on its side, so that the puppeteers can hide behind it.

2 How might you use (include potential difficulties of) this activity in your language classroom?

○ Time will be a problem in a normal language class. It may also be difficult to provide materials for a large class. (Can teachers suggest ways of organising this activity for a class of 20+?)

○ The language is relatively straightforward, particularly if the class teacher acts as the narrator. Alternatively, with older children, the narrator's lines may be put on an OHT and read aloud by the non-acting pupils.

3 Can Ts think of other uses (and other types) of puppets, e.g. sock puppets as language presenters in a roleplay?

○ Often the language of classroom instruction for an activity presents a communication problem. If a teacher uses puppets to demonstrate what to do, or the interaction in a roleplay, this can get round a lengthy and potentially frustrating explanation, or the need to translate into L1. In addition Ps also acquire a rich store of understanding of classroom language that they can respond to.

4 How may puppets allow children to take roles which they might otherwise feel embarrassed to accept?

○ Children will quite happily take on all sorts of roles for their puppet. This can get round the reluctance to take roles of different gender, age, etc.

5 How may puppets provide authenticity and motivation to a potentially dull language practice?

○ Learning lines for a puppet to enact is a far richer learning experience than merely repeating in chorus after a teacher.

• Ts sit in their groups and discuss possible next steps in the teaching sequence for the potato story. Examples may include:
- further vocabulary input;
- further potato games;
- further cross-curricular activities that generate specific language points, e.g. making a bag for potatoes and guessing how many potatoes there are in the bag.

• Finally, reorganise Ts into new groups of five or six. In order to create a positive atmosphere, start the activity with a 'potato formation game', e.g.

Groups stand in a (closed) circle. Ts all face clockwise and place their hands on the shoulders of the T in front of them.

Tell Ts to 'clean the board' (i.e. gently rub the back of the teacher standing in front of them in the circle with an imaginary cloth).

Say the TPR text you used earlier in this unit:

Dig a big hole. Take a potato. Plant it. Water it. The sun shines. Then the rain pours down. Pours down. The potato starts to grow. It grows higher and higher and higher. The leaves start to grow. They grow wider and wider and wider. The wind starts to blow. It blows harder and harder and harder and … stops. Relax.

Ts must enact/draw (with a finger) this text on the back of the T standing in front of them in the circle. Encourage them to add 'sound effects' for the 'wind'.

Ts change direction (i.e. face anti-clockwise) and you repeat the activity/text.

3.6   Bingo: using key 'potato' vocabulary

Aims
This activity provides:
- an example of *bingo* as a vocabulary consolidation game;
- practice of the procedures for playing *bingo*.

- As a first step, you may need to go through the bingo procedure with the whole group. In this case encourage a *co-operative* development of the teaching procedure: ask the teachers to help you to work out the necessary teaching steps and tasks.
- When ready, Ts follow their instructions.

3.7   Concluding/group-dynamics activity

Aims
This activity demonstrates:
- the use of rhymes in the language classroom;
- the value of *theme-based* rhymes.

- Ts work in teams of five or six and follow the instructions. The following is an example procedure for teaching a rhyme or chant or song:

Teaching procedure	What the pupils do
1 Play or say the rhyme right through without stopping.	Listen only.
2 Say the rhyme again. This time make appropriate actions and gestures as you say the rhyme.	Listen and watch. They don't repeat.
3 Say or play the rhyme again, with the appropriate actions and gestures.	Listen and do the gestures and actions. They don't speak.
4 Say or play the rhyme again, line by line, with the appropriate actions and gestures. Ask the groups to change roles and repeat this step.	Half the group repeat after you, the other half do the actions and gestures.

| 5 Play the cassette or mime the rhyme without speaking. | The class say the rhyme as best they can with the cassette, or following your mimed prompts. |

3.8 Summary: a unit outline

Aims
This activity asks teachers to:
- reflect on the teaching sequence for an *activity-centred* teaching unit;
- compare this sequence with a more traditional EFL teaching unit.

Ts refer to Unit Outlines A and B in the course notes and investigate the contrast between a more traditional approach to the use of stories in the language classroom (Outline A), with that presented so far in this unit (Outline B).

- Start the activity by organising Ts into groups of five or six. Write the sequence of the activities presented in this unit in **random order** on the board, i.e.
  play potato games
  teach 5 or 6 potato-story vocabulary items
  enactment of a 'potato response' text
  storytelling of the potato story
  potato puppet making
  potato story roleplay + language focus
  potato bingo (theme-related game)
  round-up activity (theme related)
- Within their groups Ts agree on a 'teaching' sequence for the activities.
- Next, refer Ts to Unit Outlines A and B. Divide the whole group into Group(s) A and Group(s) B (optimum group size is five or six Ts). Group(s) A work with Outline A; Group(s) B work with Outline B.
- Groups discuss the outlines. They should consider:
  - the teaching sequence in the outline;
  - the number of lessons needed to teach the content of the outline;
  - any extra steps/activities that may be needed to manage the content of the outline.
  Groups should also list:
  - vocabulary the children should be able to recognise by the end of the unit;
  - vocabulary the children should be able to produce by the end of the unit;
  - the language structure(s)/function(s) the children will be able to recognise by the end of the unit;
  - the language structure(s)/function(s) the children will be able to produce by the end of the unit.

The following are example issues that you may wish to raise during this activity:

1 Is there a 'best order' for the activities or could there be variations, e.g.
What are the factors that determine a teaching sequence?
Is it possible or desirable to maintain a fixed sequence?
What events might make it necessary to change the sequence?

2 What is the time required for each stage in the sequence, e.g.
What activities, if any, are a 'waste of time' in terms of EFL learning?
If time is tight, which should be omitted, language practice or completion of a task?

3 How does the activity-based sequence compare with a language-based EFL sequence, e.g.
Are teachers aware of the three Ps, i.e. presentation, practice and production?
Are the three Ps as relevant to teaching children as they seem to be in the teaching of adults?
How important is 'production' compared with 'doing and understanding'? In other words, can production be more readily postponed in the children's EFL classroom?

- When finished, reorganise the training group into new groups consisting of members of the 'old' Groups A and B. Allow about ten minutes for an information exchange.
- In order to bring the training group together at the end of the session, encourage a more confident teacher to organise a final game of *vegetable soup* (see page 160).

4 Adapting EFL techniques to teaching children

Theme/topic
Islands

Overall aims
This unit examines the relevance of contemporary EFL techniques to the teaching of English to younger learners. It also illustrates the crossover between primary practice and the teaching of EFL.

Study plan

	Study agenda/ activities	Preparation and resources needed	Key points	Approx. timing
4.1	Starting points: group formation	No additional materials needed	Topic-based group-dynamics activities Use of songs/rhymes as a central point for a range of activities contrasted with use as a language practice tool	20–30 minutes
4.2	Consolidation of techniques for introducing vocabulary	Sheets of A4 paper, crayons or felt tips	Consolidation of presentation techniques for teaching new words	40–50 minutes
4.3	Total 'island' response activity	No additional materials needed	In-depth study of topic-based TPR	90+ minutes
4.4	Treasure island 'EFL Techniques': a forfeit game	No additional materials needed	Identifying, listing and demonstrating EFL teaching techniques	30+ minutes
4.5	Practical task: designing a 'treasure island' game; developing a lesson plan	Making a 3D board game: card, scissors, A2/A1 size card/ paper, crayons, scrap materials, glue, etc.	Designing a game for classroom use Developing a lesson/ unit plan around a theme/topic Co-operative team work	120+ minutes

	Study agenda/ activities	Preparation and resources needed	Key points	Approx. timing
4.6	Feedback/ discussion task on primary education/EFL teaching techniques	No additional materials needed	Sharing notes on the crossover between EFL and primary education	40–60+ minutes
4.7	Round-up activity: review the chant	No additional materials needed	Relating the theme of the unit to group-dynamics activities	15–20 minutes

4.1 Starting points

Aims
This activity provides:
- further practice of group-formation activities;
- reflection on the use of songs and rhymes in EFL for younger learners.

Group-formation activities

A) ROW YOUR BOAT

Ts sit in two parallel lines facing the board, on chairs or on the floor. They sing *Row, row, row your boat* according to the instructions in the course notes.

B) FIVE FAT SAUSAGES

Ts stand or sit in circles of at least five and follow the instructions in the course notes.

Reflection and reading

- Ts follow the instructions in pairs.
- Point out to the Ts that the songs and rhymes in this book are viewed as a *whole*, and are integrated with the other tasks in any specific unit. They are not analysed for their value in terms of language exercises. As with stories, songs and rhymes provide the *starting, central* or *end point* for a range of activities that include a language teaching focus. The song/rhyme itself does not need to be seen/used as the *source* of the language focus.

4.2 Consolidation of techniques: introducing new vocabulary for Treasure Island

Aims

This activity provides consolidation of teaching procedures for presenting and teaching vocabulary.

Micro teaching

- Ts use the Treasure Island vocabulary on the page and follow the detailed instructions.

Feedback/discussion on the task

- Ts follow the detailed instructions in groups of five or six.
- Record the results of the discussions, e.g. Ts produce an information sheet on an OHT on *teaching vocabulary*.

4.3 Total 'island' response activity

Aims

This activity encourages:
- an in-depth study of TPR techniques and procedures;
- the use of a *theme* for the development of a TPR text.

Starting point

The first task is to raise the Ts' awareness of the factors that make a TPR text usable/difficult to use with children.
- Organise the Ts into groups of five or six. Say and attempt to demonstrate with actions the *total island response* text on page 51.
- Ask Ts to comment on the parts they felt were too difficult, complicated or hard to demonstrate through gesture and mime. Ts then work in their groups and re-write/simplify the text. The following is a possible simplification:
  You are on Treasure Island. You walk and you walk and you walk. You see a bridge. Walk across the bridge. You see a wide river. Swim across the river. You see a high mountain. Climb the mountain. You see a volcano. Run around the volcano. You see a dark cave. Tip-toe into the cave. You see a treasure chest. Open it up. What's inside?
- Make quick drawings of a treasure island, a bridge, a mountain, a volcano, a river, a treasure chest on the board. Using the above simplified text and your drawings on the board, demonstrate the following five

steps in a TPR activity (the content of these steps has been adapted to suit an audience of English-speaking teachers rather than beginner-level children):

1 **Explaining/confirming what is going to happen**
   - Tell Ts they are going to do a TPR task.
   - Confirm that language involved is relevant to the *island game* that they will be using later in the training session.

For the purpose of managing the task effectively, teachers will work with a partner within groups of four or six.

2 **Presentation of the text and associated actions**
   - Say the simplified text above once through without stopping, demonstrating the actions as you say the text by 'walking' with your fingers around the Treasure Island you have drawn on the board.
   - Elicit from Ts (by miming or asking) what they think is inside the treasure chest. Many groups of Ts shout 'treasure' at this point. The Ts watch and listen only for the majority of the text. They don't speak except to say what is in the treasure chest.

This *silent* (or *active*) listening stage is very important for *long-term* acquisition of the language.

3 **Guided practice of the text and actions**
   - T1 in each pair takes his/her partner's open hand and uses it as a 'Treasure Island'.
   - Say the text once more, demonstrating the associated actions on the board as you speak. Stop after each sentence. T1 of each pair repeats the actions on the hand of his/her partner without speaking.
   - Ts change roles and repeat this step.

4 **Consolidation practice of the text and actions**
   - Say the text once more, this time without demonstrating the associated actions as you speak. Stop after each sentence. T1 of each pair does the actions on the hand of his/her partner without speaking. Ts change roles and repeat this step.

Follow-up stage
Ts practise the complete TPR activity within their groups:
   - Appoint TL within each group to be the team leader. TL in each group takes your role of presenter of the text.
   - TL goes through the four steps, with the remaining Ts in his/her group taking the role of pupils (working in pairs/threes). Each group works co-operatively through this activity, giving support to their TL if he/she gets stuck.
   - Ts change roles within their groups and repeat the activity until they are confident with the procedure. You should give support where needed.

Challenge

- Ts follow the detailed instructions in the course notes and produce a large visual aid of a *How to do TPR* instruction sheet. As with previous *jigsaw* group activities, negotiate a time schedule with the Ts before the start of the activity and ensure that the time frame is followed.

4.4 Treasure Island 'EFL techniques': a forfeit game

Aims

This activity encourages teachers to identify, list and comment on practical teaching (EFL) techniques, procedures, and skills.

Ts work in groups of five or six and follow the detailed instructions in the course notes. Each forfeit relates to a technique or procedure associated with TEFL for younger learners. The chart below is a reference. Make sure Ts carry out their forfeits **in full**.

Forfeit key	Possible related teaching aims
Ask a *yes/no* question about the treasure.	Checking understanding
Draw a happy (island) face on the board, or on a friend's back, with your finger.	Assessment
Mime burying the treasure.	TPR, mime explanation
Make up and chant a four-line island rap rhyme.	Consolidation of language
Check if your partner can say *island* correctly.	Pronunciation, correction
Stand up, rub your stomach, say *Yo, ho, ho, for a bottle of rum* and sit down.	TPR (or total 'island' response)
Think of an island word. Draw it.	Visualisation of language, focusing attention, creating a personal text
Stand opposite a partner. You are your partner's mirror. Your partner must eat a large oyster, slowly and with feeling. Mirror your partner's actions exactly.	Development of drama skills, observational skills
Ask an 'open question' about the treasure island.	Checking understanding
Dictate instructions on how to find the treasure.	Dictation, listening skills, TPR, writing
Make up a difficult 'island sentence'. Make a mistake in it. Ask one of your group to correct you.	Error and correction, listening skills

≫→

Forfeit key	Possible related teaching aims
Dictate the shape of the island to your group. They follow your instructions and draw it.	Listening skills, pre-writing, picture dictation
Make up an island tongue twister. (Don't say it aloud.) Whisper it to the person sitting next to you. Ask him/her to pass it on (whisper it) to the next person in the group.	Language consolidation, listening skills, pronunciation practice
Write a quick recipe for a delicious island drink or dish. Cut up and jumble the sentences. Hand them to your group to sort into the correct order.	Reading skills
Make up a four-line island dialogue.	Assessment, speaking skills
Play *There's a ... on my island* with the rest of your group.	Vocabulary review
Teach three island adjectives to your group.	Vocabulary review
Draw an island item on your partner's back with your finger.	Developing positive group dynamics
Write an island sentence on the board, then write a simple substitution drill exercise on the board around this sentence.	Language practice and consolidation, choral drill
Play a quick island team game (such as *Touch the word on the board* or *Draw the word on the board*).	Vocabulary review
Play island *Simon says*.	TPR

Feedback

Ts stay in groups of five or six and discuss the activity, following the discussion points in their notes. Here are example responses from teachers to the last two points raised:

Discuss with others in your group how many of these techniques you would use in any one forty-minute lesson.

○ Three or four. The important point is not the technique, but the balance within the lesson – and the needs of the children.
○ It depends on the coursebook.
○ There is no set recipe for using one technique or another.
○ Different activities lend themselves to different techniques and approaches.

Are any of them **not** appropriate to teaching children?
○ They are all appropriate.
○ The writing may be too difficult for younger children.
○ The jumbled reading puzzle might be too difficult for younger children.

4.5 Practical task: designing a 'treasure island' board game for an EFL classroom

Aims
This activity asks teachers to:
- work co-operatively within a team to design a game for use with children;
- develop an associated teaching/lesson plan;
- practise procedures/techniques related to *activity-centred* teaching.

Planning and preparation

Ts follow the detailed notes. Producing the board game requires careful planning and preparation. Ensure that there is ample time allocated to this. By ways of additional information for Ts, you may wish to mention the flexibility that 'forfeit cards' can offer:

They may be designed to practise/review any given language point.

They may be designed to focus on affirmative, negative and interrogative forms.

They allow the game to be re-used many times as, for example, a 'corner activity' for pupils who finish classwork early, or for remedial practice with a small group within a class.

In other words, various sets of forfeit cards can be produced so that the board game can be played again and again throughout a language course, each time reviewing a different language point.

Note: Even though a 'set' of forfeit cards may focus on one specific language point, there should always be humorous forfeits which are **just for fun!**

Action

In terms of overall organisation of this activity:

Ts usually require at least two hours to work through all the stages of production and playing of the game. (About thirty minutes should be allocated for the playing, display and evaluation of finished projects.)

Ensure that **all** Ts participate throughout the making of the game. If necessary point out that, as with early finishers in the language classroom, work must be found for 'teachers' who finish early.

Write up key points that are mentioned with respect to the use of the board game in a language classroom.

Ts follow the detailed notes on page 58. Ensure all Ts play all of the games.

Follow-up: the importance of a language focus

- Organise the Ts into new groups of five or six for this activity. In order to provide a change of pace/atmosphere, begin with a review of *Row your boat* as a group-formation activity.

- Ask Ts for ideas on how they would follow up the board game in their classrooms in terms of a specific *language focus,* e.g. the teaching of *There is: On my island there is a mountain. On my island there is a mountain and a river ...* etc.
- Ts read the example lesson notes *Language work on can't .../ have to* and the ensuing 'comment'. Encourage Ts to discuss how they would make sure that a language focus is **seen** to be taught, e.g. by producing written exercises/activities for the children to complete in their notebook after the game has been played. This is more formally dealt with as the final task in this section.
- Ts produce brief notes on the **specific** language focus they could introduce as a follow-up activity. When ready, organise the Ts into new groups so that they may exchange ideas and information with others in the training room.

4.6 Teaching techniques: are they from EFL or primary education, or ...?

Aims

This activity encourages teachers to:
- share notes on the crossover between EFL and primary education;
- discuss the value of *techniques* in the teaching of children.

Starting points

This is a shared reading/writing task. Ts work with a partner and follow the instructions. Finally, pairs compare their conclusions with the rest of the training group. Ensure that the key points raised are displayed for the whole group.

Discussion: the top ten techniques

Ts work in pairs and follow the intructions in their books. There is an example of a completed chart on pages 179–181.

4.7 Round-up activity: review the chant *We're all going on a treasure hunt*

Aim

This activity provides a further opportunity to use a theme-related activity for *group dynamics.*
Ts sit in a circle/semicircle and follow the instructions.

The 'top 30' techniques and recipes	Examples of use in EFL	Examples from mainstream primary education	Examples from other fields
Choral drills	Repeating words and sentences, pronunciation practice	Maths tables, rhymes	Military training
Pairwork/groupwork	Question and answer practice, class surveys	Many co-operative activities across the curriculum	Management training
Roleplay	Practising and learning a dialogue	Drama work focusing on social and creative development of the child	Therapy, leadership training
Oral dictation	Testing of acquired knowledge of a text, testing listening skills	Assessment, listening/writing skills	Note taking
Picture dictation	Pre-writing activity, testing listening skills	Developing spatial awareness and linguistic accuracy	Free-time activity
Read, look up and say, check	Language consolidation, self assessment	Developing early reading skills	Preparing a speech
Pelmanism/matching games	Vocabulary games	Developing early reading/writing skills	Free-time activity
Bingo games	Vocabulary review game	Social interaction, sets in maths	Social game
TPR	Language presentation technique	Developing skills for following instructions	Recipes for cooking, driving instruction
Translating	Introducing language/language awareness	Developing awareness of similarities and differences between languages	Business and politics
Chinese whispers	Listening skills	Listening skills	Relaying messages
Mime and gesture	Presentation technique	Drama work, development of social and creative skills	Therapy, acting

179

The 'top 30' techniques and recipes	Examples of use in EFL	Examples from mainstream primary education	Examples from other fields
Chaining/combining sentences	Language/vocabulary game, language consolidation	Developing speaking/writing skills	Writing from notes
Listen and repeat	Pronunciation practice	Rote learning, consolidation	Military training
Puzzles, crosswords, charades, etc.	Language consolidation, vocabulary review	Consolidation, socialisation	Free-time activities
Questionnaires	Language form practice, question and answer	Surveys	Market research
Class and team games: *I spy, spelling bee*, etc.	Vocabulary practice	Consolidation activities, socialisation	Time fillers on long journeys, particularly for children
Substitution tables (spoken and written)	Language form practice	Assessment, consolidation	———
Comprehension questions (spoken and written)	Assessment, focusing pupils' attention on key areas	Evaluation/testing	Quiz shows
Storytelling	Presentation of language	Language development	Personal reading, social interaction
Listen and draw	Assessing listening comprehension	Pre-writing activity	Recording information
Information-gap activities	Communicative practice	Assessment, guided writing activity	Social interaction
Imagine it, draw it, describe it	Creating a personal language text	Creative art, drama and writing, oral skills	Creative work, fiction writing

The 'top 30' techniques and recipes	Examples of use in EFL	Examples from mainstream primary education	Examples from other fields
Cuisenaire rods/ *Silent way* techniques	Correction of errors, presentation of language	Concept of number	——
Finger correction	Correction of errors	Correction	——
Jumbled-up sentences	Reading comprehension	Developing reading and writing	Free-time activity
Yes/no games	Consolidation of language	Consolidation, socialisation	Quiz game
Minimal pair pronunciation exercises	Pronunciation practice	Remedial pronunciation work	Comedy sketches
Chants/rhymes for vocabulary, stress and intonation	Vocabulary consolidation, pronunciation practice	Language development	Mother and child interaction
Written gap-filling exercises	Assessment	Assessment, guided writing	——

5 A balanced teaching diet

Theme/topic
Bridges and balances (weighing)

Overall aims
This unit examines the importance of providing a *balance* in the teaching of English to younger learners. It also illustrates the balance of issues that are raised when introducing the teaching of a second language into the curriculum in the primary school.

Study plan

	Study agenda/ activities	Preparation and resources needed	Key points	Approx. timing
5.1	Starting points: group-formation activities and sorting activity	No additional materials needed	Group dynamics Factors that influence child behaviour within a lesson	30–40 minutes
5.2	Background reading challenge	No additional materials needed	In-depth study of the *balance* within the teaching situation	60–90 minutes
5.3	Practical tasks and teaching plans: preparing a teaching plan for practical work	*A science corner:* plasticine, cubes, marbles, potatoes, other non-standard weights; materials for constructing a balance (or a balance/scales) *A bridge reading corner:* Billy Goats Gruff story, other *bridge* stories/rhymes if available *A Billy Goats roleplay area:* card, scissors, cocktail sticks or straws, OHP *A bridge construction corner:* variety of scrap materials: card, pieces of wood, paper, strong glue, Sellotape	Creating *balanced lesson plans* within an activity-based context	120+ minutes

Study agenda/ activities	Preparation and resources needed	Key points	Approx. timing
5.4 Practical task: making a *lift the flap* book	A4 paper, stapler, card for the cover	Writing for a specific purpose/audience contrasted with recording (i.e. writing) language learnt	40–60+ minutes
5.5 Round-up activities	No additional materials needed	Group-formation activity	15–20 minutes

5.1 Starting points

Aims

This activity encourages:
- further use of group dynamics;
- teachers to reflect on factors that influence child behaviour within a lesson.

Group-formation activities

Ts follow the instructions in the course notes.
For the *see-saw* activity, if sitting on the floor is not practical, Ts:
- stand in two parallel lines and turn to face a partner;
- stretch their arms out so that the palms of their hands are touching their partner's;
- push their partner's arms back and forth in harmony with others in their own line, singing the rhyme as they do so.

Sorting activity

Ts first work with a partner. When ready, pairs join to form groups of four or six and exchange information/explain their sorting criteria.

5.2 Background reading challenge

Aims

This activity encourages an in-depth study of the *dynamic balance* within the teaching situation.
- Ts follow the detailed instructions to produce a large illustrated information sheet on *A balanced teaching diet*. As with previous *jigsaw* group activities, negotiate a time schedule with the Ts before the start of the activity and ensure that the time frame is followed.

- The reading heavily favours an *activity-based* approach. If appropriate to your training situation, ask one group of Ts to re-write a section/sections of the reading passage from the point of view of a teacher who favours a *language-based* approach to the teaching of English to children.

Feedback

- When ready, organise a whole-group feedback on the activity.
  Ts sit in a circle or semicircle.
  The following are examples of issues that you may wish the Ts to consider in response to the points listed in the reading, and some comments on the issues:
  1 Do coursebooks (the Ts are familiar with) provide a 'balanced teaching diet' for children?
     - Most coursebooks say they provide a balanced input/practice in the 'four skills'. However, these skills are usually viewed in terms of **language** only and not in terms of the overall development of the child. In reality, training for reading, listening, speaking and writing is an extremely long-term process that not only relates across the curriculum, but extends into all areas of home and social life. Therefore the learning of the 'four skills' in an EFL context needs to be put into perspective.

  2 Can Ts name one or two cross-curricular themes that they feel are particularly useful to exploit in an EFL classroom with eight-year-old beginners?
     - Topics that relate to the children and their immediate environment are very useful (*ourselves, food, family, mini-creatures, school, colour, shapes, our town*, etc.). Aspects which generate very simple language points within authentic contexts are particularly useful, e.g.
       Ourselves: numbers, colours, verb to be, ... have got ...
       Food: like/don't like, my favourite is ...

  3 What do Ts understand by 'variety and change of pace' within a language lesson?
     - A lesson plan which incorporates stages such as group formation, movement activity, practical task, a quiet time (reflect, write) and formal practice, etc. Here it is important that there is an obvious link in terms of *content* within the stages of the lesson.

  4 Do coursebooks (Ts are familiar with) take mixed-ability classes into consideration?
     - Generally speaking, most coursebooks seem to aim for the average pupil and follow a linear learning progression. It is usually up

to the teacher to adapt materials to suit mixed-ability classes. This often means the production of extra materials. It also implies careful organisation of children and space so that information and learning can be shared by the children themselves.

5 Do Ts think it is feasible to adapt their own classroom space to the learning needs of the children and specific activities they may wish to do?
   o This may be desirable, but not always feasible. Some classrooms are just too small and/or classes too large to alter easily. However, change of classroom space should not be ruled out because of inconvenience or lethargy. There is very little to be lost through experimentation.

6 In the EFL classroom (Ts are familiar with), do Ts feel there is enough importance attached to adequate recycling and review?
   o In general, coursebooks tend to provide new language input in each unit, and Ts follow along. It is interesting to compare 'consolidation and review' units in a coursebook with the preceding learning material. In all events, recycling and review is very important. It is equally important to provide new contexts and activities for this review. Children get bored very easily when confronted by old items in new clothes.

7 What, if anything, do Ts think **they** have learnt from making a visual aid for *A balanced teaching diet*?
   o The balance between activity content and the need to complete a language syllabus can provide a great deal of stress for the teacher, particularly where end-of-year formal tests are seen as a measure of success. Therefore, in a more traditional situation, moving the balance towards 'activities' may well be seen as a long-term process. In more open situations, there is more opportunity to provide a balanced teaching diet in terms of cross-curricular content and language focus.

5.3 Practical tasks and teaching plans

Aims
This activity provides teachers with:
- a hands-on experience of organising and doing a series of cross-curricular tasks related to the theme of 'bridges';
- ideas/resources across the curriculum related to the theme of 'bridges' that teachers can use in **their** EFL classroom;
- a hands-on experience of lesson planning in terms of organisation of classroom space and time, developing a language focus from a practical task and developing an activity-centred teaching plan.

Starting points

- Ts work in teams of five or six. Find out how many teachers provide a *choice* of activities in their class. Discuss advantages and disadvantages. The following are examples of issues that Ts may wish to consider, and some comments on the issues:

  1 Do Ts at present provide a choice of activities for the pupils in their class, or does the whole class always work on the same learning content at the same time?

     o Many teachers use the same content with all the children and, where feasible, provide individual attention to slow learners. It is very useful to build up a resource bank of supplementary materials – games, puzzles, short reading texts, etc., which can be stored or filed according to a language syllabus. This can be used by early finishers as well as providing extra practice for slower learners. More able pupils may also be encouraged to make their own games and puzzles based on commercial/your examples.

  2 Do Ts feel it is feasible (or desirable) to provide a choice of activities in an EFL classroom?

     o In addition to teacher preparation, providing a choice of activity requires 'learner training' for the children. For example, learning how to work independently, learning how to share knowledge with peers, etc. This is highly worthwhile, but should not be seen as a short-term process, i.e. it may take half the school year before 'learner choice' of activities works effectively.

TOPIC WEB FOR 'BRIDGES AND BALANCES':

An example completed topic web is shown opposite.

Practical work

Ts follow the detailed instructions in the course notes.

Creating a teaching plan for a practical task

- Ts set up work areas in the training classroom according to the instructions in the course notes. Ensure, if feasible, all four topics are covered within the training group.
- Ts complete a practical task within their group, then produce a teaching plan according to the instructions.

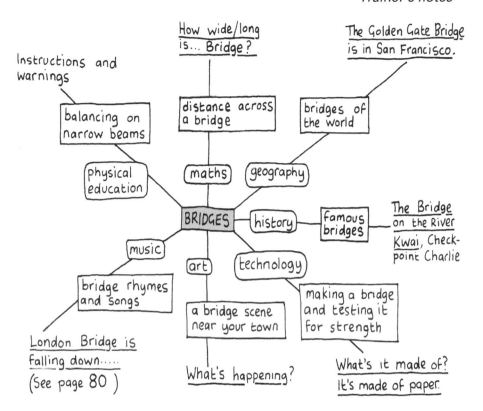

How wide/long is... Bridge?

The Golden Gate Bridge is in San Francisco.

Instructions and warnings

balancing on narrow beams

distance across a bridge

bridges of the world

physical education

maths

geography

BRIDGES — history — famous bridges

The Bridge on the River Kwai, Checkpoint Charlie

music

art

technology

bridge rhymes and songs

a bridge scene near your town

making a bridge and testing it for strength

London Bridge is falling down.....
(See page 80)

What's happening?

What's it made of?
It's made of paper.

Reflection and feedback

At the end of this activity, Ts sit in a circle or semicircle and discuss the activity they have completed. The following are examples of issues that Ts may raise/consider in response to the work they have done, with some comments on the issues:

1 What have you learned about bridges?
   ○ There are many different types of bridges. Making bridges from different materials is a very challenging activity with lots of science and technology concepts involved. In this sense, it is extremely valuable as teaching content with children.

2 What have you learnt about using the topic of *bridges* as a springboard for producing and practising specific language points?
   ○ Here again, since the content is valid and interesting, there is a lot of motivation for using (and learning) the language needed.

3 Were the language points generated by practical tasks comparable to those commonly found within a traditional EFL syllabus for children?
   ○ The order of points may not match that of many coursebooks, but the language points themselves certainly fit within a traditional language syllabus.

4 Would these activities have been the same if you had started with a language point and then looked for a range of practical tasks to provide 'extension practice'?
   ○ Almost certainly not. This is a topic which is not usually integrated into EFL coursebooks. It is more likely that a dialogue or roleplay would be used as a further practice activity.

5 Has participation in this series of practical activities helped your own understanding of how to exploit a practical task in an EFL classroom?
   ○ It has created much more awareness of the need to organise – and the feasibility of doing so. In most EFL classrooms it would require a great deal of learner training to set up a choice of practical tasks. However, if one practical task (only) is used in a lesson, then it may be feasible to integrate this into a more traditional language programme.

5.4 Practical task: making a 'lift the flap book' – *Where's the troll?*

Aims
This activity asks teachers:
- to write for a specific purpose and an audience;
- to compare the value of writing *as an author* with the writing offered in most language teaching texts (i.e. recording language structure);
- to share ideas on the ideal age/stage for introducing writing into a language course for young learners.

● Ts work in groups of five or six and follow the detailed instructions in the course notes.

Feedback

The following are examples of issues that Ts may raise/consider in response to the points listed in the book and some comments on them:

1 How can this type of activity be used in the language classroom?
   ○ This is a very practical activity. It needs little preparation or extra materials. If the pupils work in teams, the more able children can help the slower ones. Work can also be completed at home.

2 How can this type of activity be used to motivate children to *write* in English?
   ○ Publishing a book (however simple) is highly motivating. It is a permanent record of achievement. The children's own books are those which are most often re-visited by the children themselves if made available within the class.

3 How can this type of activity be used to encourage older children to write and read for younger children?
   o It is feasible in some EFL teaching situations to invite older children to read to younger classes. Similarly, creating a book to read to younger children is a highly motivating task for older children. Moreover, the purpose and audience for the book is very clearly defined.

4 How does this type of writing activity differ from typical writing activities in EFL coursebooks that you are familiar with?
   o Many writing activities in EFL coursebooks are designed to:
      – consolidate spoken language;
      – provide written evidence of progress in language learning;
      – check listening or reading comprehension by requiring fixed and predetermined written responses.
   o There are very few opportunities to encourage 'authorship' within EFL learning.

5 At what age/stage do you feel writing should be introduced into a language course?
   o Wherever/whenever the teacher feels it is appropriate. English is a written as well as spoken language. It is best learnt as such. In most cases, the children themselves are anxious to produce a written record of their learning.

Display and keep the finished books as an ongoing training/classroom resource.

5.5 Round-up activities

Aims
This activity provides:
– a further example of *topic-linked* group-dynamics activities;
– resource material for teachers' own classrooms.

A) LONDON BRIDGE

Ts follow the instructions in the course notes. To start the activity, organise the Ts into two large groups. Groups sit facing each other.
Group 1 sings *London Bridge is falling down* with accompanying gestures.
Group 2 continues by singing *falling down, falling down* with similar gestures.
Group 1 continues by singing *London Bridge is falling down* with accompanying gestures.
Group 2 ends the verse with *my fair lady* with accompanying gestures.

Group 2 starts Verse 2 with *Build it up with bricks and stones* with accompanying gestures.

Group 1 continues Verse 2 with *bricks and stones, bricks and stones* with similar gestures, and so on.

(See page 259 of the Resource file for the complete song.)

B) BRIDGE RACE

Note: Play this game with care. Ensure that teachers are aware of the safety factors before starting.

- Ts sit in two parallel lines (L1 and L2), that run at right angles away from the board. If feasible, teachers remove shoes and sit on the floor. If not, Ts sit on their chairs in the lines. They turn to face a partner in the opposite line, stretch out their legs so that their feet touch those of their partner to form a long bridge of legs and feet.
- Choose vocabulary related to *Billy Goats Gruff*, e.g. *goat, bridge, grass, green, troll, trip trap, walk, three, big*. Assign each pair (i.e. T1 from L1 and T1 from L2) one of the words.
- Make up a short story that includes the *Billy Goats* words you have assigned, and slowly tell it to the group, e.g.
  *When I went shopping last week I wore my high heels. I live in the country near a beautiful **bridge**. It's a lovely area, full **of green** fields and there are lots of animals. Anyway, I walked down the road, **trip trap**. Suddenly three animals, I mean **goats** ...*
- When the pair of teachers hear their word (e.g. *goat*) they must stand up, run down the bridge of legs (without stepping on anybody), write or draw their word on the board, and return to their original place by running back along the bridge. Remaining team members shout and clap encouragement: *Come on, come on, come on!*
- First T back scores a team point. Award a bonus point for neatness (or correct spelling!).
- Continue the game until most/all Ts have had their word included in your story.

6 Storytelling, comprehension, errors and correction

Theme/topic
Jack and the Beanstalk, growing

Overall aims
This unit examines the concept of listening and reading comprehension in TEFL for younger learners, and the role of errors in the language learning process. It also discusses the issues raised by the correction of errors made by children in the language classroom. In order to give practical examples for discussion, the unit starts with a series of activities and tasks that generate an authentic content in which errors might occur.

Study plan

	Study agenda/ activities	Preparation and resources needed	Key points	Approx. timing
6.1	Starting points	A4 sheets of paper, pens, crayons, etc.	Group dynamics Writing own action game	30–40 minutes
6.2	Storytelling and comprehension	No additional materials needed	The difference between *checking* and *teaching* comprehension Active storytelling activity Writing comprehension questions	40–60 minutes
6.3	Practical tasks	Discuss with Ts. Prepare materials accordingly: *Physical education (PE):* tape measure, stop-watch, string *An art and craft area – making a beanstalk, and leaf collage:* leaves, paints, aprons, glue, Sellotape, sheets of white and coloured paper (esp. green and red), string	Producing and trying out *activity-based* lessons	120+ minutes

≫→

	Study agenda/ activities	Preparation and resources needed	Key points	Approx. timing
6.3 contd		*A puppet/roleplay area – making puppets from paper plates:* paper plates, rods/ sticks, Sellotape, crayons & felt tip pens, scissors *A maths corner – measuring (estimating) the height of trees and tall buildings:* rulers, graph paper, tape measures, string, etc. *A science corner:* jars, seeds, soil, water, filter paper *A technology corner: giant* objects, (wrapping) paper, card, Sellotape, glue, stapler, ruler/tape measure		
6.4	An 'errors and correction' beanstalk	String, Sellotape, scissors, sheets of white, green, and red paper; Baroque music on cassette	Predicting errors in a specific context Ways of correcting errors Listing *errors* and practising *correction* techniques Evaluation of correction techniques	40–60 minutes
6.5	Errors and correction: how it feels to correct and be corrected	Prepare/learn several long and difficult sentences in L3	Making errors as a learner Discussing the effect of correcting errors	40–60+ minutes
6.6	Round-up activity: chant	No additional materials needed	Group-formation activity	10–15 minutes

6.1 Starting points

Aims

This activity encourages teachers:
- to take part in a further group-formation activity;
- to produce their own 'story-based' action game.

Group-dynamics activity (action game)

- Ts work in pairs. T2 is an *actor*. T1 is a *mirror*. T2 in each pair *leads* the action, while T1 mirrors T2's actions. Say the script below, encouraging the teachers to *act out* the growing seed.

You're a tiny, tiny, seed. Curl up really small. The sun shines. The rain pours down. The seed starts to grow. Now, uncurl, really slowly. Now slowly stand up. Stretch your arms up. Slowly. The plant grows higher and higher and higher. Now the leaves start to grow wider and wider and wider. Now the wind starts to blow. The plant sways in the wind. The wind blows harder and harder and harder and stops. Relax.

- Ts change roles and repeat.
- Ts stand in a large circle, all facing the same direction (clockwise).
- Ts touch, with a finger, the back of the person standing on their left in the circle. (It may be easier to ask them first to put their hands on the shoulders of the person on their left in order to produce the correct distance between each teacher.)
- Repeat the action game. Ts must draw, using a finger, the *seed*, the *growing plant*, the *actions* and the *scene* within the action game as you say it – on the back of the person standing in front of them in the circle.
- Ts in the circle now turn 180 degrees to face the other way. Repeat the action game.
- Ts sit down so that they can work individually within groups of four or five. They take a sheet of blank paper and divide it into four equal squares. Re-tell the action game; Ts illustrate and write key lines in each of the four squares. They may help each other at this stage.
- Groups find a *rap tune* or *jazz chant* for this action game and say it to the whole training group. They use the script above to help them if necessary.

Producing your own action game

- Ts work in groups of four or five to write an action game script that links with the theme of *Jack and the Beanstalk*.
- When they are ready, ask groups to try out their action game with others in the training group. Decide on factors that make an action game usable in the classroom, e.g.
  It is short (normally no more than six lines).
  It contains actions/content that can be demonstrated easily.
  It contains language that can be demonstrated easily.
  It contains language/actions that are relevant to the topic/theme of the unit.
  It can be acted out within the classroom/limited space.
- Finally, Ts vote on the most appropriate action game.

6.2 Storytelling and comprehension

Aims
This activity encourages teachers to:
- discuss the difference between *checking* and *teaching* comprehension;
- take part in an active storytelling activity;
- produce comprehension activities.

Introduction

- Ts work with a partner and follow the instructions in the course notes.

Storytelling: Jack and the Beanstalk

- Ts sit in a semicircle. Give an *active* reading of *Jack and the Beanstalk* (see page 267), encouraging the Ts to participate in the story. You may wish to elaborate the story, or use a commercial version.
- After the storytelling Ts work with a partner and do the comprehension activity in the book. The completed table below shows 'correct' teacher response to the sorting activity.

Questions which have only one 'right' answer.	Questions which encourage the listener/reader to 'construct' his/her own meaning from the text.
1 Was Jack rich or poor?	2 Draw and describe Jack's house.
4 How many beans did Jack get?	3 What colour was Jack's cow?
6 What did Jack do when he heard the giant coming?	5 How tall was the giant? What size shoes did he wear?
8 How did Jack escape from the giant? What happened to the giant?	7 How much does one golden egg weigh? How much money is it worth?
10 What did the giant say when he chased Jack?	9 What did Jack's mother buy with one golden egg?
11 Jack and his mother lived happ	12 You have a hen that lays golden eggs. What would you do?

Feedback

The section below contains potential issues that teachers may raise or that you may wish teachers to discuss:

1 Agree which of the above questions you usually associate with reading/listening comprehension in TEFL. Discuss the possible teaching aims of questions 1, 4, 6, 8, 10 and 11.
   ○ These questions test factual comprehension.
   ○ There is only one right or wrong answer.
   ○ They are easy to grade or mark in a test.
   ○ They are useful for consolidating language *form*, but do not necessarily check the children's understanding of the text.
   ○ In their native language, many children learn how to answer this type of question. They learn what the teacher wants them to say – rather than risk expressing their own opinions.
   ○ They do not encourage children to 'construct' meaning.

2 Discuss the possible *teaching* aims of questions 2, 3, 5, 7, 9 and 12, and whether these aims are achievable in the *language* classroom with children.
   ○ These questions ask children to respond to the text, and not only to copy it.
   ○ There is no **one** right or wrong answer. Often the answer can be given in a non-verbal form, such as a drawing.
   ○ These kinds of questions are difficult to grade in a traditional sense. However, in overall educational terms, it is of much more value to encourage children to construct meaning with a text than to merely test a mechanical response to grammar form and sentence content.
   ○ Children are encouraged to express their **personal** understanding of, and reaction to the text. This may be very different from the teacher's (and other children's) understanding and reaction. This is a healthy view of learning, whatever the language.
   ○ They encourage children to 'construct' meaning, to stretch their ability to use English to express personal opinions and thoughts – not merely a mechanical repetition of language from the text.

• Ts write sets of comprehension questions for the *Billy Goats Gruff* story (page 268) and for *Incy Wincy Spider* (page 147). Here the aim is for Ts to write questions that:
   – are feasible for **their** pupils to respond to (verbal and non-verbal response);
   – encourage children to 'construct' meaning from the text;
   – consolidate and practice **specific** (predetermined) language forms, but not necessarily predetermined language content;
   – encourage children to take 'risks' with language (or find alternative means of communication) in order to express personal ideas and opinions.

- As a final task, ask Ts what they feel **they** have learnt from this activity with respect to teaching/testing of reading and listening comprehension in the language classroom.

6.3 Practical tasks

Aims
This activity provides teachers with the opportunity to produce and participate in an activity-based lesson.

- Ts work in a team of five or six and draw a cross-curricular topic web for the theme of *growing*. See page 239 of the Resource file for an example. When they have finished, Ts in their groups set up *work areas* in the training classroom according to the instructions. Ensure, if feasible, that up to four topics are covered within the training group.
- Ts complete a practical task within their group, then produce a teaching outline according to the instructions. Make sure the teaching outlines include:
  - the *language focus* for the work area. This point is particularly important. Experience has shown that teachers may get so enthused with the *activity* content that they ignore the need to demonstrate overtly that a *language syllabus* has also been taken into account. In this respect, for each practical task encourage Ts to choose (a) language point(s) that typically arise(s) in Year 1 of traditional children's EFL courses, e.g. the verb *to be, this/that is, have got ..., how much/many*, personal pronouns, present continuous, *like/don't like*, etc.
  - the stages within the teaching outline. Example stages for an activity-based outline are listed in the course notes. By way of comparison, copy and write up the stages of a teaching outline from the Teacher's Guide of a language-based children's EFL coursebook you are familiar with.
  - the time involved. Ensure Ts are aware that a practical task is not viewed in isolation. It is an integral part of a unit which may consist of two to four (or more) fifty-minute lessons.
  - the importance of creating a balance of activities within a teaching outline. This training course provides a balance of active, reflective, passive, practical, group, pair, individual, etc. activities. The teaching outline should reflect this balance.
  - the organisation of the children and the space in the classroom. Encourage Ts to discuss the feasibility of setting up a choice of 'work stations' for the children within **their** language classroom. (It may be useful for Ts to draw a rough plan of their classroom layout, and to consider how work stations might be introduced.)
  Ensure the outline suits the **participants'** teaching situation. Remind

Ts of the need to relate their outline to the teaching situation that
they are familiar with.
- Finally, Ts copy and display their teaching outlines. Spend time discussing how they might work in **their** teaching situation.

6.4   An 'errors and correction' beanstalk

Aims
This activity encourages teachers to:
- predict errors in a specific context;
- consider ways of correcting errors;
- list errors and practise correction techniques;
- evaluate correction techniques.

Introduction

- Ts work in groups of five to:
  - list likely *errors* that may arise within the children's practice and
  processing of the language focus generated by the practical task
  above;
  - describe *how/if* these errors should be or need to be corrected;
  - consider if young learners are likely to make more/fewer errors than
  adults;
  - consider if young learners require a different approach to correction than adult learners.

Action

Ts make an '*errors beanstalk*' following the instructions in the course
notes.
- While teachers are working, make a '*corrections beanstalk*' relating to
the following issues:
if to correct
why to correct
when to correct
what to correct
how to correct
who should do the correcting

- Write one issue per leaf. List related factors on the appropriate leaves, e.g.

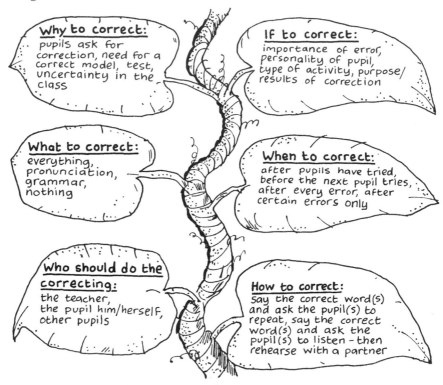

- When completed, Ts examine and discuss the issues on your beanstalk.
- As a next stage, play some music (ideally Vivaldi's *Four Seasons*). While the music is playing, Ts walk around the training room (not in a circle). When you stop the music, Ts find (and greet) a partner. T1 takes the role of a teacher (T). T2 takes the role of a pupil (P). Pairs choose a leaf on the teachers' *errors beanstalk*. P constructs a sentence making the type of error that is mentioned on this leaf. T decides whether to correct, and which correction technique to use.
- Ts change roles and repeat this step.
- At the end of this stage, Ts discuss:
  - what happened;
  - what decisions were made concerning errors;
  - what correction techniques were used.

Here are some example points raised by teachers during the discussion of the *error and correction* activity. This is not an exhaustive list:

What happened?

- ○ Mostly the teacher said the correct words and I repeated them.
- ○ I usually wanted the teacher to correct me, but perhaps that is because I am a teacher.

○ I didn't like to be corrected. It made me very afraid of speaking in case I made a mistake.

What decisions were made concerning errors?
○ I decided if the error was really important. For example, could I understand the sentence?
○ I don't like to let the pupil think something is correct when it isn't, so I always corrected everything.

What correction techniques were used?
○ Listen and repeat after me.
○ Finger correction.
○ Mime and gesture.

● Finally, Ts consider the *errors and correction beanstalks*. They construct and complete an *errors and correction table* on the board. Discuss the methods of correction they and you are most acquainted with, and have found the most useful.

6.5 Errors and correction: how it feels to correct and be corrected

Aims
This activity provides:
– the experience of how it feels to *make errors* as a learner;
– the opportunity to discuss the effect of correcting errors.

How it feels as a learner

● Ts sit in a semicircle or in rows. Use the long sentences you have prepared in L3 (see page 127 of the Trainer's guidelines) in the following ways:
● Say one of the sentences and choose teachers to repeat after you in front of the rest of the group. Correct all errors.
● Say another of the sentences. Ask the training group to repeat it in chorus after you. Then choose teachers to repeat the sentence on their own in front of the rest of the group.
● Organise the teachers into pairs. Say another of the sentences. Ask the teachers to take turns with their partners to say this sentence to each other. Encourage them to help and support and correct their partners if necessary. You may repeat the sentence to the whole group, but do not correct any of the teachers yourself. You may choose competent teachers to go round the group to help weaker ones.
● Before you say another of the sentences, organise the teachers into teams of four or five. Allow them up to five minutes to discuss *learning/error correction* strategies that will help them to say the next

sentence correctly. Ask each team in turn how they would like you to present/say the sentence, and agree on one manner of presentation for the whole training group. Present/say the sentence and encourage the teachers to comment on the result.

How you feel as a teacher

- First, ask Ts to summarise their viewpoints on *correction of errors*. Write up key points.
- Ts then:
  - underline the correction techniques listed in the book that they associate with their teaching;
  - discuss the techniques **they** find most effective and give their reasons.
- Reorganise the Ts into new groups of five:
  Assign a number (from 1–5) to each T within their existing minigroups.
  Tell Ts to re-group according to their new number, i.e. all the (new) number 1s sit together, the (new) number 2s sit together and so on.
  Participants (in their new groups) share the points raised in their 'old' groups.

Feedback

- Individual children respond differently to correction by a teacher. Ts stay in their groups and discuss the *effect* of the various correction techniques on young learners for each of the various lesson stages mentioned in the book.
- When they have finished, groups share their comments with the rest of the training group. If time is available, as an optional activity, encourage the groups to produce and display an information poster on *errors and correction*.

6.6 Round-up activity: chant – *Fee, fi, fo fum*

Aim
This activity provides a further opportunity to participate in a topic-based group-formation activity.

- Ts follow the instructions in the course notes. Create a suitable space for them to move around in.

7 Classroom management and organisation

Theme/topic
Goldilocks and the Three Bears, bears (in general)

Overall aims
This unit examines the role and importance of classroom management and organisation in the teaching of children. It offers practical advice to teachers, and gives them the opportunity to try out management ideas in the training room as well as in the language classroom.

Study plan

	Study agenda/ activities	Preparation and resources needed	Key points	Approx. timing
7.1	Starting points: organising classroom space	Copies of pages 269 and 270	Making the most effective use of the space available in your training room Topic-linked group dynamics	15–20 minutes
7.2	Arrangement of desks and chairs in the classroom	No additional materials needed	Changing of seating arrangements to suit teaching purpose	15–20 minutes
7.3	Consolidation of storytelling techniques: Goldilocks and the Three Bears	Bring in bears (soft toys), bowls, spoons, porridge	Active storytelling Follow-up steps in storytelling	45–60 minutes
7.4	Organisation of the teaching space in your classroom	*For storytelling*: carpet squares, cushions, pillows, shoe boxes, glue, Sellotape, soft material, scraps of wool, paper bags (for paper bag puppets) and other realia linked to *Goldilocks and the Three Bears* story, copies of *Goldilocks and the Three Bears* books	Improving your own classroom space Organising classroom space for various practical activities Trying out the activities	120+ minutes

≫→

	Study agenda/ activities	Preparation and resources needed	Key points	Approx. timing
7.4 contd		*For writing*: pens, pencils, felt tips, brushes, OHP transparencies and pens, paper of various types, colours and sizes *For construction:* shoe boxes, other boxes or cartons, scraps of string, wool, scissors, glue, Sellotape, Blu-tack, pieces of cloth of various colours, straws, small rods *For the home corner:* recipes for porridge and rice pudding, ingredients for porridge/bear food, ingredients for honey sandwiches, bowls, spoons, paper plates, knives, forks		
7.5	Management of time	No additional materials needed	Examining your own use and misuse of classroom time Sharing notes with other teachers: suggesting ways of improving your own use of classroom time	40–60+ minutes
7.6	Management of children	No additional materials needed	Reading task on classroom control Discussing your own ideas related to class control Observation of other teachers in the classroom	60–90+ minutes open-ended
7.7	Round-up activity: bear rhymes and games	No additional materials needed	Group-formation activity	15–20 minutes

7.1 Starting points

Aims

This activity provides teachers with the opportunity to:
- participate in a further topic-linked group dynamics activity;
- examine the use of the space available in the training room.

'Bear' group formation

- Ts follow the instructions in the course notes.

7.2 Seating arrangements in the classroom

Aims
This activity encourages teachers to:
- consider a variety of potential seating arrangements within their training room/classroom;
- discuss the advantages of specific organisation of classroom space.

Looking at your training space

- Ts work in groups of four or five and follow the instructions in the course notes.

Looking at your teaching space

- Ts work with a partner or small group and match a list of teaching statements/purposes to the seating arrangements illustrated in the book. The following is an *example match*:

Class in rows. Teacher at front of class.
Formal testing
Useful when all the children are doing the same thing at the same time

Class in a horseshoe/U-shape, seats behind the desks.
Teacher at the front centre of the U.
Facilitates introduction of new material
Useful for choral work
Facilitates large/whole group discussion
Encourages P–P interaction within language practice activities

Class in a horseshoe shape/U-shape, desks against the wall, seats in the space created by moving the desks against the wall. Teacher at the front centre of the U or mobile.
Facilitates roleplay and game playing
Makes it easy to attract all the children's attention easily
Facilitates a wide range of communicative activities
Facilitates the demonstration of new visual aids, such as flashcards

Class in circle or diamond shape. Teacher in the circle/diamond.
Creates the impression of the teacher as an equal in the group
Facilitates P–P communication in a whole-class discussion/activity
Provides an informal setting for feedback on an activity or task

Class in groups of five or six. Groups in space in the classroom. Teacher mobile or at a selected place in the room.
Allows for several different activities to take place at the same time
Encourages peer teaching and sharing of information
Encourages social interaction among the children
Facilitates the handling of children who finish early or allows for remedial work within the class
Facilitates the planning and practice of roleplays

Class in pairs. Teacher mobile or at a selected place in the room.
Encourages interaction between children
Facilitates child-initiated dialogue practice
Facilitates the playing of communicative games
Facilitates the use of self-access materials

- When ready, reorganise Ts into new groups. Ts explain which classroom seating arrangement **they** use most or least often.

7.3 Classroom management: storytelling as a starting point

Aims
This activity encourages teachers to:
- participate in active storytelling;
- develop a cross-curricular topic web around the theme of the story.

- Ts work in groups of six or seven and follow the detailed instructions in the course notes. If necessary, for an example of a topic web for the three bears, refer Ts to page 240 of the Resource file.
- For the storytelling stage, encourage Ts who have the roles of the three bears (within their group) to play the roles of the bears' bowls, chairs and beds, too. This avoids a long period of non-participation.

7.4 Organisation of the teaching space in your classroom

Aims
This activity encourages teachers to:
- improve their own classroom space;
- organise classroom space effectively for various practical activities;
- try out practical activities they may use with their own class;
- develop teaching plans for a specific practical activity.

- Ts follow the detailed instructions in the course notes.
- Organise feedback sessions at appropriate times within the activity, as well as at the end.

7.5 Management of time

Aims
This activity provides teachers with the opportunity to:
- examine their own use and misuse of classroom time;
- share notes with other teachers;
- to improve their own use of classroom time.

Introduction

- Ts work individually on the questions in the text. They then share ideas on how to improve their use of time. Here are some example responses from teachers to the discussion points. This is not an exhaustive list:

1 What makes the greatest demand on your time? Is it possible to get rid of, or share (with parents, other teachers, children) some of this demand?
   - Preparing for lessons.
   - Keeping all the children occupied all of the time.
   - Badly behaved children.
   - Testing and marking.

2 What puts you under pressure with respect to time? Is there any practical way of relieving this pressure or improving the situation?
   - Having to finish a book and cover the syllabus by the end of term.
   - Setting out and putting things away at the end of each lesson.

3 Do you invite other adults or older students/teenagers to help you? If so, do they know what is expected of them?
   - Not usually, I don't like parents in the class.
   - I always encourage parents to come into class.
   - Lots of parents learn with their children.
   - It would be a good idea for parents or older students from the secondary school to come and help, but I haven't done it yet.

4 Do you have regular meetings with other teachers, or with teachers from other schools to share ideas and problems?
   - We sometimes have meetings at school.
   - I'd love to meet with teachers from other schools, but it isn't practical.

5 Does your school organisation support your classroom organisation? Are there ways in which they could support you further?
   - We don't get much support, just pressure to keep the room tidy and quiet.
   - We get a lot of support from parents.
   - Support from the school is essential.
   - I always ask for help if I need it.

Your suggestions

- Ts work at first in pairs, then in one of two teams. They follow the detailed instructions in the book.
- The table below contains example responses from teachers. It is not an exhaustive list.

Time eaters	Best suggestion for saving time	Other suggestions for saving time
Registration	Children take the register	Self registration
Late arrivals	Have a 'late arrivals' desk	Give them nine lives – like a cat
Classroom reorganisation	Train children to do this	Ask parents to help
Too many new words to teach	Be realistic in your teaching aims: ten words maximum in one hour	Encourage children to take words home to *teach their parents*
Taking out and putting away materials	Children do this	Ask parents to help
Preparing materials for practical work	Children do this, in or out of class	Ask parents to help
Preparing teaching aids	Ask children to do this for you for homework	Ask parents to help
A few low-ability children in the class	Organise some activities in mixed ability teams; encourage more able children to support the rest of the team	Have a choice of activities on offer to suit different abilities
Missing items or materials	Adapt your lesson plan	Imagine them; ask children to draw or make them
Review and consolidation	Integrate into your lesson	Prepare work cards for the children to do at home/free moments in the class
Tests and marking them	Children work in teams and correct each other's work; use an OHT for reference	Help children to devise their own tests
Copying/writing	Prepare work cards for the children to take home and complete	Have a special *writing corner*
Correcting homework	Children work in teams and correct each other's work; use an OHT for reference	Ask older children in the school to do this as a *pair conference* activity (older child sits with younger child)

Time eaters	Best suggestion for saving time	Other suggestions for saving time
Lots of cutting and sticking	Children glue a 'bits and pieces' envelope inside their exercise book; they take their cut-outs home for completion	Ask fast finishers or parents to help
Complex practical tasks	Assign clear roles within groups so that materials can be collected, stored, etc. materials trolley	Organise your storage space with priority equipment easily at hand; use a

7.6 Management of children

Aims
This activity encourages:
- extensive background reading on classroom control;
- teachers to explain their own ideas on class control;
- teachers to critically observe other teachers in the classroom.

Reading and writing task

- Ts work in groups of five or six and follow the detailed instructions in the course notes.

Your teaching

- Ts follow the instructions in groups of five or six.

Observation and feedback

If observation is feasible:
- Discuss and list the key issues that are related to classroom management. Encourage the Ts to list specific points rather than generalisations.
- In groups of five or six, Ts prepare a practical observation sheet that incorporates the key issues. There is an example on pages 272-3. This should be adapted to suit the needs of the training group.
- Groups compare their observation sheets with those of others in the training group and design/produce a consensus sheet.
- Ts try it out and modify its design after practical experience.
- Have regular feedback sessions on all observation carried out.

7.7 Round-up activity: bear rhymes and games

Aims

This activity provides a further opportunity for teachers to participate in theme-based group-formation activities.

Ts work in one of three teams. Teams follow the detailed instructions in the course notes.

8 Visual and other teaching aids

Theme/topic

Hallowe'en, other festivals and special days

Overall aims

The main body of this unit offers teachers the opportunity to practise the selection and preparation of a variety of teaching/visual aids for the topic of Hallowe'en (and other festivals). It also asks teachers to prepare lesson plans that incorporate these teaching aids.

Study plan

	Study agenda/ activities	Preparation and resources needed	Key points	Approx. timing
8.1	Starting points	No additional materials needed	Topic-linked group dynamics	5–10 minutes
8.2	Reading task: *Speaking English with pictures*	No additional materials needed	Shared reading task Ways to improve the visual impact of your classroom	45–60 minutes
8.3	Planning for *Hallowe'en* as a topic in the language classroom	Provide, if available, reference texts on the production of teaching aids, OHP transparencies or large sheets of paper	Listing visual/teaching aids to support a wide range of learning areas Deciding who should produce or supply these aids: teacher, child, school, parents	20–30 minutes
8.4	Practical tasks	Ts should read sections B–E of the Resource file in advance. Concertina book: sheets of A1, A2 or A3 paper, crayons, glue, scissors, etc. Teaching aids: paper, scrap materials, glue, crayons; other items as requested by teachers	Producing teaching aids to help and encourage children to speak within the topic of *Hallowe'en* Producing a teaching plan that incorporates the use of these teaching aids	120+ minutes

	Study agenda/ activities	Preparation and resources needed	Key points	Approx. timing
8.5	Reading task: video	Where available, bring in a selection of children's EFL videos, promotional and informational leaflets concerning these videos and videos for native-speaking children (e.g. *Postman Pat*) If appropriate, provide viewing time, or assign viewing of specific videos prior to the training room activities	Shared reading task Shared production of an advertising pamphlet for a children's EFL video	90–120 minutes
8.6	Round-up activity: spell competition	No additional materials needed	Producing a shared *illustrated spell* and casting it on the group	15–20+ minutes

8.1 Starting points

Aims

Further practice of topic-based formation activities.

Ts follow the instructions and play *The witch is in her cave* and *Witch models*.

8.2 Reading task 1: visual aids

Aims

This activity encourages teachers to:
- share a reading task on teaching/visual aids;
- focus on the visual impact of **their** classroom.

- Ts work in pairs and complete the reading task.
- In terms of visual aids, highlight the importance of factors such as:
  - attraction and friendliness to children;
  - clarity and size;
  - display at children's eye level;
  - encouragement of children to make teaching aids for the classroom and to display them, showing that the T values their work;
  - frequent change of aids according to the topic/theme/unit being studied;
  - involvement of the children, even with visuals T has provided.
- Challenge teachers to improve their/your training environment.

8.3 Planning for Hallowe'en

Aims
This activity encourages teachers to:
- list visual/teaching aids that support a wide range of learning areas;
- discuss ways of encouraging pupils, parents, other teachers to produce their teaching aids.

- Ts work in teams of five/six and follow the instructions in the course notes. For the production of the topic web, if necessary, Ts may use the web on page 241 of the Resource file as a guide. In addition, ensure that Ts highlight the part(s) of the web that they think can be completed in English. In this respect, Ts need to state the specific language point they wish to focus upon. They also need to discuss, within their group, the general teaching sequence they might use to integrate the practical task and language focus in a language classroom situation. As previously stated in this book, it is important that:
  - the task has 'whole learning' value to the children completing it;
  - the task can realistically be achieved within a language classroom and its associated limitations;
  - the teacher has a specific and predetermined language focus (in terms of production by the children) in mind throughout the task, and that this language focus is relevant to a traditional EFL language syllabus;
  - at the end of the task, there is evidence of the completion of *language practice*, as well as physical evidence of the final product of the task itself.

For the activity concerning visual and other teaching aids, ask Ts to make a large *teaching aids cauldron* for the training room.

If feasible provide the reference texts mentioned, and others you may be familiar with.

Ensure that **all** teachers within a group participate in this activity. Some teachers are highly critical of their own artistic skills and will need encouragement and support from others in their group. Your own willingness to join various groups and take part in the activity may also provide encouragement to more cautious teachers.

Early finishers should be set new tasks, such as preparing the display space within the training room – so that the whole training group is involved all the time.

- When Ts have finished, organise a whole group feedback on the activity, e.g. Ts say which aids:
  - are most/least useful for their teaching situation;
  - are easy to make/find;
  - are difficult to make/find;
  - teachers must make/find;

- parents might make/find;
- pupils can make/find.

8.4 Practical tasks

Aims

This activity encourages teachers:
- to produce a *concertina book* and discuss the use of this activity in the language classroom;
- to produce teaching aids to support the teaching of vocabulary;
- to produce an illustrated teaching plan for a Hallowe'en topic;
- use (in teaching simulation) of a teacher-devised lesson plan.

Making a witch concertina book

Ts work in a team of five or six and follow the detailed instructions in the course notes.

In terms of management of this activity ensure that:
- a time frame is established at the beginning of the activity and is adhered to;
- **all** teachers participate actively throughout the activity. In other words, the groups themselves must find additional/alternative tasks for teachers who finish early or are unwilling to do specific things.

In terms of making *concertina books* ensure that:
- there is an *editor* for each group;
- the group makes a rough plan for its book **before** working on the actual book;
- the groups realise the importance of *planning* (for themselves and for children) in the making of books in the classroom, e.g. when folded sheets of paper are bound together into a book, the page order becomes a critical issue.

In terms of a *concertina book*, it is practical to work on separate sheets of paper, then glue these onto the concertina, rather than risk making mistakes on the concertina itself.

Producing teaching/visual aids for Hallowe'en/festivals

A) PREPARATION

- Ts follow the detailed instructions in the course notes. Ensure that they keep in mind that the aids are for a class of twenty ten/eleven-year-old children, and that they distinguish between aids that merely introduce new vocabulary and those that support the development of dialogue/conversation/discourse in English.
- Before moving onto the 'production' stage, recommend Ts to read

sections B–E of the Resource file. This is useful as background reading and a source of practical ideas for the next stage of this activity.

B) PRODUCTION

Ts follow the detailed instructions to produce four *teaching/visual aids/notes* related to the theme of *Hallowe'en* that will encourage *speaking*. Ensure that you negotiate a time schedule with the Ts before the start of the activity and ensure that the time frame is followed.
If feasible, ensure that various aids are produced, e.g.
flashcards
audio aids (on cassette)
OHTs
board game
cue cards
books (semi-completed for children to complete/illustrate)
language games and puzzles

C) DISPLAY AND FEEDBACK

Ts make, display and discuss the teaching aids they have produced.

8.5 Reading task 2: video

Aims
This activity encourages teachers to:
– share a reading task on the use of video;
– produce an advertising pamphlet for a children's EFL video.

Preparation

Note: If appropriate, provide viewing time prior to this activity, or assign the viewing of specific videos, and the reading of associated materials to Ts or to groups.
● Ts work in teams of six and discuss children's EFL videos they are familiar with.
● When they have finished, Ts work with a partner within their team and complete the reading/writing task in the book. Completed passages are shared with the rest of the team and with the whole training group.

Action

Ts produce in their teams a promotional pamphlet (A4, A3 or A2 size) for a commercial EFL video for children. Ts will need commercial promotional material as a reference source for this activity.

Feedback

Ts display and explain their pamphlet to other teams in the training group.

If Ts are interested, encourage further viewing and evaluation of EFL and non-EFL children's videos.

Detailed teaching procedures for the use of video in an EFL situation lie outside the scope of this book. Interested teachers may wish to read further, e.g. *Video* (Cooper, Lavery and Rinvolucri, OUP) or *Video in Language Teaching* (Jack Lonergan, CUP). Such Ts may be encouraged to produce a summary sheet on how such activities can be adapted to suit children in the language classroom.

8.6 Round-up activity: spell competition

Aims
This activity provides a further example of topic-based formation activities.

Ts follow the detailed instructions in the course notes.

9 Content and curriculum

Theme/topic
The house that Jack built, buildings

Overall aims
This unit likens the idea of the *construction* involved in building a house to that of *constructing a curriculum*. Ts examine contemporary EFL coursebooks for children and are encouraged to *build* part of a curriculum. The relationship between language and activity is stressed throughout. Although short in length, the content of this unit needs a lot of time with respect to evaluation of coursebooks and course curricula.

Study plan

	Study agenda/ activities	Preparation and resources needed	Key points	Approx. timing
9.1	Starting points: group-formation activities; topic web for *Sing a song of sixpence*	No additional materials needed	Topic-linked group dynamics Comparing a potential activity-centred curriculum with a language-centred curriculum	40–60 minutes
9.2	The House that Jack Built	Large sheets of paper, crayons	Active participation in *The House that Jack Built* Producing a *house that Jack built* poster of own teaching situation Producing a *wall* to represent the curriculum of this coursebook	60–90+ minutes
9.3	The content and curriculum of a children's EFL coursebook	A selection of current children's EFL coursebooks and supplementary materials	Producing an activity-oriented curriculum Discussing key points related to the curriculum Producing a shared curriculum	90–120+ minutes

⟫→

	Study agenda/ activities	Preparation and resources needed	Key points	Approx. timing
9.4	Games children play	No additional materials needed	Discussing the reasons for integrating games/ play into the curriculum Sharing ideas for games/play in the language classroom	40–60 minutes
9.5	Round-up activity	No additional materials needed	Producing a humorous *house* rhyme based on traditional examples	15–20+ minutes

9.1 Starting points

Aims
This activity provides a further example of a topic-based formation activity.

House/castle group-formation activities

Ts follow the instructions in the course notes.

Sing a song of sixpence topic web

- Ts work in a team of five or six and follow the instructions.
  For the production of the topic web ensure that Ts highlight the part(s) of the web that they think can be completed in English. In this respect, Ts need to state the specific language point they wish to focus upon. They also need to discuss, within their groups, the general teaching sequence they might use to integrate the practical task and language focus in a language classroom situation. As previously stated in this book, it is important that:
  - the task has 'whole learning' value to the children completing it;
  - the task can realistically be achieved within a language classroom and its associated limitations;
  - the teacher has a specific and predetermined language focus (in terms of production by the children) in mind throughout the task, and that this language focus is relevant to a traditional EFL language syllabus;
  - at the end of the task, there is evidence of the completion of *language* practice as well as physical evidence of the final product of the task itself.

- When they have finished, refer the Ts back to the topic webs they have produced so far in this course:
Ts extract the language focus they have highlighted in each web. Ts compare this with language that is presented in a language-based language course.
Ts discuss in their teams the feasibility/advantages/disadvantages of developing a curriculum based on language that is generated from topic and theme centres, as compared with working from a predetermined language curriculum and adding extension (practical) tasks where time and facilities permit.

Below are extracts from example tables completed by teachers:

Activity-based curriculum

Advantages	Disadvantages
Provides 'whole learning' context for language Suits mixed-ability groups Allows for a rich language input Allows for Ps to develop their own language texts from the results of practical tasks Provides a highly motivating context for language to develop from Provides authentic contexts for language Motivates children to take risks with language and to look for language they want to use rather than repeat predetermined language from a textbook Encourages social interaction and peer teaching Encourages success at the individual child's own cognitive and language skill level	May be difficult to organise in the language classroom Requires a lot of preparation time Requires confidence to take risks with discipline Activities may take up too much time; consequently there is little time left for language focus and practice Needs language confidence and fluency from the teacher Activities need to be carefully selected so that the language generated can be matched to that of a traditional EFL curriculum Requires much planning in order to maintain a consistent progress in terms of language development May require co-operation from other teachers

Language-based curriculum

Advantages	Disadvantages
Easy to organise in the language classroom Requires little preparation time Requires little risk-taking in terms of management techniques with children Activities are pre-planned and can usually be completed on the page; consequently there is a lot of time left for language focus and practice Language is predicted and cassettes are usually available; teacher can teach from the book Easy to demonstrate what is to be taught and learned in terms of a traditional EFL curriculum	Provides very little 'whole learning' context for language; many of the contexts are artificial and not related to the children's interests or potential use of language in the real world Unsuitable for mixed-ability groups; assumes that all children learn (and want to learn) the same thing at the same time, in the same manner and at the same pace Provides a very limited language input Discourages Ps from developing or constructing their own language texts; encourages fixed (and known) response and language practice Provides a stereotyped and non-personalised context for language to develop from Discourages children from taking risks with language Encourages children to use language they feel the T wants them to use rather than search for their own ideas Encourages fixed group interaction and teacher-led learning Encourages success for the bright and motivated child, and failure for those whose cognitive and language skill level may not yet be ready to handle the language content presented in the text

9.2 The House that Jack Built

Aims
In this activity, teachers:
- actively participate in *The House that Jack Built*;
- produce a *House that Jack Built* poster of their teaching situation;
- produce a *wall* to represent the curriculum of this coursebook.

The rhyme

- Ts work in teams of five or six. Say the rhyme below.
  This is the house that Jack built.
  This is the malt in the house that Jack built.
  This is the rat that ate the malt in the house that Jack built.
  This is the cat that killed the rat that ate the malt in the house that Jack built.

This is the dog that chased the cat that killed the rat that ate the malt in the house that Jack built.
This is the cow that kicked the dog that chased the cat that killed the rat that ate the malt in the house that Jack built.
This is the woman that milked the cow that kicked the dog that chased the cat that killed the rat that ate the malt in the house that Jack built.
This is the man who married the woman that milked the cow that kicked the dog that chased the cat that killed the rat that ate the malt in the house that Jack built.
And this is Jack.

- When the rhyme finishes, Ts in each team have about a minute and a half only to draw as many of the characters and locations in the rhyme as they can on sheets of A4 size paper. When the time is up, they have a further thirty seconds to attach (pin, Sellotape or Blu-tack) their pictures to the board or notice board (as quickly as possible) and return to their original places. Give points to the first team to finish.
- Repeat this step if necessary to allow all the groups to finish.
- Appoint one T from each group as a monitor. Retell the rhyme to the whole training group in *the plural* (if there is more than one copy of a particular animal, etc.), e.g. *These are the cats that ate the rats that ate the malt in the houses that Jack built.* The monitors must rearrange the pictures and display them in the correct sequence around the room.
- When they have finished, Ts choose a character/item and stand beside or under it. In a large training group there will be several Ts for each picture. You point to each character/item in turn and the rhyme is then retold by the characters themselves.
- Ts move to a new character of their choice and retell the rhyme.
- When they have finished, Ts work in new groups of five or six. They discuss how this, or a similar activity, could be used with low-level younger learners. Include the following questions in the discussion:
  What vocabulary, if any, needs to be pre-taught?
  Where might this rhyme be presented:
  – in a traditional *language curriculum*?
  – as part of a topic/theme in L1?

Reading and illustrating task

Ts read the text on page 114, then work co-operatively with a partner to follow the instructions. Make sure that large size paper is available for this activity.

Producing a 'curriculum wall' for your training course

Ts work in groups of four or five and follow the detailed instructions in the course notes. Encourage Ts:
- to look back through the book and their notes;
- to share ideas and information with others in their group;
- to display their finished work and to look at the posters made by other groups.

9.3 The content and curriculum of a children's EFL coursebook

Aims
In this activity, teachers:
- produce an activity-oriented curriculum;
- discuss key points related to the curriculum;
- produce a shared curriculum.

- Ts work in teams of five or six and follow the detailed instructions in the course notes.
  With respect to Table 1:
  Teams use the stated curriculum from a contemporary coursebook to complete the structure, function and vocabulary sections of this table in their book. Experience has shown that this activity usually requires Ts to 'fill the gaps' in the table in terms of:
  - potential language input from the teacher;
  - potential use of an action game;
  - potential use of 'practical' tasks or stories, songs, etc.
- When they have finished, Ts compare their completed table with that of the curriculum in the coursebook and discuss the reasons for, and implications of the differences, e.g.
  Action games, where provided within a coursebook, are usually not linked to the topic (if there is one) of a particular unit.
  - This implies that the action game is a 'cherry on the cake' and not an integrated learning step in a teaching unit.

Practical tasks (where suggested within a coursebook) usually require all the children to do the same task at the same time.
  - Such tasks are often not relevant or challenging to the range of abilities and interests usually found within any group of children. Many teachers see these tasks as the final activity in a unit, rather than the starting point from which language can authentically be generated.

Language input from the teacher (where suggested) is often the counterpart of language output expected of the children.
  - Few coursebooks encourage a rich language input from the teacher.

Instead they focus on teaching children 'language formulae' in the early part of the course, irrespective of the children's interests, motivation, skills, confidence, needs. The role of a rich and authentic language input from the teacher plays a very minor part when compared with the apparent desire to teach *What's that?* or *My name is ....*

With respect to Table 2:
Ts are encouraged to start with practical topics/teacher language input and relate them to a traditional grammar-based language sequence that can be found in many contemporary coursebooks, i.e. teachers are encouraged to develop an *activity-based syllabus* that generates a reasonably traditional language syllabus.

Remind Ts that the topics or themes and tasks they choose:
- should have 'whole learning' value to the children completing them;
- should be realistically achievable within a language classroom and its associated limitations;
- should have a specific and predetermined language focus (in terms of production by the children) – and this language focus should be relevant to a traditional EFL language syllabus.

There should be evidence at the end of the practical activity of the completion of *language* practice – as well as evidence of the final product of the task itself.

- When ready, Ts in their own group join with another group of Ts and share the curriculum they have decided on.
- Allow 15–25 minutes for discussion within the larger groups to select the most promising ideas for a curriculum.
- When Ts are ready, organise a whole group feedback:
  T1 and T2 from each group write the final selections on the board. This may then be transferred to A4 paper, and photocopied for the rest of the group.

9.4 Games children play

Aims
This activity encourages teachers:
- to share their 'best' games with each other;
- to discuss the role of games/play in the curriculum;
- to integrate specific games into the 'curriculum' they have developed in this unit.

Preparation

Ts work in teams of six and follow the instructions in the course notes. Encourage Ts to take opposing viewpoints to stimulate discussion if necessary.

Here are some points you may wish to raise:

1 Play has a key role in the learning process for children.
   ○ Although play obviously has a key role in the emotional, social, intellectual and language development of children, it has a relatively minor role in the more formal classroom. Aside from formulaic games, play is also largely overlooked in contemporary EFL coursebooks for children.

2 Play is a source of motivation, interest and enjoyment.
   ○ Play is often considered as the first step to loss of control by the teacher. It is often overlooked as a means of class control. Motivation and interest in play can have a key role in maintaining a natural and mutually respected code of discipline.

3 Parents may become anxious if children say they have 'played' in the language lesson.
   ○ Many parents are over-anxious for their children to 'learn' as much as possible at school in as short a time period as possible. They may overlook the value of play in the learning process (and their own negative learning experience in a formal learning situation) in favour of the more traditional language learning activities such as choral drills, copying from the board and completion of repetitive exercises. Parents must therefore be kept informed of the *relevance* and *reason* for play. Unconvinced parents will also need to see concrete evidence (i.e. written or spoken by their child) that language learning is taking place.

4 Teachers may reject coursebooks which place a high priority on 'play'.
   ○ Most coursebooks omit the word *play* from promotional literature, although recently *fun* has become an acceptable term to include. Many teachers may feel threatened by an overemphasis on the value of play in the learning of a language – since this can give rise to noise and overexcitement in the classroom – without any apparent associated evidence that language learning is taking place. Should teachers therefore only consider play where it is possible to produce evidence (such as completed written exercises) that the play has performed a teaching/learning function?

5 For children, inside and outside the classroom, playing is a source of language, and a context for language use.
   ○ When in a new foreign language situation, children will often happily play with new friends, using gesture and the odd key word as a form of communication. The play/game itself provides the main content and form of communication. There seem to be very few barriers between children who do not speak the same language where play is concerned. What implication does this have for the more formal teaching situation?

6 The content of play/games should be linked to the overall theme/topic of the lesson.
   ○ It is all too easy to have a bag of games to fill the dead moments in a lesson, or to use as a prize for good behaviour. However, with a little careful consideration a game can be adapted to link, in terms of vocabulary, language form or topic, to most themes or course-book units.

7 Games/play are an essential part of a curriculum, not a time filler or reward.
   ○ As stated in points 1 and 2 above, play has a key role in the learning process for children and provides an excellent source of motivation, interest and enjoyment.

8 Games/play should encourage group support and not merely competition between children and groups.
   ○ Children enjoy competitive games and these can serve as a motivation for successful participation. However, if only competitive games are played, or too much value is given to 'winning', the more able children will receive much praise at the expense of the weaker pupils in the class. It is therefore extremely important to provide co-operative as well as competitive play and games within the classroom.

9 Children should be encouraged to decide/bring/choose the games they want to play in English.
   ○ The playing of familiar and popular games **in English** is a valuable source of authentic language input. Similarly, children will be highly motivated to acquire language so that they can play their favourite game successfully in English.

10 The play/game I enjoyed playing when I was a child was _____. It is/isn't possible to use this game in my language teaching.
   ○ It is very easy to forget the games we used to play. Children are usually very ready to take part in any game that 'teacher used to play when he/she was a child'. A teacher's emotional commitment to a traditional game is an excellent justification for bringing it to his/her teaching situation.

Action

Ts work in teams of at least six and share their favourite games with each other. This activity may best be done outside.

Feedback

Ts discuss how the games shared in this activity can be integrated into the curriculum they have planned in this unit. This is a further opportunity for emphasising the value of adapting a game to suit the specific language and theme needs of a particular lesson or coursebook unit.

9.5 Round-up activity: house/home rhymes and chants

Aims

In this activity, teachers produce a humorous *house* rhyme based on traditional examples.

Ts work in teams of five or six and follow the detailed instructions in the course notes.

10 Observation, assessment and records

Theme/topic
Faces, face shapes, wanted posters

Overall aims
This unit introduces some of the key issues involved in assessment. Teachers are encouraged to make assessment decisions with respect to their own teaching situation, and the training course they are about to complete.

Study plan

	Study agenda/ activities	Preparation and resources needed	Key points	Approx. timing
10.1	Starting points: group-formation activities	No additional materials needed	Topic-linked group dynamics	10–20+ minutes
10.2	Making a 'wanted poster'	Poster size sheets of paper, crayons, felt tips, scrap materials for decorating the picture, etc.	Profiling activity involving drawing and writing positive statements	20–30+ minutes
10.3	Testing, evaluation and assessment	No additional materials needed	Shared discussion on assessment Reading of letter from a *teacher* to an *inspector* concerning assessment Discussion of the content of the letter Shared writing of the inspector's reply	60–90+ minutes
10.4	Profiling	No additional materials needed	Discussion on the value of profiling in the assessment of children and of yourselves as teachers/trainees	20–30+ minutes
10.5	Constructive assessment: *classroom research*	No additional materials needed	Discussion on *classroom research*	20–30+ minutes

≫→

	Study agenda/ activities	Preparation and resources needed	Key points	Approx. timing
10.6	Round-up activity	No additional materials needed	Producing a teaching procedure for a *skipping rhyme* *The hokey cokey*	10–15 minutes

10.1   Starting points

Aims
This activity provides:
– a further example of topic-based group-formation activities;
– an introduction to the theme of the unit.

A) PLEASE MR CROCODILE

Ts follow the instructions in the course notes.

B) WHO IS IT?

Training group divides into three equal groups and follows the instructions in the course notes.

C) DRAW MY FACE

- Use the following action game script:
  First, draw one large round face. Now, draw two large round eyes. Next, draw two little cup-shaped ears. Now, draw a medium-sized, triangle-shaped nose. Next, draw a large heart-shaped mouth. Finally, draw the hair and a beard.
- Ts stand in a large circle, all facing the same direction (clockwise).
- T1 stands beside you, outside (or in the centre of) the circle.
- Ts touch, with a finger, the back of the person standing on their left in the circle. (It may be easier to ask them first to put their hands on the shoulders of the person on their left in order to produce the correct distance between each person.)
- Give the action game instructions. Ts must draw, using a finger, the face as you (or T1) say it on the back of the person standing in front of them in the circle.
- Ts in the circle now turn 180 degrees to face the other way. Repeat the action game instructions.
- Ts sit down so that they can work individually within groups of four or five. They take a sheet of blank paper.

- T1 in each group gives *draw a face* instructions. The other Ts in the group draw.
- Ts describe the face they have drawn, and give other personal details of the face to a partner.

10.2 Making a 'wanted poster'

Aims

This activity introduces the idea of a *personal profile* for assessment purposes. It also introduces the importance of *positive* evaluation and assessment.

Ts work in pairs and follow the instructions in the course notes.
As a way of starting this activity, ask T1 in each pair to look at his/her partner (T2) carefully for ten seconds, then to close his/her eyes. T1 (eyes closed) describes T2 from memory (in as glowing terms as possible). Ts change roles and repeat this step.

10.3 Assessment

Aims

In this activity, teachers:
- distinguish (if appropriate) between testing, evaluation and assessment;
- share their views on testing/evaluation/assessment;
- read and discuss a letter from a *teacher* to an *inspector* concerning assessment;
- share the writing of the inspector's reply.

Introduction

- Ts first work with a partner and agree on the meaning of *testing, assessment* and *evaluation*. Below are example definitions:

Testing
A means of checking learning that has taken place with respect to a specified teaching content or input, often by means of a particular task. The results are usually concrete and can be expressed quantitatively, e.g. as a mark or percentage.

Evaluation
A global view of achievement of the teaching and learning process over a period of time, e.g. analysis of the success or failure of a teaching approach, coursebook, pupil response, motivation, etc.

Assessment

An attempt to analyse the learning that a child has achieved over a period of time as a result of the classroom/teaching/learning situation. Assessment does not need to be based on a particular task, nor is it usually expressed as a mark or percentage. It may include subjective (teacher) opinion of the achievement of a child in terms of attitude, participation, socialisation, general cognitive and physical development, etc. Assessment may also be expressed 'relatively' in that the progress of an individual child can be measured against his/her individual starting points and abilities rather than compared against the skills and abilities of other children – as in the traditional testing situation.

- When ready, Ts work in a team of five and discuss their personal experience of testing, evaluation and assessment. Ts are also asked how they would like to be assessed (or tested) on their performance during this training course. Organise whole-group feedback on this section, writing up key points on the board.
- For the next activity, Ts return to their teams and write possible ways of assessing and testing children's work and progress. This activity also encourages Ts to discuss the purpose and effect of the various means of assessment and testing. In this respect, the following points are examples of those that may be raised or discussed.

Ways of testing which:
may be shared with the child.
- ○ In a test situation, there are many factors that can affect children's performance, such as problems at home or with friends, health, motivation, etc. It would therefore seem valuable to give children the chance to talk about their performance in a specific test. In terms of assessment, chatting or conferencing with a small group of children in order to exchange your views with theirs can provide valuable insights to both linguistic and social/cognitive problem areas and to children's needs.

provide accurate information about the child's ability in English.
- ○ A specific test may be viewed as just one indication of learning and not a definitive measure of achievement. Young children often seem to show remarkable progress within a short span of time. Inability to perform at one given moment in a course does not mean that the child is ignorant. Ideally, children should be given many opportunities to succeed throughout the course in many different types of 'test', and that success by a child should always be valued by the teacher.

provide necessary information to the teacher for in-school purposes.
- ○ A record of achievement over a long period is likely to give a more accurate picture of the ability of a child. Ideally, such a record or profile should include copies of class work, ongoing teacher comment,

comment from the child and parent – and not merely a list of test marks.

may be shared with the whole class, verbally or as a 'performance list'.

○ Teachers need to consider carefully the effect of ranking children. While public evidence of positive achievement may motivate the successful children to maintain their standard, it may also serve to destroy the confidence of the less able child, or the child who does not perform well in a test situation.

may motivate/demotivate a weaker learner.

○ Most children respond positively to success and praise. It is therefore important to set children tasks **at their own level** – so that they have the opportunity to succeed.

require children to work individually/allow(s) children to work co-operatively with others in the class.

○ Co-operative tasks, whether they are the shared completion of a formal test, or the tackling of a group project, demonstrate, for example, a child's ability to:
 – make a valid contribution to a task;
 – interact with others;
 – make effective use of the skill of their partners.
 In this way, children may **learn** from the testing and assessment situation. It is our aim to support children in their development, not to condemn them their weaknesses.

provide information about what the child **can** do rather than what he/she can't do.

○ Teachers who view children in terms of what they **can** do rather than what they can't do are liable to transmit this positive attitude to their class. As previously mentioned, children are more likely to build on 'success' than on 'failure'.

may be useful for parents.

○ Since parental support is a key factor in the learning situation, it is essential to involve parents in the ongoing assessment of their children's progress. Additionally, parents may reveal valid reasons for their children's problems at school.

may be useful for a child's future teachers.

○ A list of poor test results is liable to colour a teacher's attitude to a particular pupil in a new class. A profile of a child's work would seem to present a far more useful and positive background, not only to the ability of the child, but also to the type of work carried out in a previous class.

Reading task

Ts share the reading of the letter on pages 121–122 with a partner.

Discussion

Ts work in groups and exchange comments and personal experience related to the letter. They consider the issues raised in the book.

Co-operative writing task

Ts work co-operatively with a partner to write the inspector's reply.

10.4 Profiling

Aims
This activity provides:
- a discussion on *profiling* in the assessment of children;
- a discussion on the *profiling* of teachers/trainees.

● Ts discuss *profiling*. The following are examples for the profiling key words and phrases:
Conferencing with children
Discussing with children how they feel about their work. Finding out their likes, dislikes, interests, etc. Sharing your feelings about their work with them. Negotiating what you both feel the next steps might be.

Keeping samples of work done in a folder
Making copies or keeping originals of children's work. These provide a very clear indication of progress and areas for further work. Each child has his/her own folder where sample work is stored.

Discussion with parents/keeping parents informed about the course and their children's progress
Parents need to be informed of, and involved with, their children's progress. There should be space in the profile for parents' comments on the work their children do at home, and the comments parents hear from their children with respect to the work done in class.

Negotiating with the children about work done, and setting targets
Children are partners in the learning-teaching process. They should be informed of the purpose of their learning, and their opinions with respect to this should be valued and taken into consideration. They should be asked to set themselves realistic learning targets to be achieved within a specific time frame. With respect to learning English these targets might include saying ten new words, asking a question in English, writing five English words on a picture, finding a label with English words on, etc. Achievement, or non-achievement of targets should be discussed with the child at the appropriate time, and new targets negotiated.

Self and peer evaluation
Sharing the responsibility for assessment with the children. Showing the children that their and their classmates' opinion on their work/progress has validity. Teachers should not necessarily be seen as the judge and jury in the learning situation.

Passing on of a 'profile folder' to the next teacher
Profiles should be transferred to the next class along with the child. It is very important for new teachers to have an overall picture of the children in the class. Any radical change in behaviour or performance may therefore be easy to spot and the reasons for this change potentially easier to diagnose.

- If not already included as part of the course, ask Ts what activities, work, etc. they feel they would like to include in their *profile* as trainees on the course.

10.5 Classroom assessment and Research

Aims
This section encourages Ts to undertake classroom research projects as a next step following the end of their training programme.

Introduction

Whilst an in-depth study of classroom (action) research lies outside the scope of this book, we feel that classroom research is a particularly appropriate response to teachers who may be looking for ways of acting on/reflecting upon the ideas and approaches they have encountered during this training course.

- As a starting point to this section, draw the following learning cycle on the board for discussion and comment by the group:

Where:
UI stands for
  unconscious ignorance
CI stands for
  conscious ignorance
CC stands for
  conscious competence
UC stands for
  unconscious competence

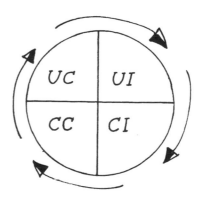

If appropriate, explain that in terms of learning, the crucial step is for learners to be able to accept, or to become *aware* of their 'ignorance'. When this acceptance and awareness occurs, it is usually followed by the wish to become competent – and the accompanying motivation 'to learn'. At this stage it is crucial for the teacher to offer support and encouragement to the learner.

- As a next step, Ts work in pairs or groups. Encourage them to share their existing experience/knowledge of classroom research. Highlight the fact that classroom research encourages Ts to examine specific aspects of their own teaching situation/classroom in a systematic and reflective manner.

Procedure

- Ts read steps A to D. Allow them time to make a written statement and plan for steps A and B.
- Finally, organise Ts into new pairs/teams. Ts explain their own steps A and B to their new partners. Where feasible, ask Ts to 'exchange contracts' to carry out the research and report on steps C to E to their partner(s), either by mail or by phone.

10.6 Round-up activity: assess your skipping and hokey cokey skills

Aims
This activity:
- demonstrates a teaching procedure and tune for a *skipping rhyme*;
- provides an 'end of course' group-formation activity.

Ts follow the detailed instructions for both group-formation activities.

RESOURCE FILE

Introduction

This resource file has five sections:
Section A contains cross-curricular topic webs for each of the ten units in the book.
Section B reviews the types of TPR activities that are suggested within this book.
Section C offers a wide range of practical ideas for reading and writing activities.
Section D provides examples of songs and rhymes for the topics of each of the ten units in the book.
Section E contains ten games which may be adapted to integrate within a wide range of topics and potential language aims.

A Ten topic webs

The following ten topic webs show how activities can be developed in a language/primary classroom around the theme of each of the ten units in this book. These 'webs' should be adapted to suit your own teaching style and situation. The topic webs also give examples of language that can be generated through each of the activities. Although not intended as a language course, it is interesting to compare this language with the language aims of more traditional language courses. As a further activity, teachers may wish to:
- draw up a checklist of language points that they wish their language course to cover;
- match this checklist to the language points that are generated through the activities suggested in the topic webs;
- add/adapt activities so that both checklists cover more or less the same language points.

Note: Since a given activity may generate a range of language points, it is important to decide **before** the activity the language point you wish the children to use (in terms of *production*). There are some additional topic webs in the Trainer's notes.

A.1 Spiders and mini-creatures

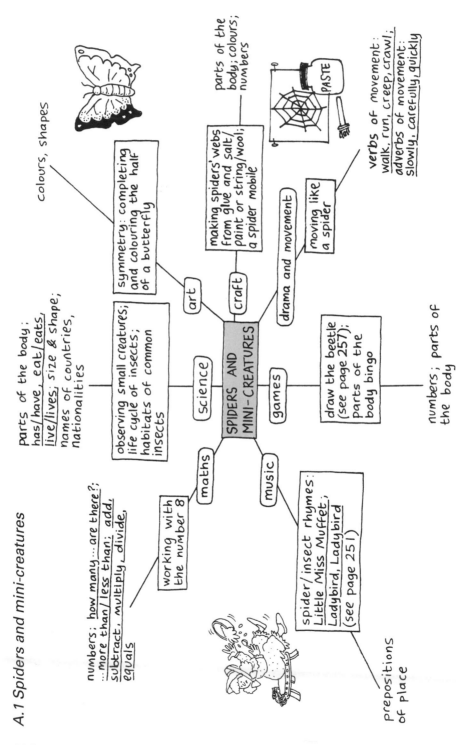

colours, shapes

parts of the body; colours; numbers

verbs of movement: walk, run, creep, crawl; adverbs of movement: slowly, carefully, quickly

symmetry: completing and colouring the half of a butterfly

art

making spiders' webs from glue and salt/ paint or string/wool; a spider mobile

craft

PASTE

moving like a spider

drama and movement

parts of the body; has/have, eat/eats, live/lives; size & shape; names of countries, nationalities

observing small creatures; life cycle of insects; habitats of common insects

science

SPIDERS AND MINI-CREATURES

games

draw the beetle (see page 257); parts of the body bingo

numbers; parts of the body

numbers: how many...are there?; more than/less than; add, subtract, multiply, divide, equals

working with the number 8

maths

music

spider/insect rhymes: Little Miss Muffet; Ladybird, Ladybird (see page 251)

prepositions of place

234

A.2 Circus

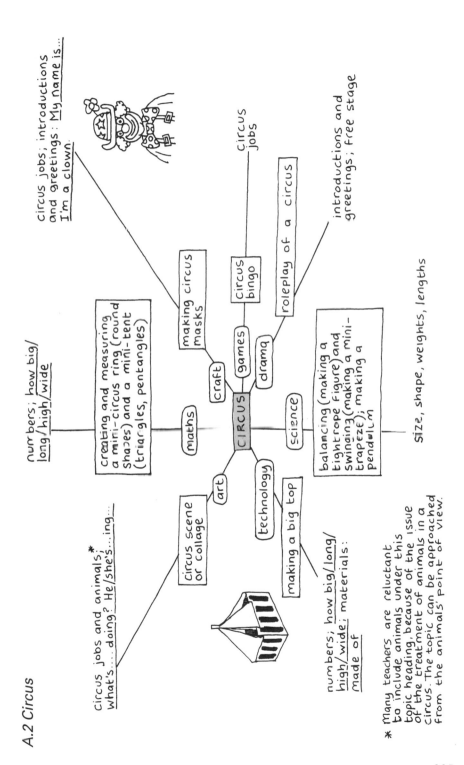

circus jobs; introductions
and greetings: <u>My name is</u>....
<u>I'm a clown</u>.

numbers; how big/
long/high/wide

creating and measuring
a mini-circus ring (round
shapes) and a mini-tent
(triangles, pentangles)

making circus
masks

circus jobs

circus
bingo

introductions and
greetings; free stage

roleplay of a circus

CIRCUS

maths

Craft

games

drama

science

art

technology

circus jobs and animals;
what's.....doing? He/she's.....ing....*

Circus scene
or collage

making a big top

balancing (making a
tightrope figure) and
swinging (making a mini-
trapeze); making a
pendulum

size, shape, weights, lengths

numbers; how big/long/
high/wide; materials:
<u>made of</u>

* Many teachers are reluctant
to include animals under this
topic heading, because of the issue
of the treatment of animals in a
circus. The topic can be approached
from the animals' point of view.

235

A.3 Potatoes/vegetables

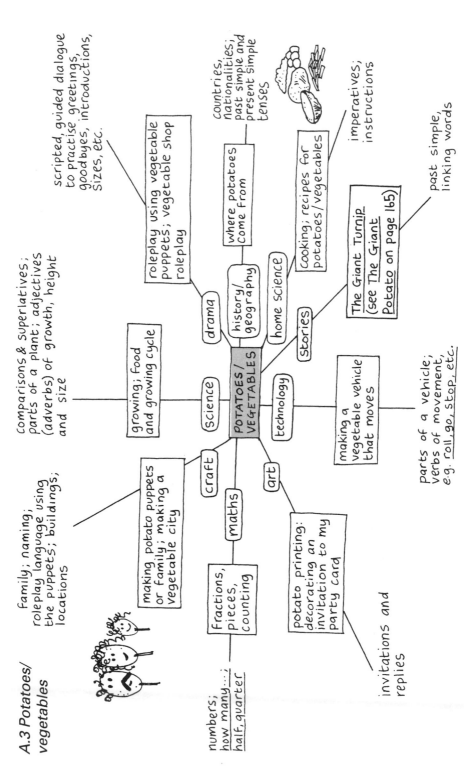

POTATOES/VEGETABLES

drama — roleplay using vegetable puppets; vegetable shop roleplay
— scripted, guided dialogue to practise greetings, goodbyes, introductions, sizes, etc.

history/geography — where potatoes come from — countries, nationalities; past simple and present simple tenses

home science — Cooking; recipes for potatoes/vegetables — imperatives; instructions

Stories — The Giant Turnip (see The Giant Potato on page 165) — past simple, linking words

Science — growing; food and growing cycle — comparisons & superlatives; parts of a plant; adjectives (adverbs) of growth, height and size

technology — making a vegetable vehicle that moves — parts of a vehicle; verbs of movement, e.g. roll, go, stop, etc.

art — potato printing; decorating an invitation to my party card — invitations and replies

maths — Fractions, pieces, counting — numbers; how many...; half, quarter

craft — making potato puppets or family; making a vegetable city — Family; naming; roleplay language using the puppets; buildings; locations

A.4 Islands

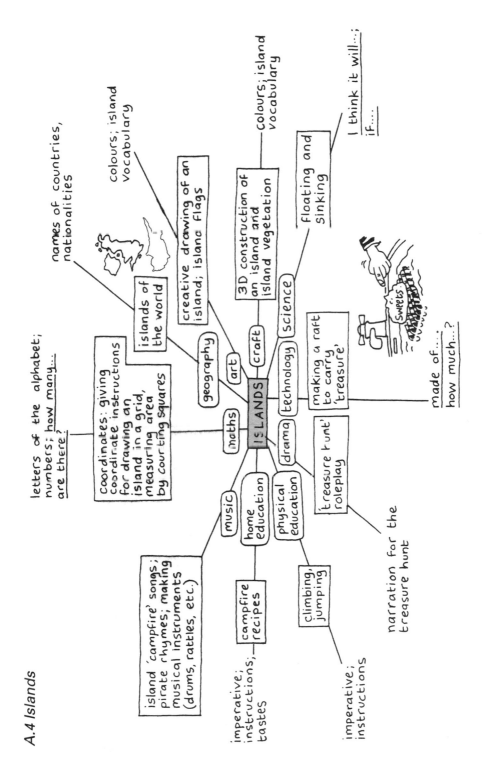

ISLANDS

geography
- islands of the world — names of countries, nationalities

art
- creative drawing of an island; island flags — colours; island vocabulary

craft
- 3D construction of an island and island vegetation — colours; island vocabulary

science
- floating and sinking — I think it will...; if...
- making a raft to carry 'treasure' — made of...; how much...?

technology
- treasure hunt' roleplay

drama
- narration for the treasure hunt — imperative; instructions

physical education
- climbing, jumping — imperative; instructions

home education
- campfire recipes — imperative; instructions; tastes

music
- island 'campfire' songs; pirate rhymes; making musical instruments (drums, rattles, etc.)

maths
- coordinates: giving coordinate instructions for drawing an island in a grid, measuring area by counting squares — letters of the alphabet; numbers; how many... are there?

237

A.5 Bridges

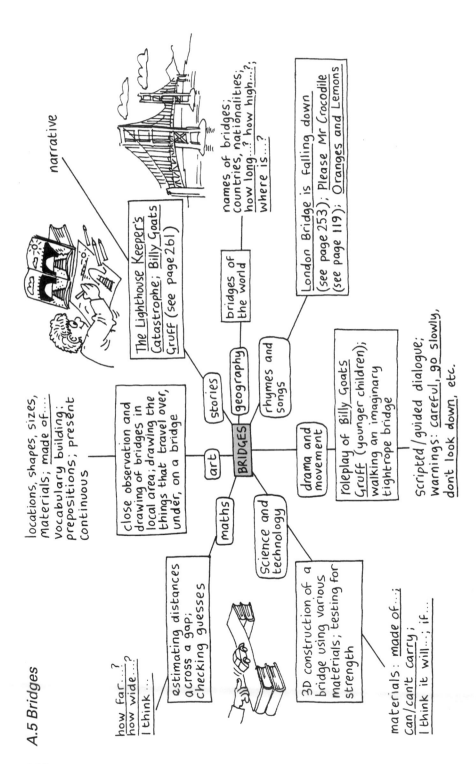

narrative

stories

The Lighthouse Keeper's Catastrophe; Billy Goats Gruff (see page 261)

geography

bridges of the world

names of bridges; countries, nationalities; how long...? how high...?; where is...?

rhymes and songs

London Bridge is falling down (see page 253); Please Mr Crocodile (see page 119); Oranges and Lemons

BRIDGES

art

close observation and drawing of bridges in local area; drawing the things that travel over, under, on a bridge

locations, shapes, sizes, materials; made of...; vocabulary building; prepositions; present continuous

drama and movement

roleplay of Billy Goats Gruff (younger children); walking on an imaginary tightrope bridge

Scripted/guided dialogue; warnings: careful, go slowly, don't look down, etc.

maths

estimating distances across a gap; checking guesses

how far...? how wide...? I think....

Science and technology

3D construction of a bridge using various materials; testing for strength

materials: made of...; can/can't carry; I think it will...; if....

A.6 Jack and the beanstalk / growing

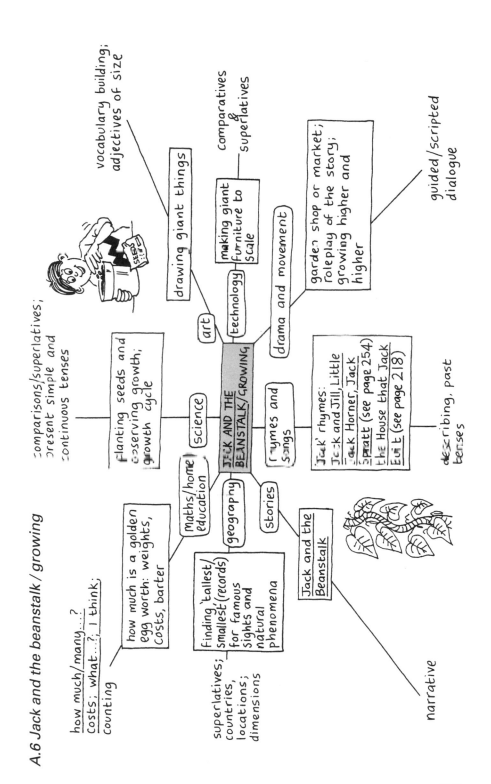

JACK AND THE BEANSTALK / GROWING

art
- drawing giant things
  - vocabulary building; adjectives of size

technology
- making giant furniture to scale
  - comparatives & superlatives

drama and movement
- garden shop or market; roleplay of the story; growing higher and higher
  - guided/scripted dialogue

science
- planting seeds and observing growth; growth cycle
  - comparisons/superlatives; present simple and continuous tenses

maths/home education
- how much is a golden egg worth: weights, costs, barter
  - how much/many...? Costs; what...?; I think; counting

geography
- finding 'tallest', 'smallest' (records) for famous sights and natural phenomena
  - superlatives; countries, locations; dimensions

stories
- Jack and the Beanstalk
  - narrative

rhymes and songs
- Jack rhymes: Jack and Jill, Little Jack Horner, Jack Spratt (see page 254), the House that Jack Built (see page 218)
  - describing, past tenses

239

A.7 Goldilocks and the three bears / bears (in general)

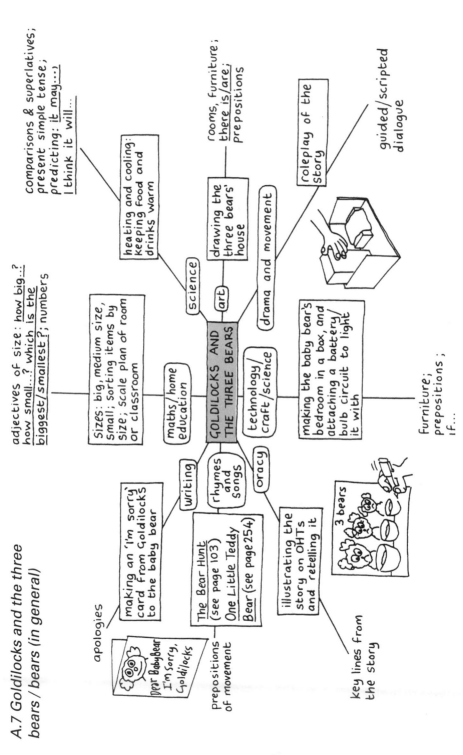

comparisons & superlatives;
present simple tense;
predicting: it may...;
I think it will...

heating and cooling:
keeping food and
drinks warm

rooms, furniture;
there is/are;
prepositions

roleplay of the
story

guided/scripted
dialogue

science

drawing the
three bears'
house

art

drama and movement

adjectives of size: how big...?
how small...? which is the
biggest/smallest?; numbers

Sizes: big, medium size,
small; sorting items by
size; scale plan of room
or classroom

maths/home
education

**GOLDILOCKS AND
THE THREE BEARS**

technology/
craft/science

making the baby bear's
bedroom in a box, and
attaching a battery/
bulb circuit to light
it with

Furniture;
prepositions;
if...

writing

rhymes
and
songs

oracy

making an 'I'm sorry'
card from Goldilocks
to the baby bear

The Bear Hunt
(see page 103)
One Little Teddy
Bear (see page 254)

illustrating the
story on OHTs
and retelling it

3 bears

apologies

Dear BabyBear
I'm Sorry,
Goldilocks

prepositions
of movement

key lines from
the story

240

A.8 Hallowe'en / festivals

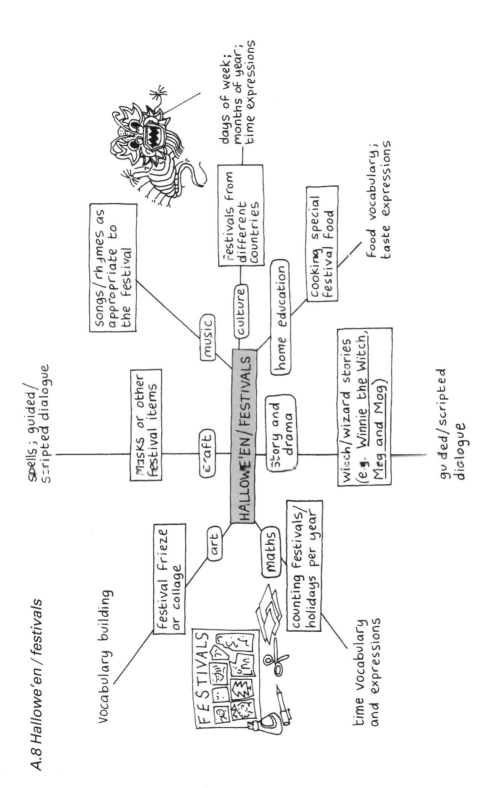

Vocabulary building

spells; guided/scripted dialogue

songs/rhymes as appropriate to the festival

days of week; months of year; time expressions

Food vocabulary; taste expressions

Masks or other festival items

Festivals from different Countries

Cooking special festival food

music

culture

home education

craft

Story and drama

Witch/wizard stories (e.g. Winnie the Witch, Meg and Mog)

guided/scripted dialogue

HALLOWE'EN / FESTIVALS

Festival Frieze or collage

art

maths

counting festivals/holidays per year

FESTIVALS

time vocabulary and expressions

A.9 The house that Jack built / buildings

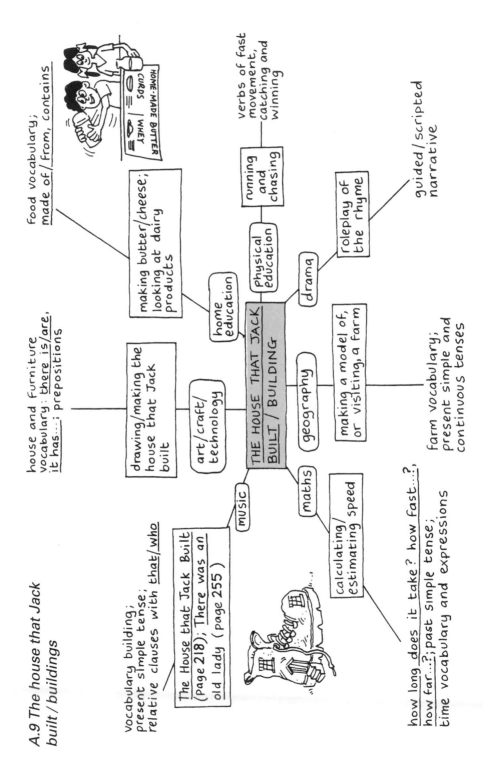

THE HOUSE THAT JACK BUILT / BUILDING

home education — making butter/cheese; looking at dairy products
Food vocabulary; made of / from, contains

art/craft/technology — drawing/making the house that Jack built
house and furniture vocabulary; there is / are, it has...; prepositions

music — The House that Jack Built (page 218); There was an old lady (page 255)
vocabulary building; present simple tense; relative clauses with that / who

maths — calculating/estimating speed
how long does it take? how fast...? how far...?; past simple tense; time vocabulary and expressions

geography — making a model of, or visiting, a farm
farm vocabulary; present simple and continuous tenses

physical education — running and chasing
verbs of fast movement, catching and winning

drama — roleplay of the rhyme
guided / scripted narrative

A.10 'Wanted'

parts of the body;
present simple tense

past simple tense; place and
area names; relative clauses,
e.g. a place where/a bandit who....

Face vocabulary;
comparatives;
shapes, sizes

WHO CAN DO 20 JUMPS?

	JUAN	MARIA	MIGUEL	ANGEL	PILAR
20					
10					
0					

action verbs;
can, might, will

making identikits or
further wanted posters

close observation
and drawing of
faces (human and
animal)

personal/class chart
of can do, e.g. sit ups,
hops, jumps, etc.

large numbers
how much....?

Calculating
rewards

the 'wild west': famous
outlaws, cowboys, places

charades of
famous people or
pupils in the class

who is it?
expressions

Cowboy songs

WANTED

art — Science — physical education — maths — drama — geography — music

243

B Total physical response activities

The following section reviews the practical ideas included within the book with respect to the use of TPR in the children's language classroom.

Note: While these TPR tasks refer to spoken texts, the same activities can be done with written texts, e.g. Read and draw/act, etc.

A) LISTEN AND DRAW (OR COLOUR)

Create a text that requires the Ps to draw. Depending on your teaching purpose, this text may be given in various verb forms/tenses, e.g.
Imperative: *Draw a big round head. Draw a large body.*
Narrative in the present simple tense: *This animal has a large head. It has a large body ...*
Narrative in the present continuous: *The tiger is standing under a tree. The snake is crawling in the grass ...*
Narrative in the past simple tense: *The tiger stood under a tree. The snake crawled in the grass ...*

Note: This activity is not intended to 'introduce' the tenses. However, it offers Ps the opportunity to consolidate the language *form* through doing a practical task.

Depending on ability, Ps may go on to describe their drawings, or narrate the action in the drawings.

B) LISTEN AND ACT

Create a text that requires the Ps to do actions, or interact with each other, e.g.
   Incy Wincy Spider climbs up the spout ...
   The slippery snake slithered slowly through the long grass ...
Depending on ability, Ps may go on to narrate the actions to a partner.

C) LISTEN AND MAKE

Create a text that requires the Ps to follow instructions while making or constructing a model, etc., e.g.
Pick up a piece of plasticine. Make a large round head. Make two eyes ...
Depending on ability, Ps may go on to describe their models, or give similar 'making' instructions to a partner.

D) LISTEN AND MOVE

Create a text that requires the Ps to follow instructions and move/place various objects, e.g.

Put your pencil on your desk. Put your pen next to the pencil, on the left. Put your pencil sharpener ...
Depending on ability, Ps may then give similar instructions to a partner.

E) LISTEN AND MATCH

Create a text based on, e.g. objects/animals in the coursebook that requires the Ps to:
– first draw/outline (in the air with a finger);
– then identify the objects/animals, etc.
   For example, *This animal has a big head. It has a long body.*
Depending on ability, Ps may then give similar instructions to a partner.

F) LISTEN AND PLAY

Create a text that requires the Ps to play a game. This may be a board game (with written instructions), or a game which asks the Ps to move within the classroom. Example games are:
   What's the time, Mr Wolf?
   Pin the tail on the donkey.

G) LISTEN AND SING

Many traditional rhymes and songs can be used, or adapted and used as *action rhymes*. In terms of TPR, the focus is very much on encouraging the Ps to make appropriate actions in response to the words. In this respect, consider dividing the Ps into two or four teams:
Teams 1 and 2 sing. Teams 3 and 4 do the actions.
Teams sing/act alternate lines.
Teams sing the text as a 'round':
– Team 1 sings line 1. Teams 2–4 are silent.
– Team 1 sings line 2. Team 2 sings line 1. Teams 3–4 are silent.
– Team 1 sings line 3. Team 2 sings line 2. Team 3 sings line 1. Team 4 is silent, etc.

H) LISTEN AND SPEAK

Create a text that requires the Ps to speak, e.g.
   Turn to a friend. Ask your friend for a pencil. Say thank you.

I) LISTEN AND WRITE

Create a text that requires the Ps to write, e.g.
   Take a pencil and a piece of paper. Write your name at the top. Write the date ...
Depending on ability, Ps may then give similar instructions to a partner.

Resource file

J) LISTEN AND CARRY OUT A TASK

Create a text that requires the Ps to carry out a sequence of simple tasks, e.g. *When you get home, first switch on the television. Then write the name of the programme on a piece of paper. Next, find two …*

C Reading and writing activities

This first section provides an example questionnaire that aims to find out how children in your classes feel about themselves as readers. It should be adapted and translated into L1 as necessary to suit your particular teaching situation. The children may respond in their native language.

NAME: _____

What do you feel about reading?

I think reading is/isn't important because _____.
_____.

I read a lot/little because _____
_____.

I enjoy/don't enjoy reading because _____
_____.

I think I read books because it helps

1 _____

2 _____

3 _____

I think I am a very good/average/bad reader because _____
_____.

What, where and when do you read?

I usually read at school/at home/both because _____
_____.

I usually read _____ hours/minutes every week/day.

My favourite book is _____ because _____
_____.

I also like to read _____ because _____
_____.

I like stories which:

make me laugh	☐	are about animals	☐
make me cry	☐	are about space	☐
make me think	☐	are about adventures	☐
make me _____	☐	are about _____	☐
are about people	☐	are about _____	☐

The following section gives a range of practical ideas that promote reading and writing (and pre-reading/pre-writing). Although for the purpose of this book we have used the topics of *animals* and *classroom* to provide a context for these ideas, the majority of these examples may be adapted to suit a wide variety of topics and language points.

C.1 Alphabet/letter codes

A) LETTER SHAPES

With a small class, where space is available:

Ps stand in small circles (in groups) of four or five.

Ps hold hands and take a slow, deep breath.

Call out this sequence of six letters: S–P–I–D–E–R, one at a time. Ps form the shape of each letter after you say it by linking arms, or hands, etc. with the rest of their group.

Ask (or tell) Ps which word they spelt.

This example is related to revision of names of 'mini-creatures':

With a large class, where, for example, the desks are in rows and are difficult to move, Ps turn to a partner, and form the letter shapes by linking hands/arms with their partner. Alternatively, letters can be drawn, with a finger, on the back/palm of the hand of a nearby pupil.

B) ANIMAL ALPHABET

Ps find an animal for each of the letters of the alphabet, e.g.
A is for antelope.
B is for _____ (bear).
C is for _____ (cat).
D is for _____ (dog).
E is for _____ (elephant).
F is for _____ (fox).
G is for _____ (giraffe).
H is for _____ (hippopotamus).
I is for _____ (ibex).
J is for _____ (jackal).
K is for _____ (kangaroo).
L is for _____ (lion).
M is for _____ (monkey), etc.

C) WRITING IN CODES

This is an example of an alphabet key. Ps must find the names of the animals and/or where they come from.

| **Secret key**
A = 1, B = 2,
C = 3,... | 12–9–15–14
comes from
Africa

(Space for Ps
to draw the
animal.) | 11–1–14–7–1–18–15–15
comes from
1–21–19–20–18–1–12–9–1

(Space for Ps
to draw the
animal.) |

More able Ps may produce their own code puzzles or messages.

C.2 Signs, notices, labels

A) MAKE A MOBILE

In this example, Ps make a mobile for parts of the body (based on the song *Head, shoulders, knees and toes*):

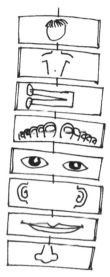

B) MAKE SIGNS FOR THE CLASSROOM

In this example, Ps make signs for the most common instructions or warnings you give during a lesson, e.g.

1 Put your hand up.

2 Put your hand down.

3 Stand up.

4 Sit down.

5 Line up.

6 Be quiet.

7 Sit up straight.

8 Don't talk.

C) MAKE WORD LABELS

Ps may make word labels for common classroom items. In addition, encourage Ps to label the main parts of any drawings they may do during a lesson.

C.3 Dictionary activities

A) CREATING A WORD BANK

Discuss with the pupils (in L1 if necessary) the need for each of them to create their own *word bank* as an effective way of learning and retrieving English words. Agree on the best format for their *word bank*, e.g.
- use a loose-leaf file, so pages can be added/re-sequenced if necessary;
- make a cover design of (the pupil's) personal choice;
- sort the words by *topic/theme* pages;
- illustrate the words, or find picture cut-outs;
- make it bilingual, and illustrate the pages (for interest, etc.).

Allow the students homework or class time to start their individual *word banks*.

B) DICTIONARY WORD GAMES AND PUZZLES

The following are a selection of popular word/dictionary related puzzles that are suitable for near-beginner level pupils. By extracting vocabulary from any given unit in a coursebook, teachers may prepare their own 'puzzle bank'.

Word sorting activities

Ps sort the words on the left under the headings on the right:

Africa	ear	
America	Europe	**colours**
Asia	eye	**parts of the body**
black	gorilla	**continents**
blue	head	**animals**
body	leg	
brown	lion	
cheetah	nose	
crocodile	red	

Encourage Ps to add **one** word to each list.

Sort the animals, e.g. *panda, elephant, fox, hippopotamus, whale, giraffe, bushbaby, kangaroo:*

alphabetically	**biggest to smallest**	**Africa/Asia**
bushbaby	whale	elephant
_____	_____	_____
_____	_____	_____
_____	_____	_____
_____	_____	
_____	_____	
whale	_____	

Ps sort these words into an *is/isn't* (or *has/doesn't have*, etc.) table:
Example: *rabbit, dog, cat, lynx, tiger, cheetah, jaguar, elephant, rhinoceros, gorilla, kangaroo, whale*

Pets		Cats		Country	
... is a pet	... isn't a pet	... is a cat	... isn't a cat	... comes from Africa	... doesn't come from Africa

Ps may then add **one** word they know to each list.

Letter recognition activities
Ps solve this 'body' puzzle:
Clues

3 letters	4 letters	8 letters
ear	body	shoulder
eye	head	
leg	knee	
toe	neck	
	nose	
	tail	

Word search activities
Ps write these continents in alphabetical order: *America, Europe, Asia, Africa, Australia.*

Ps then find the continents in the word search.

A_____a
A_____a
A_____a
A_____a
_____e

a	u	s	t	r	a	l
u	u	o	a	u	a	v
s	r	s	m	r	s	e
t	o	i	e	o	i	u
r	a	e	r	p	c	r
a	f	r	i	c	a	o
l	s	h	c	o	g	p
i	f	i	a	d	i	e
a	r	o	a	o	d	c

Ps may then, for example:
- find two animals for each continent;
- make their own *word search*.

Alternatively, Ps make (finish) their own *word search* using words you provide, or their own selection, e.g.

pet, dog, rabbit, cousin, Africa, Europe, Asia, America.

			l	s		
			c	a		
			o	c		
			r	a		
			e	t		
			i	l		
			t	i		
			l	r		
			c	o		

Word building activities

Ps piece the parts of the words (or pictures) together to make 'whole' animals:

cro	gu	ar	_____
e	co	roo	_____
ja	ga	phant	_____
kan	le	dile	_____

C.4 Instructions

A) INSTRUCTION CARDS

Make a series of instruction cards that review the language Ps are studying, and require the Ps to complete a practical task. For example:

```
Draw a big round head.
Draw two little eyes.
Draw two little ears.
Draw a big round nose.
Draw a wide mouth.
Colour your picture.
What is your animal?
```

More able pupils can be asked to make their own instruction cards, using the cards you have prepared as a guide. Ps may illustrate these cards as appropriate.

B) ILLUSTRATED CLASSROOM INSTRUCTIONS

Ps illustrate common classroom instructions, or make additional illustrations for the instructions in their coursebooks.
(See also 'signs' on page 249.)

Shhh... Quiet.
Readers at work.

C.5 Lists

A) SHOPPING LISTS

Ps sort words you provide, and make 'shopping lists' of:
- food words for animals;
- colour words for animals;
- habitat words for animals;
- sounds animals make, etc.

In each case, the list is treated as a series of 'target' words to learn.

Help more able Ps to add to the 'shopping lists' with their own words.

B) MISSING WORDS IN A LIST

Each list has one missing animal that is in the other two lists.

Ps scan (alphabetically) and find/write the names of the missing animals.

Anteater	Anteater	Anteater
Bear	Bear	Bear
Duck	Duck	Duck
Giraffe	Frog	Frog
Iguana	Giraffe	Giraffe
Lion	Iguana	Iguana
Newt	Lion	Newt
Panda	Newt	Panda
Quetzal	Panda	Quetzal
Tiger	Tiger	Tiger
Wolf	Wolf	Wolf
Yak	Yak	Yak
Zebra	Zebra	Zebra

C) WORD CHAINS

Example: *lionsandtigersandjaguarsandcheetahsarecats*

Ps circle the animals. If a word chain is constructed as above, more able Ps may then be encouraged to make sentences or phrases from the parts of a word chain, e.g. *Lions and tigers are cats*.

More able Ps may also make their own word chains.

C.6 Messages and letters

A) NOTICE BOARD/POST BOX

To start the notices off, pin messages for/from selected pupils on the notice board, e.g.

> Maria, how do you spell ... (picture)?
> Ana, what's your favourite animal?

Ps go on to pin up their own messages for their friends on a regular basis.

B) LETTER TO A CHARACTER IN THE COURSEBOOK

At the end of a unit, Ps may be encouraged to write a few appropriate words or a comment to one of the characters in the unit. Where necessary, support this writing by providing a model for the Ps to copy and use as a guide.

C) LETTER TO AN ANIMAL PARK/ZOO IN BRITAIN OR THE USA FOR INFORMATION/'ADOPT AN ANIMAL'

This is a long-term but highly worthwhile project. Children are strongly motivated by the authentic nature of the *purpose* of this project. The correspondence involved, and materials that zoos/animal parks will send, provide highly motivating authentic reading and writing opportunities.

C.7 Invitations/greetings

A) BIRTHDAY CARD/BIRTHDAY GREETINGS

Show birthday/greetings cards in English. (Or make them using local birthday/greeting cards and 'over-writing' the text with English.)

Encourage Ps to make their own birthday and greetings cards. Provide the model for a short birthday/greetings text.

B) INVITATION CARD

Show invitation cards in English. (Or make them using local invitation cards and 'over-writing' the text with English.) Example:

> Please come to my party on Saturday.
> Love ___

Encourage Ps to make their own invitation cards. Provide the model for the text.

C) THANK-YOU CARD

Show thank-you cards in English. (Or make them using local thank-you cards and 'over-writing' the text with English.) Examples:

> Dear ___
> Thank you very much for my ___.
> Love, ___

Encourage Ps to make and illustrate their own thank-you cards. Provide the model for the text.

C.8 Brief description/narrative

A) JIGSAW TEXT

Ps copy out sentences from a description/text/dialogue that they are studying onto strips of paper – one sentence per strip.

Ps work in groups. P1 in each group shuffles the sentences; the remaining Ps piece them together.

B) TRANSPARENCY TEXT

Following a picture story or TPR activity, Ps work in groups of four or pairs to recreate as much of the story/text as they can onto an OHP transparency.

They illustrate the text and re-tell/re-enact the story in their own words while showing the OHT to the remainder of the class.

C.9 Songs/rhymes/poems

A) ILLUSTRATING THE TEXT

Example: *Incy Wincy Spider*

Ps work in groups of four or pairs to copy the text. Each pupil in a group copies one or two lines onto a small sheet of paper and creates an illustration for this text.

Each pupil then glues his/her illustration + text onto a suitable size sheet of paper. The group staples the sheets together to produce a mini-book.

B) CREATING A TUNE FOR THE TEXT

Example: *Incy Wincy Spider*
Ps work in groups of four or pairs to:
- copy the text;
- create a tune for the rhyme;
- rehearse singing it;
- teach the tune to the rest of the class and sing it.

C.10 Making books/publishing

A) CONCERTINA BOOK

Following a picture story (e.g. *Goldilocks and the Three Bears*, *The Hungry Caterpillar*, *Where the Wild Things are*) or TPR activity, Ps make a 'concertina' or similar book in groups of four or pairs. This might, e.g.
- re-tell the story with key lines and illustrations;
- continue the story;
- focus on one of the characters in the story.

B) 'LIFT THE FLAP' BOOK

This is based on the *Where's Spot?* series, e.g.
Write the question *Is the elephant under the tree?*
Ps work in groups of four. Each child folds a sheet of A4 paper into two. On the top half, pupils draw an animal of their choice. On the bottom half:
- P1 draws the elephant in a car. Under this picture P1 writes *No. (The elephant isn't under the tree.) The elephant is in the car.*
- P2 draws the elephant up a tree. Under this picture P2 writes: *No. (The elephant isn't under the tree.) The elephant is up the tree.*
- P3 draws the elephant in a swimming pool. Under this picture P3 writes *No. (The elephant isn't under the tree.) The elephant is in a swimming pool.*
- P4 draws the elephant under a tree. Under this picture, P4 writes *Yes. The elephant is under the tree.*

All Ps take another half sheet of A4 and use it as a 'flap' to cover the picture/location of the elephant. On top of the flap they write *Is the elephant under the tree?* (**Note:** Any question that generates a series of similar, simple *yes/no* responses may be used.)

Finally, groups staple their 'book', and swap and read their finished products. All finished books are kept for future use.

D Songs and rhymes

This section of the Resource file provides a list of traditional rhymes and songs that have been 'adapted' to suit the theme of each of the ten units in this book.

In terms of teaching procedure, consider alternatives to merely 'singing and acting out' the songs/rhymes, e.g. Ps may:
- make small paper/card cut-outs for the key vocabulary, placing the cut-outs on an OHT to re-enact the rhyme/song;
- make puppets (paper bag, card, paper plates, sock, etc.) and re-enact the rhyme/song;
- copy the text and illustrate it;
- divide a sheet of A4 paper into sections. Ps then draw a picture in each section to show the action/story in the rhyme/song.

D.1 Spiders and mini-creatures

LITTLE MISS MUFFET

Little Miss Muffet
Sat on a bucket,
And ate a chocolate ice-cream.
Along came a spider
And sat down beside her,
And made poor Miss Muffet scream: Aaaaah!

LADYBIRD, LADYBIRD

Ladybird, ladybird, fly away home.
Your house is on fire and your children have gone.
All except one – and her name is Ann.
She is hiding under the frying pan.

D.2 Circus

CIRCUS RING

The clown is in the ring.
The clown is in the ring.
Eee ay addio, the clown is in the ring.
The clown throws a pie.
The clown throws a pie.
Eee ay addio, the clown throws a pie.
We all start to laugh.
We all start to laugh.
Eee ay addio, we all start to laugh.

(Played as in Unit 8, page 105, *The witch is in …*)

CIRCUS THIS IS THE WAY ...

This is the way a fire-eater breathes,
A fire-eater breathes, a fire-eater breathes.
This is the way a fire-eater breathes
In the circus ring in the evening. (fire-eater actions)

This is the way a trapeze artist swings,
A trapeze artist swings, a trapeze artist swings.
This is the way a trapeze artist swings
In the circus ring in the evening. (trapeze artist actions)

D.3 Potatoes/vegetables

ONE POTATO ...

One potato, two potatoes, three potatoes, four,
Five potatoes, six potatoes, seven potatoes, more.

Ps stand in pairs, groups of four or in a large circle. They take turns to 'count' the potatoes by placing closed fists (i.e. potatoes) one on top of the other as the rhyme proceeds, e.g.

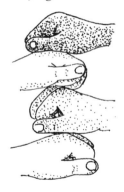

As the last word is said (i.e. *more*) all Ps try to slap each other's hands before they can be removed from the pile of 'fists'.

FIVE FAT FRENCH FRIES

Five fat French fries frying near the door.
My dog ate one, and then there were four.
Four fat French fries frying for my tea.
My cat ate one and then there were three.
Three fat French fries frying near the zoo.
An elephant ate one, and then there were two.
Two fat French fries frying in the sun.
I ate two and then there were none.

(Played as in Unit 4, page 47, *Five fat sausages ...*)

D.4 Islands/water

JACK AND JILL

Jack and Jill went up the hill
To get a pail of water.
Jack fell down and broke his crown
And Jill came tumbling after.

Jack got up and ran off home
As fast as he could caper.
He went to bed and fixed his head
With vinegar and brown paper.

THERE'S A HOLE IN MY BUCKET

There's a hole in my bucket, dear Lisa, dear Lisa,
There's a hole in my bucket, dear Lisa, a hole.
Well fix it, dear Mona, dear Mona, dear Mona,
Well fix it, dear Mona, dear Mona, fix it.
With what shall I fix it, dear Lisa, dear Lisa,
With what shall I fix it, dear Lisa, with what?
With Scotch tape, dear Mona, dear Mona, dear Mona,
With Scotch tape, dear Mona, dear Mona, with tape.
With what shall I cut it, dear Lisa, dear Lisa,
With what shall I cut it, dear Lisa, with what?
With scissors ...

Ps work in two teams to 'extend' or adapt the song:
Team 1 makes suggestions for repair items.
Team 2 asks where to get these items/how to do the repair.

D.5 Bridges/green fields

LONDON BRIDGE

London Bridge is falling down, falling down, falling down,
London Bridge is falling down, my fair lady.
Build it up with bricks and stones, bricks and stones, bricks and stones,
Build it up with bricks and stones, my fair lady.

ONE MAN WENT TO MOW

One man went to mow, went to mow a meadow,
One man and his dog went to mow a meadow.

Two men went to mow, went to mow a meadow,
Two men, one man and his dog went to mow a meadow.

Three men went to mow, went to mow a meadow,
Three men, two men, one man and his dog went to mow a meadow.
(up to ten)

D.6 Jack ...

JACK SPRATT

Jack Spratt will eat no fat,
His wife will eat no lean.
And so between the two of them,
They lick their two plates clean.

LITTLE JACK HORNER

Little Jack Horner
Sat in a corner,
Eating a big plum pie.
He stuck in his thumb
And pulled out a plum,
And said 'What a good boy am I.'

D.7 Goldilocks, bears and porridge

GO TO THE WINDOW

Go to the window. Peep in.
Knock at the door. Creep in.
Walk to the kitchen. Step in.
Put a spoon in the porridge. Tuck in.

ONE LITTLE TEDDY BEAR

One little, two little, three little teddy bears,
Four little, five little, six little teddy bears,
Seven little, eight little, nine little teddy bears,
Ten little brown teddy bears.

D.8 Festivals

WE WISH YOU A MERRY CHRISTMAS

We wish you a merry Christmas, we wish you a merry Christmas,
We wish you a merry Christmas and a Happy New Year.

HERE WE GO ROUND THE MULBERRY BUSH

Here we go round the mulberry bush, the mulberry bush, the mulberry bush,
Here we go round the mulberry bush on a cold and frosty morning.

D.9 This is the ... (extending rhymes)

THIS IS THE WAY

This is the way we clap our hands, clap our hands, clap our hands,
This is the way we clap our hands on a cold and frosty morning.

This is the way we stamp our feet, stamp our feet, stamp our feet,
This is the way we stamp our feet on a cold and frosty morning.

THERE WAS AN OLD LADY ...

There was an old lady who swallowed a fly.
I don't know why she swallowed a fly. Perhaps she'll die.
There was an old lady who swallowed a spider.
She swallowed the spider to catch the fly. I don't know why ...
There was an old lady who swallowed a bird.
She swallowed the bird to catch the spider,
She swallowed the spider to catch the fly. I don't know why ...
There was an old lady who swallowed a cat ... etc.

ONE FINGER ONE THUMB

One finger, one thumb, keep moving,
One finger, one thumb, keep moving,
One finger, one thumb, keep moving, and off to town we go.
One finger, one thumb, one arm, one leg, keep moving,
One finger, one thumb, one arm, one leg, keep moving.
One finger, one thumb, one arm, one leg, keep moving, and off to town
we go.
One finger, one thumb, one arm, one leg, one hand, one foot, keep
moving,
One finger, one thumb, one arm, one leg, one hand, one foot, keep
moving,
One finger, one thumb, one arm, one leg, one hand, one foot, keep
moving, and off to town we go.
One finger, one thumb, one arm, one leg, one hand, one foot, stand up,
sit down, keep moving,
One finger, one thumb, one arm, one leg, one hand, one foot, stand up,
sit down, keep moving,
One finger, one thumb, one arm, one leg, one hand, one foot, stand up,
sit down, keep moving, and off to town we go ...

D.10 'Profile' songs

SHE IS WEARING PINK PYJAMAS

She is wearing pink pyjamas and a hat.
She is wearing pink pyjamas and a hat.
She is wearing pink pyjamas, wearing pink pyjamas.
She is wearing pink pyjamas and a hat.

He is eating green bananas and a cake.
He is eating green bananas and a cake.
He is eating green bananas, eating green bananas.
He is eating green bananas and a cake.

THIS OLD MAN

This old man, he played one, he played knick-knack on my thumb.
With a knick-knack paddiwack, give a dog a bone,
This old man came rolling home.

This old man, he played two, he played knick-knack on my shoe.
With a knick-knack paddiwack, give a dog a bone,
This old man came rolling home.

This old man, he played three, he played knick-knack on my knee.
With a knick-knack paddiwack, give a dog a bone,
This old man came rolling home.

This old man, he played four, he played knick-knack on my door.
With a knick-knack paddiwack, give a dog a bone,
This old man came rolling home.

E 'Top ten' games

The final section of the Resource file contains ten games which may be easily adapted to a variety of topics and language points.

A) SIMON SAYS

Rules:
Ps must follow the instruction if it is preceded by *Simon says*.
Ps must not follow the instruction if it is **not** preceded by *Simon says*. Ps who follow this type of instruction are out of the game.

These are three examples of *Simon says* that focus on numbers.
Simon says count to ten. Simon says count from six to nine. Simon says count from ten down to five. Count from one to ten. Simon says count from one to ten …

Simon says draw number one (in the air). Simon says draw number three.
Draw number five. Simon says draw number five ...
Simon says touch number one. Simon says point to number seven. Point
to number six. Simon says point to number six ...

B) THIS IS THE WAY YOU ...

Procedure:
Ps work in teams or whole class to sing and act out the song to the tune
of *This is the way you brush your teeth ...*

This is an example of *This is the way you ...*, again related to numbers:
This is the way you count to ten, count to ten, count to ten.
This is the way you count to ten, on a cold and frosty morning:
one two three four five six seven eight nine ten.

C) BEETLE

This is an example of 'beetle' related to the topic of 'mini-creatures':
- Ps need a die and a pencil.
- Ps take turns to throw the die:
  1 = the beetle's head   2 = the beetle's eyes and nose
  3 = the beetle's ears   4 = the beetle's mouth
  5 = the beetle's legs   6 = the beetle's tail

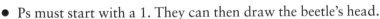

- Ps must start with a 1. They can then draw the beetle's head.
- Ps must then throw a 2 and they can draw the beetle's eyes and nose.
- Ps must then throw a 3, and so on.
- The winner must draw the complete beetle and describe it, e.g. *This is the beetle's head. These are the beetle's eyes*, etc.

This game may be adapted to other vocabulary sets.

D) BINGO

Here is an example of bingo related to *numbers* and *parts of the body:*
- Draw this grid on the board. Ps copy it.

- Ask Ps for words they can remember from the unit. Write them on the board.
- Ps choose any six words and write them in their grid. You write **all** the words on small pieces of paper and put them in a bag or box.
- Take out the words from the bag one by one, naming them. Ps cross them off their grid. The first child to cross off all six words wins – and becomes caller for a repeat game.

This game may be used for many vocabulary sets.

E) PELMANISM

This is an example of the game related to numbers:
- Make simple flashcards for each of the numbers 0–10. Ps copy them in groups of four to six to produce one complete set per group.
- Produce a similar set of word cards for each of the numbers, i.e. the numbers written in words. Ps copy them in groups of four to six to produce one complete set per group.
- Ps place their two sets of cards face down and mix them up. Within their groups, Ps then take turns to turn over **two** cards at a time. They try to find cards that match, i.e. the word and matching number. The child who collects the most pairs is the winner.

This game may be used for many vocabulary sets.

F) ADD-A-WORD

This is an example of the game related to revision of parts of a spider:
- Ps work in two teams (T1 and T2). You say the first sentence, e.g. *This spider has a body.*
- Teams confer. P1 from T1 must add a word to this sentence, e.g. *This spider has a round body* or *This spider has a body and a head.*
- Teams score a point for each correct sentence.

G) SPIDER'S WEB

This is an example of the game related to revision of mini-creatures:
Note: Over-excitement in this game can lead to injuries! For the sake of
safety, place all chairs **against** the wall so that they cannot tip over backwards during the game.
- Ps sit in a circle. Each pupil sits on his/her own chair. Remove any
  additional chairs. The teacher stands.
- Choose any four 'mini-creatures'. Assign each pupil the name of a
  creature: one per pupil. In other words, in a group of fifteen, there may
  be four pupils who are *spiders*, four pupils who are *flies*, four who are
  worms, and three who are *ladybirds*.
- Name one of the creatures, e.g. *spiders*. All the pupils who are *spiders*
  must stand up and then sit down on a different seat. The teacher must
  also sit down. In other words, five people (four pupils and the teacher)
  will try to sit down on four seats. The pupil who doesn't find a seat is
  the next *caller* of the items.
- The game continues in this way for two or three minutes. If the caller
  says *spider's web* **everyone** must stand up, find a different seat and sit
  down on it.

H) CREEPY-CRAWLY

This is an example of the game related to revision of names of mini-
creatures:
- Prepare a *creepy-crawly*. A plastic insect is ideal, but any 'soft' alternative, e.g. made of plasticine, is OK.
- Form large circles of six to ten pupils. (You may need to do this activity outside.) P1 receives the *creepy-crawly* you have prepared.
- P1 walks around the outside of the circle with the creepy-crawly, and
  suddenly gives it to P2, who is standing as part of the circle. P1 shouts
  creepy-crawly, and begins to run around the outside of the circle while
  the pupils in the circle pass the creepy-crawly from one to the other
  round the circle, saying *Yuk, a creepy-crawly* as they do so. P1 aims to
  run around and reach the original starting position (P2) before the
  pupils can pass the creepy-crawly right around the circle and back to
  P2. If P1 succeeds, the pupil holding the creepy-crawly when P1
  arrives is the new *creepy-crawly holder* for a repeat game. Anyone
  dropping the creepy-crawly automatically becomes the new creepy-
  crawly holder.

I) CHINESE MIMES

This is an example of the game related to revision of mini-creatures:
- Organise Ps in equal team lines. P1 in each team line is the leader of the
  team. Teams face the back of the room, except for the leaders who turn

to face you. Non-leaders must **not** turn round to see what you are doing. No talking is allowed during this game.

- Give a short mime instruction to the P1s, e.g. mime drawing (with your finger) and colouring a mini-creature, or do a mini-creature action. Leaders must convey these gestures (without speaking) to the next pupil in their team line, as follows:
  P1 taps P2 on the shoulder.
  P2 turns to face P1 (remainder of team must **not** look round).
  P1 passes on (= imitates) your mime as closely as possible to P2.
  It is now P2's turn to pass on the mime to P3 in their line. The game continues until the last pupil (PX) in the line receives the mime.
- The PXs demonstrate their interpretation of the mime to the whole class and say what they think it is. P1s show their original mime, and teams discuss (in L1) 'what went wrong'!

J) ANIMAL TWISTER

This game is based on the commercial game of the same name.

- Prepare, or ask children to prepare, several sets of six 'animals' on A4 sheets of paper, one for each animal (e.g. lion, tiger, elephant, gorilla, crocodile, snake).
- Check Ps can recognise the names of the six animals you have prepared.
- Ps stand in groups. Groups create space for their group. Hand out sets of the six 'animal' sheets of paper you have prepared. Groups place the sheets of paper *strategically* so that the game proceeds with fun.
- Give *Twister* instructions, e.g. *Put your right hand on a lion. Good. Now put your left foot on an elephant. Good, now put your left elbow on a crocodile*, etc.
  Demonstrate with gesture which part of the body needs to touch which animal.
- Give instructions that are possible, but *difficult* to achieve. Ps must not remove a part of the body from an animal until you give the instruction.
- Encourage confident Ps to give the *Twister* instructions.

There are countless children's games which can be adapted to the language classroom. It is well worth spending thirty or forty minutes with your colleagues swapping 'top ten' games.

Appendix

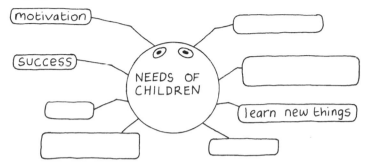

Spidergram A – the needs of children

Storyscript for *Jack and the Beanstalk*

Once upon a time there was a boy called Jack. He lived with his mother in a little house. They were very, very poor. They had one old cow and two old hens. One day they had nothing to eat. Jack's mother said, 'We need some food. Take the cow to the market and sell her.'

Jack took the cow to the market. He sold the cow to an old man. The old man didn't have any money. He gave Jack five magic beans for the cow. Jack ran home. He showed his mother the magic beans. She was very angry and she threw the beans out of the window. That night Jack and his mother had nothing to eat. They went to bed very hungry. While they were asleep the beans started to grow. They grew higher and higher and higher. The leaves on the beanstalk grew wider and wider and wider. The next morning Jack looked out of the window and rubbed his eyes. The beanstalk grew right up into the sky. Jack put on his boots and climbed up the beanstalk. He saw a castle. He ran into the castle and into the kitchen. He heard footsteps. Enormous footsteps. Jack was very frightened and he hid behind a sofa. A giant came into the kitchen. The giant had a magic hen. He put the hen on the table and said, 'Lay, little hen, lay.' The hen laid big golden eggs. Then the giant ate an enormous breakfast. He put his head on the table and went to sleep. When the giant was snoring very loudly, Jack crept out and stole the magic hen. He ran out of the castle and climbed down the beanstalk. The giant woke up and chased after Jack, shouting:

Fee, fi, fo, fum
I smell the blood of an Englishman.
Be he alive or be he dead,
I'll grind his bones to make my bread.

Jack climbed down the beanstalk as fast as he could. When he got to the bottom, Jack cut down the beanstalk with an axe. The giant crashed to the ground and was killed. Jack kept the hen. His mother was very happy. They had lots and lots of big golden eggs and they lived happily ever after.

Storyscript for *Billy Goats Gruff*

Once upon a time there were three billy goats. Big Billy Goat Gruff, Medium-size Billy Goat Gruff, Small Billy Goat Gruff. They lived in a big field, near a deep river. They loved to eat grass. Green, green grass. The greenest grass of all grew on the other side of the river. There was a narrow bridge across the river.

One day Small Billy Goat Gruff decided to cross the bridge. Now, an ugly troll lived under the bridge. The troll heard Small Billy Goat Gruff walking on the bridge, trip, trap, trip, trap. 'Who's walking on my bridge?', he shouted. And he jumped onto the bridge. He stood in front of Small Billy Goat Gruff. 'I'm going to eat you,' he said to Small Billy Goat Gruff. 'Don't eat me, I'm too small,' said Small Billy Goat Gruff. 'Eat my brother, Medium-size Billy Goat Gruff. He's much bigger than me.' The troll looked at Small Billy Goat Gruff. 'You're right. You're too small to eat.' And he let Small Billy Goat Gruff cross the bridge. Trip, trap, trip, trap.

Medium-size Billy Goat Gruff saw his brother eating the green, green grass. He decided to cross the bridge. The troll heard Medium-size Billy Goat Gruff walking on the bridge, trip, trap, trip, trap. 'Who's walking on my bridge?', he shouted. And he jumped onto the bridge. He stood in front of Medium-size Billy Goat Gruff. 'I'm going to eat you,' he said. 'Don't eat me, I'm too small,' said Medium-size Billy Goat Gruff. 'Eat my brother, Big Billy Goat Gruff. He's much bigger than me.' The troll looked at Medium-size Billy Goat Gruff. 'You're right. You're too small to eat.' And he let Medium-size Billy Goat Gruff cross the bridge. Trip, trap, trip, trap.

Big Billy Goat Gruff saw his brothers eating the green, green grass. He decided to cross the bridge. The troll heard Big Billy Goat Gruff walking on the bridge, trip, trap, trip, trap. 'Who's walking on my bridge?', he shouted. And he jumped onto the bridge. He stood in front of Big Billy Goat Gruff. 'I'm going to eat you,' he said. 'Eat me! I'm much too big,' said Big Billy Goat Gruff. And he lowered his head and charged the troll. Bang! Big Billy Goat Gruff hit the troll in the stomach. 'Ouch!' said the troll. And Big Billy Goat Gruff threw the troll into the water. 'Bye, bye, troll,' said Big Billy Goat Gruff and he walked across the bridge, trip, trap, trip, trap. So the three billy goats got to the green, green grass. 'Mmm, delicious, green, green grass,' they said.

Classroom grid

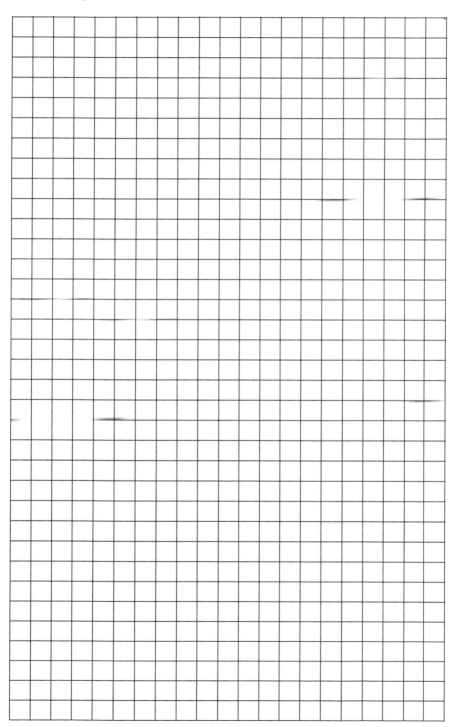

Appendix

Classroom furniture cut-outs

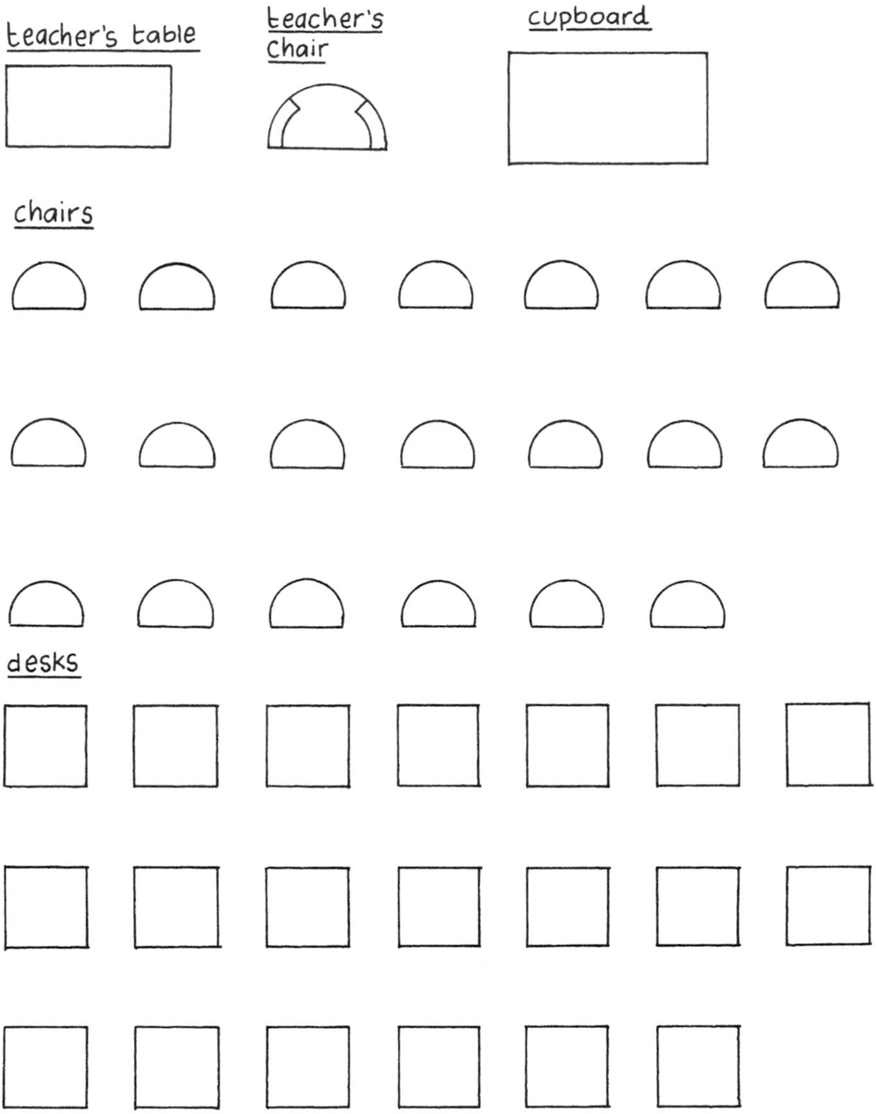

<u>teacher's table</u>

<u>teacher's chair</u>

<u>cupboard</u>

<u>chairs</u>

<u>desks</u>

© Cambridge University Press 1995

Spidergram B – action taken by the teacher

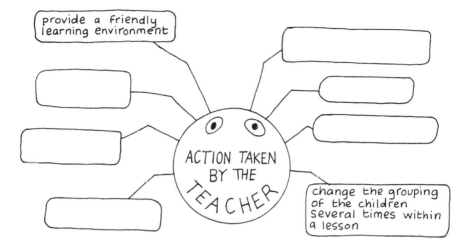

Example observation sheet

Classroom layout
Desk/chairs organised:
in rows ☐ in a horseshoe ☐ in groups ☐ in pairs ☐ other (draw it):

Types of activities	Done?	Time spent (minutes)
registration	☐	....
checking homework	☐	....
presenting new language	☐	....
using coursebook	☐	....
action game(s)	☐	....
practical tasks	☐	....
story/song	☐	....
language practice	☐	....
review/consolidation	☐	....
language games	☐	....
assigning homework	☐	....
other	....	
	....	

Management of time	Time spent (minutes)
starting/ending the class	....
disciplining	....
organising children and space	....
socialising with the children	....
teacher talking	....
children speaking	....
children listening (to text/cassette)	....
controlled language practice	....
free use/production of language	....
reading activities	....
writing/copying activities	....
children working independently	....
other	....
	....

Total lesson time .... minutes
Estimate of total time 'well spent' .... minutes
= .... per cent
Estimate of total time 'spent
non-productively' .... minutes
= .... per cent

Management of children

problem   *teacher solution*

General comments

Further reading

GENERAL/BACKGROUND

Donaldson, M. (1978) *Children's Minds*, Fontana.
Pollard, A. and Tann, S. (1987) *Reflective Teaching in the Primary Classroom*, Cassell.
Wells, G. (1985) *Language, Learning and Education*, NFER/Nelson.

RESOURCE BOOKS

Edited by Brumfit, C., Moon, J. and Tongue, R. (1991) *Teaching English to Children – from Practice to Principle*, Nelson.
Halliwell, S. (1992) *Teaching English in the Primary Classroom*, Longman.
Various authors, *The "Bright Ideas" Series*, Scholastic Publications.
Various authors, *Teacher Resource Series*, Bel Air Publications.

READING AND WRITING

Ellis, G. and Brewster, J. (1991) *The Storytelling Handbook for Primary Teachers*, Penguin.
Garvie, E. (1989) *The story as a vehicle*, Clevedon: Multilingual Matters.
Gawith, G, (1990) *Reading Alive*, A & C Black.
Hall, N. (1987) *The Emergence of Literacy*, Hodder and Stoughton.
Johnson, P. (1990) *A book of one's own*, Hodder and Stoughton.
Meek, M. (1988) *How texts teach what readers learn*, The Thimble Press.

SONGS AND GAMES

Brandreth, G. (1984) *Everyman's Book of Children's Games*, J.M. Dent and Sons.
Graham, C. (1978) *Jazz Chants for Children*, OUP.
Opie, I. and P. (1969) *Lore and Language of Schoolchildren*, OUP.
Wright, A., Betteridge, D. and Buckby, M. (1984) *Games for Language Learning*, CUP.

This Little Puffin, Finger Plays and Nursery Games, Puffin.

CLASSROOM RESEARCH

Rudduck, J. and Hopkins, D. (1985) *Research as a basis for teaching (Readings from the work of Laurence Stenhouse)*, Heinemann Educational.

PERIODICALS

Child Education (Monthly: Scholastic Publications)
Junior Education (Monthly: Scholastic Publications)

PICTURE BOOKS SUITABLE FOR THE YOUNG LEARNER'S LANGUAGE CLASSROOM

Burningham, J. *Granpa*, Picture Puffin.
Carle, E. *The very hungry caterpillar*; Picture Puffin.
Flournoy, V. and Pinkney, J. *The patchwork quilt*, Picture Puffin.
Foreman, M. *War and peas*, Picture Puffin.
Hill, E. *Where's Spot?*, Picture Puffin.
Hutchins, P. *Don't forget the bacon*, Picture Puffin.
Kinmont, P. and Cartwright, R. *Mr Potter's pidgeon*, Pocket Puffin.
Korky, P and Thomas, V. *Winnie the Witch*, OUP.
Lionni, I. *Fish is fish*, Picture Puffin.
Nicoll, H. *Meg and Mog*, Picture Puffin.
Rosen, M and Blake, Q. *You can't catch me*, Picture Puffin.
Sendak, M. *Outside over there*, Picture Puffin.
Sendak, M. *Where the wild things are*, Picture Puffin.
Smith, M. *Kimi and the watermelon*, Picture Puffin.
Sutton, F. and Dodd, L. *My cat likes to hide in boxes*, Picture Puffin.
Wilde, O. and Foreman, M. *The selfish giant*, Picture Puffin.
Waddell, M. and Dupasquier, P. *Going West*, Picture Puffin.

Index